P9-DNN-241

2,635 HOME HINTS AND TIMELESS TIPS

TRIED-AND-TRUSTED TECHNIQUES FOR EVERYDAY TROUBLES

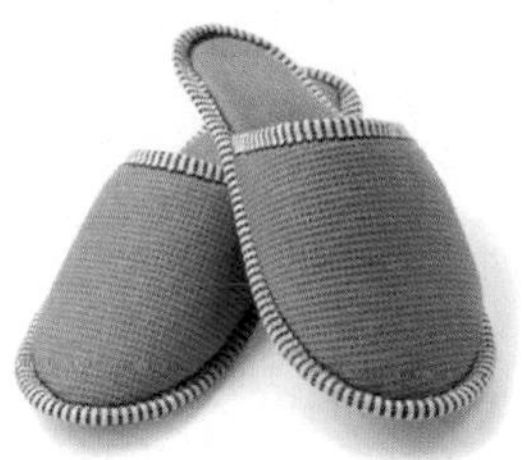

Reader's Digest
New York | Montreal

A READER'S DIGEST BOOK

ISBN 978-1-62145-490-8 (ppb)
ISBN 978-1-62145-489-2 (hc)
ISBN 978-1-62145-491-5 (e-pub)

We are committed to both the quality of our products and the service we provide to our customers. We value your comments, so please feel free to contact us.

Trusted Media Brands, Inc. Adult Trade Publishing
44 South Broadway
White Plains, NY 10601

Printed in The United States of America
1 3 5 7 9 10 8 6 4 2

NOTE TO OUR READERS
The information in this book should not be substituted for, or used to alter, medical therapy without your doctor's advice. For a specific health problem, consult your physician for guidance.

WARNING
All do-it-yourself activities involve a degree of risk. Skills, materials, tools, and site conditions vary widely. Although the editors have made every effort to ensure accuracy, the reader remains responsible for the selection and use of tools, materials, and methods. Always obey local codes and laws, follow manufacturer's operating instructions, and observe safety precautions.

Contents

Good health . . . naturally 8

Beauty and body care 60

continued...

Contents continued...

Smart housekeeping 86

Home cooking 124

Style and comfort 164

Gardening with nature 204

Yesterday's top tips for today's busy lifestyles

Almost every day, new—and usually expensive—consumer products appear that promise to make our lives easier and simpler. But are they all really necessary? Despite their initial hype, few of them live up to expectations.

Our grandparents' generation had abundant knowledge about how to solve everyday problems easily, inexpensively and effectively, without running to the store—whether the issue was storing fresh produce, making skin look younger, relieving headache pain or getting laundry whiter. Wouldn't it be a shame if all that expertise was lost to future generations?

To prevent that from happening and to preserve yesterday's top tips for today's busy families, we have gathered a wealth of traditional wisdom to create this book. Home Hints and Timeless Tips is a comprehensive collection of the best time-honored solutions from past generations. From your medicine cabinet to your freezer, your vegetable patch to your morning shower, here are clever suggestions and solutions that show you how to apply the good old ways from the good old days to improve the way we do things now.

It's not about harking back to a nostalgic past, but about presenting old-fashioned ideas in such a way that they can easily be used in today's world. It makes the wealth of our collective experience—built up over generations—accessible to people who need a helping hand today. It's advice that is proven, timely, economical and environmentally friendly.

And all these clever solutions, useful hints, practical tips and helpful remedies from days gone by have been researched and tested for their practical applications in the 21st century. They can offer alternatives to expensive products or the use of chemical additives and you'll often find the ingredients close at hand in your kitchen cabinets.

Organized into six chapters that focus on health, beauty, home management, cooking, home decor and the garden, this book is packed with more than 2,635 practical hints and tips that our parents and grandparents trusted and relied on. Every tip is guaranteed to help make life easier as well as less expensive. And each entry is presented alphabetically within each chapter, making the solutions easy to find.

Home Hints and Timeless Tips takes a step back into the past to help you achieve a more rewarding way of living today—because many of the old ways still work best!

Note to readers

The creators of this work have made every effort to be as accurate and up-to-date as possible. Many traditional home remedies use plant substances. Plant-based products (infusions, tinctures, capsules, essential oils) may cause immune reactions and should therefore be used with care. Pregnant women and anyone taking prescription drugs or undergoing surgery should consult a doctor before using herbal medicines. Essential oils should not be used by children under the age of two. For a specific health problem, consult your physician. Health advice in this book should not be substituted for or used to alter treatment without your doctor's advice. The writers, researchers, editors and publishers of this work cannot be held liable for any errors, omissions or actions that may be taken as a consequence of information contained within the book. The mention of any products in this book does not imply or constitute an endorsement by Reader's Digest.

Good health . . . naturally

Most of us regularly use over-the-counter pills and potions to treat our illnesses. In the past, people turned to plants and natural products for relief. Today, clinical science supports many such remedies, confirming that a variety of ailments will respond to nature's help alone.

Acid reflux

The searing pain of heartburn can be brought on by eating spicy, fatty or acidic foods, or just by eating too much too quickly. Luckily, it is easy to combat—or to avoid altogether.

When stomach acid backs up into the esophagus, you feel the burning pain of acid reflux. At the first sign of heartburn, try one of these natural solutions.

GOOD TO KNOW

Causes of acid reflux

A trapdoor of muscular tissue called the lower esophageal sphincter usually keeps stomach acid just where it belongs—in the stomach. However, heartburn occurs when the sphincter allows the contents of your stomach to flow back into the esophagus, causing a burning pain behind the breastbone. This is known as acid reflux.

HOME remedies

- Baking soda can neutralize excess stomach acid (don't use it if you have high blood pressure). Stir 1 teaspoon (5 ml) in a glass of warm water and drink.
- Try a tonic: Steep 1 tablespoon (15 g) each dried gentian root and dandelion root in 1 cup (250 ml) of boiling water.
- Drink ginger tea: Boil 1½ teaspoons (7 ml) fresh ginger or ½ teaspoon (2 ml) powdered ginger in 1 cup (250 ml) water for 10 minutes before drinking.
- Chew a licorice tablet before meals. This encourages mucin production in the esophagus, providing a protective barrier against stomach acids.
- Seasoning food with fennel seeds or peppermint makes it more digestible and soothes heartburn.
- Eat a piece of dry white bread or toast to neutralize stomach acids, or 1 tablespoon (15 ml) dry oatmeal.
- Sleep with your upper body slightly elevated at night to prevent acid from entering the esophagus.

PREVENTION

- Eat sensibly, avoiding foods, drinks and combinations you know give you heartburn—perhaps fatty or acidic foods, chocolate or wine.
- Avoid alcohol, nicotine and caffeine; they increase gastric acid secretion, which can cause heartburn.
- Eat slowly and always opt for smaller, more frequent portions.
- Watch your weight. If you are carrying excess pounds (kilos), this increases pressure inside your stomach, which can lead to acid reflux and heartburn.
- Eat early in the evening to give your stomach time to digest the meal—this takes about 3 hours. If you go to bed shortly after eating, stomach acid can flow back into your esophagus.

WHEN TO CONSULT A DOCTOR If you are a frequent victim of heartburn, seek professional advice.

Back pain

Most people are affected by back pain at some point in their lives. Spending long periods slumped in front of a television or peering at a computer puts our musculoskeletal systems at greater risk. While good posture is no longer associated with moral superiority as it once was, it's still one of the best ways to prevent back pain.

In addition to good posture, lifting and carrying things correctly and using a chair with a backrest can help keep your back healthy. However, exercise is the top tip for a strong back. Not only will it help you to control your weight (being overweight is linked with back issues), but physical activities such as walking, swimming or cycling will strengthen back muscles, taking pressure off your joints and tendons.

GOOD TO KNOW

Salty relief

The benefits of salt have been known for centuries as a disinfectant and preservative as well as a condiment. It can also be used to make a handy heat pack. Warm 1 cup (250 g) salt in a pan; pour it into an old, thick sock. Tie off the end and apply to the painful area.

HOME remedies

If you suffer acute back pain, a short period of bed rest may help, but more than a couple of days will do more harm than good. Gentle exercise, such as cycling or swimming, improves circulation and helps prevent further problems.

- Apply heat to a sore back. Good choices include compresses made with rosemary or thyme tea; warmed wheat bags (available from health food stores or pharmacies); salt packs (*see "Salty relief," above*); heat packs (from pharmacies); or infrared light treatment.
- Take hot oil baths with rosemary or thyme extracts to soothe pain, followed by massages with hand-warmed massage oil. Oils that contain lavender, rosemary and ginger are found to be particularly effective.
- When you can, bathe in a natural hot spring. It can be just as good for your psyche as for your back.
- Rub your back with spirits of lemon balm. To prepare, steep 1 cup (200 g) fresh lemon balm leaves for 10 days in a tightly sealed container with 1 quart (1 L) of rubbing alcohol, and leave in a warm place. Strain and dilute with water in a 4:1 proportion.
- Try a hot wheat pack. Boil about 2 pounds (1 kg) wheat grains until soft. Put the hot mixture into a cloth bag and place on your sore back for 15 minutes.
- Ease soreness with a hot bath to which you have added 1 cup (250 g) Epsom salts. These magnesium-rich salts promote relaxation, relieve pain and have a mild sedative and antispasmodic effect.

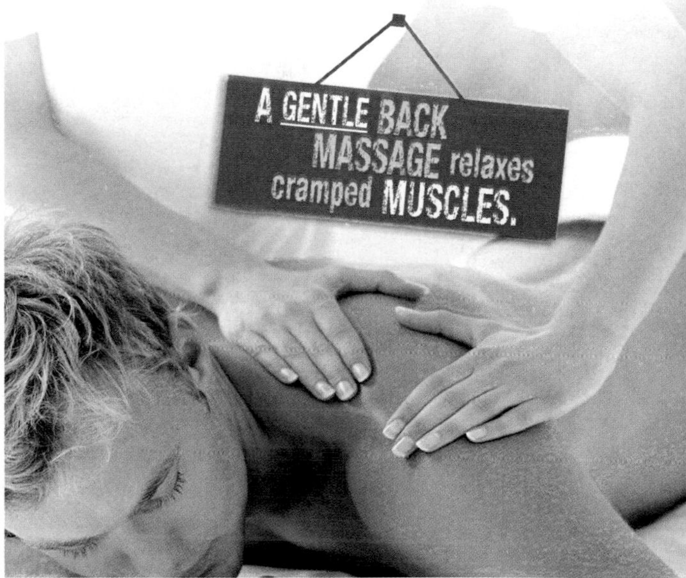

The "child's pose" in yoga, which stretches the hips, thighs and ankles, can help to relieve back pain.

• Place a thick cushion under your legs at night so that your thighs point straight up and your knees are bent at a right angle in order to take strain off your spinal column.

PREVENTION

• Don't carry lopsided loads. Lift heavy weights with your knees bent and always keep your back straight.
• Keep your back warm. Avoid exposing it to cold and drafts.
• Replace a saggy mattress. Don't penny-pinch when you buy a new one. It should be made from high-quality materials and neither too hard nor too soft.
• Avoid sitting in chairs without proper back support. Replace old, worn-out chairs.
• Use a wedge pillow to encourage erect posture while sitting.
• If you have a sedentary occupation, change your sitting position frequently and stand up and stretch every 30 minutes.
• Avoid high heels—wear comfortable shoes as often as you can.

WHAT is lumbago?

Lumbago is actually a blanket term for mild or severe pain in the lower back (or lumbar region). It differs from "normal" back pain in that it can happen suddenly. A cold draft, jerky movement or combination of bending and twisting can trigger an abrupt pain deep in your back muscles. However, a slipped disc has similar symptoms, so if there's no improvement after a few days consult a doctor. First, try this remedies.

• Large adhesive bandages used with compounds like capsaicin, which stimulates circulation, continue to warm muscles for a long time. Don't use them on irritated skin.

MAKING a wrap

Moist heat is helpful for lumbago. Here are two wraps that might ease back pain.

1 Mix together 10 drops of lavender oil, 8 drops each chamomile and cedar oils, 4 drops each juniper and clary sage oils and 1 cup (250 ml) body lotion.
2 Pour 2 tablespoons (30 ml) on a cloth soaked in hot water, wring out and apply it to the painful area.
3 Spread a dry cloth over it and cover with a blanket. Repeat several times daily.

For a verbena wrap:
1 Stir together a handful of crushed fresh verbena leaves, 1 egg yolk, 1 tablespoon (15 ml) flour and 2 tablespoons (30 ml) warm water.
2 Fold a cotton towel to fit the painful area. Spread with the mixture and warm over a steaming pot.
3 Place a hot wheat bag (*see page 11*) on an exercise mat, lay the cotton towel over it (with the verbena side facing up), and lie down with your lower back on it.
4 Cover up with a blanket and lie for as long as possible on the hot underlay.

Rub your back with spirits of lemon balm.

Bladder and kidney disorders

The kidneys and bladder are part of the urinary system, which transports harmful waste products out of the body. For correct functioning, a good fluid intake is essential, so drink plenty of liquids to avoid a bladder infections or kidney stones.

BLADDER weakness and incontinence

Do you check where the toilets are at the mall when you get there? Or try to avoid sneezing or laughing because you are not sure you'll stay dry? You're probably suffering from bladder weakness or incontinence. Both men and women suffer from this embarrassing condition, but the physical stresses of childbirth and a decrease in estrogen at menopause make women three times more susceptible.

Frequently, there's a psychological component to a weak bladder, so stress reduction programs such as yoga or autogenic training may help.

The problem isn't new so there are many time-tested solutions, including the following teas, that can help to strengthen bladder muscles.

- Linden flower, cornsilk and horsetail are good for incontinence and can be combined to make tea. Drink three cups daily.
- Raspberry leaf tea is a very good treatment for bladder weakness that may be experienced during the late stages of pregnancy, as it helps to strengthen both the uterus and the bladder. Raspberry leaf is also available in tablet form.

PREVENT kidney stones

It has been said that the pain of passing a kidney stone is comparable to that of giving birth. Stones might pass in a few hours, but sometimes it takes days. It's best to try to avoid developing them.

Dehydration is a key factor. Lack of fluids prevents mineral salts in urine from being dissolved, causing them to clump together as grit and slowly form kidney stones. To be sure your kidneys are well irrigated and healthy, drink plenty of herbal and fruit teas, water and diluted fruit juice.

- Limit your intake of cocoa, coffee, rhubarb and spinach. They contain oxalate, which adds to the formation of calcium oxalate, a common type of kidney stone.
- Drink enough fluids to be sure you produce about 2 quarts (2 L) of urine a day. Most fluids are all right, but avoid cola, beer and black tea.
- Salt and meat can aggravate kidney stone formation. Consume them in moderation.

HOME remedies

If grit or small stones have already formed in your kidney, the following home remedies may help to flush them out.

- Teas or tinctures made with the herbs cornsilk, buchu and marshmallow.
- The citric acid in lemon inhibits the crystallization of calcium oxalate. Drink the juice of half a lemon in a glass of warm water each morning.
- The soothing properties of heat and warm baths or a hot water bottle placed on the lower abdomen at bedtime may ease kidney or bladder pains.

WHEN TO CONSULT A DOCTOR If you are experiencing serious pain in the kidney region and/or a buildup of urine, contact a doctor immediately.

Drinking cranberry juice every day can prevent a urinary tract infection (UTI).

To keep your bladder and kidneys healthy, drink about 2 quarts (2 L) of liquids a day.

TREAT bladder infections and UTIs

About 50 percent of women will experience a bladder or urinary tract infection (UTI) at some point in their lives, and many will have multiple infections. Women suffer from the problem more often than men because their urethra is shorter, so bacteria can enter the bladder more easily.

Dehydration is often a factor, but there are a host of traditional remedies to combat pain and the continual urge to urinate. Bear in mind that these remedies are most effective when applied early.

- Hot cornsilk tea can help flush out the bacteria causing inflammation and soothe the pain. Strip the fine hair from a corn cob and steep in 1 cup (250 ml) boiling water.
- Take a high-strength cranberry supplement or drink two large glasses of cranberry juice a day to relieve the infection. Cranberry may also help to prevent infections from occurring.
- Heat reduces the pain caused by a bladder infection or UTI. Place a warmed wheat bag between your legs or over your bladder, or soak in a hot bath.

WHEN TO CONSULT A DOCTOR If your UTI is extremely painful or is not noticeably better after 3 days, consult a doctor.

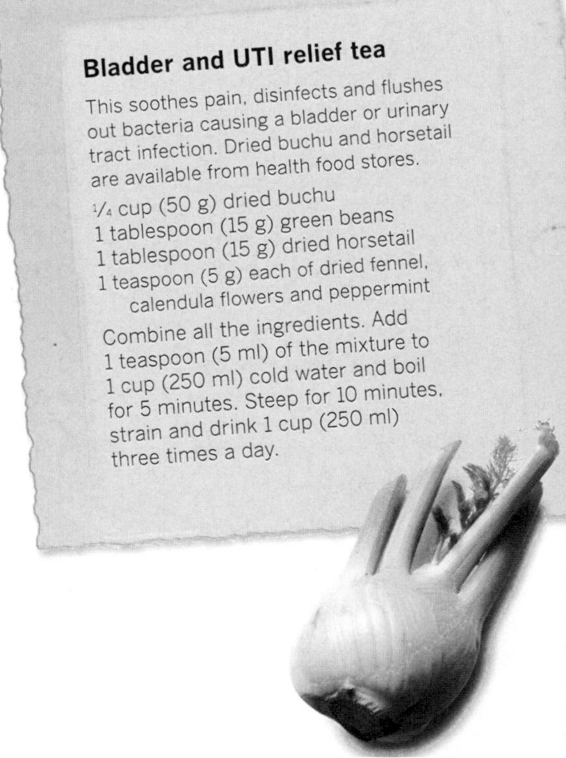

Bladder and UTI relief tea

This soothes pain, disinfects and flushes out bacteria causing a bladder or urinary tract infection. Dried buchu and horsetail are available from health food stores.

1/4 cup (50 g) dried buchu
1 tablespoon (15 g) green beans
1 tablespoon (15 g) dried horsetail
1 teaspoon (5 g) each of dried fennel, calendula flowers and peppermint

Combine all the ingredients. Add 1 teaspoon (5 ml) of the mixture to 1 cup (250 ml) cold water and boil for 5 minutes. Steep for 10 minutes, strain and drink 1 cup (250 ml) three times a day.

Blood pressure

Age, weight gain, lack of exercise, smoking and alcohol abuse are just a few of the lifestyle factors that can subject your heart and circulatory system to tremendous strain. That, in turn, causes damage to blood vessels, sending your blood pressure soaring. The good news: It's never too late to do something about it.

Regular exercise and gentle endurance sports such as cycling, Nordic walking and swimming can help both low and high blood pressure.

HIGH BLOOD PRESSURE

High blood pressure is one of the main risk factors for having a stroke. It requires monitoring and, often, medical treatment. Make sure that you get your blood pressure checked regularly at a pharmacy or by your doctor and seek medical treatment if it consistently measures 140/90 or above. Many plants contain ingredients that can lower blood pressure effectively, relax the muscles of your blood vessels and have a calming effect on your nervous system. With a little help from nature, it's easy to bring slightly elevated blood pressure under control or complement conventional medical therapy if your blood pressure is very high.

GOOD TO KNOW

Green tea

The health effects of green tea have been touted for 4,700 years, since Chinese emperor Shennong claimed it was useful for treating a range of ailments. The tea is rich in antioxidants that have benefits for the cardiovascular system, and drinking it regularly over the long term may help to prevent high blood pressure. To optimize the health benefits, use water that's not quite boiling—about 160°F (70°C) is ideal and allow it to brew for 5–6 minutes. Drink a few cups of this tasty and healthy beverage every day.

HOME remedies

To help to reduce mild high blood pressure, try the following remedies. Consult your doctor first if you are already taking prescription medication.

- Drink lime flower or nettle tea three times daily.
- Other plants that help to regulate blood pressure include olive leaves, passionflower, valerian, yarrow, hawthorn, skullcap and bilberry. However, it is best to take them in a tincture form that has been prescribed for you by a qualified herbalist.
- Chew a clove of raw garlic every day or add one to salad dressings and other dishes. Raw garlic and onions contain a substance called allicin, which helps to keep blood vessels elastic, lowering blood pressure.

Regular exercise is beneficial whether you have high or low blood pressure.

NUTRITION for high blood pressure

- Enjoy fresh asparagus. This vegetable acts as a natural diuretic and can lower blood pressure by removing excess salt and water from the body.
- Reduce salt consumption, as too much salt raises blood pressure. Season food with fresh herbs instead.
- Avoid alcohol, nicotine and coffee—they may increase blood pressure.
- Eat fresh, oily fish such as sardines or salmon once a week. They contain valuable fish oils that may lower blood pressure.
- Use plant oils for cooking and frying.
- Use butter or margarine sparingly, especially if you are predisposed to high blood pressure or high cholesterol.
- Cut out saturated fats, but eat plenty of fruits, vegetables and whole grains.

LOW BLOOD PRESSURE

Fatigue and exhaustion, feeling faint or even actually fainting, especially just after getting up from a lying or sitting position, are typical symptoms of extremely low blood pressure. Make sure you get your blood pressure checked regularly by your doctor or at a pharmacy.

HOME remedies

- Drink more. Dehydration reduces blood volume, which can lower blood pressure.
- Drink black tea; it's a stimulant. But don't let it steep for longer than 3–5 minutes.

- Have a shot glass of rosemary wine with a meal at midday and in the evening to help boost blood circulation. To make it, pour about 3 cups (750 ml) white wine over a heaping tablespoon (20 g) fresh rosemary leaves. Strain and bottle after 5 days.
- Indulge a sweet tooth with licorice. Eat one small piece a day, no more than 1 tablespoon (15 g). The active ingredient in it, glycyrrhizin, can have undesirable side effects if consumed in large quantities.
- Soak 30 raisins in water overnight, they may help to regulate blood pressure. Eat the raisins in the morning and drink the water.
- Alternate hot and cold water during your morning shower. This practice has long been a tradition in some parts of Europe. It forces blood vessels to contract then expand, and helps blood pressure to return to normal. Begin with warm water. Then after 2 minutes, turn the temperature to cold for 15 seconds. Repeat the procedure three times, ending with cold water.
- Get moving. Physical activity increases blood pressure, so try a regime of light exercise such as walking, swimming or exercise program from your doctor.

Brush massage

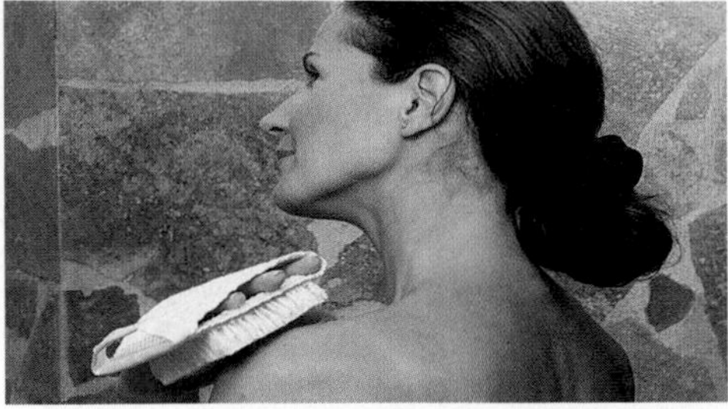

1. Massage may help those with high blood pressure to cope with stress. Start with a natural-bristle brush on the back of your right foot and brush your right leg up to the buttock using a circular motion, first on the outside, then the inside. Repeat on the left leg.

2. Brush your buttocks, upper body and arms, again using a circular motion.

3. Finally, ask your partner to massage your back using the same technique.

Breath problems

Halitosis is unpleasant. Luckily, much can be done to prevent it. If you've failed the breath test and people back away when you stop to chat, rely on these remedies from the herb garden to freshen your breath quickly.

You can't usually tell if you have bad breath and people are often reluctant to point it out. An easy test is to hold cupped hands in front of your mouth, exhale into them, then move your hands quickly to your nose to check the exhaled breath.

HOME remedies

- Use mouthwash regularly after brushing your teeth. Add two drops of chamomile, peppermint, clary sage or lemon balm oil to a glass of water and rinse your mouth with it, but avoid swallowing it.
- For morning breath, rinse your mouth with cider vinegar—1 teaspoon (5 ml) in a glass of water—as soon as you get up.
- For persistent bad breath, chew fresh parsley or mint leaves—both will freshen breath in an instant.
- Mix together dill, anise and fennel seeds and chew a few of them occasionally.
- If stomach problems are what are causing your bad breath, you could try this old and trusted home remedy: Chew on a coffee bean, which will neutralize the acid smell. But be sure not to swallow it.
- Both apples and yogurt taste good, freshen your breath and are a healthy snack.
- When you're on the go, suck on a peppermint or eucalyptus candy.

Gargle regularly with lemon water to avoid developing bad breath or a dry mouth.

Anise mouthwash

one Bring 2 tablespoons (30 ml) anise seeds to a boil in about # cup (100 ml) water and let cool.

two Strain the mixture through a coffee filter and squeeze out the seeds.

three Mix the strained liquid with about # cup (50 ml) vodka and about # cup (50 ml) rosewater and pour the solution into a dark bottle.

four After brushing your teeth, add a dash of the anise mouthwash to a glass of water and rinse your mouth thoroughly.

PREVENTION

If digestive disorders or gum disease are the cause of your halitosis, a visit to the doctor or dentist should provide a solution. Otherwise, brush regularly, and clean the spaces between your teeth with dental floss.

- Avoid smoking—a prime cause of halitosis.
- If you drink a lot of coffee (which can also cause bad breath), rinse your mouth frequently.
- Eat and drink on a regularly —halitosis often occurs when your stomach is empty.
- People who eat yogurt regularly are less prone to halitosis than people who don't.

Burns and scalds

Burns are the result of direct contact with a hot object, while scalds are produced by hot fluids or steam. Both damage the skin's tissues, causing blisters or charred skin, and should be treated the same way.

There are major distinctions between first-, second- and third-degree burns. Only first-degree burns and scalds should be treated at home. For more serious burns, see a doctor immediately. First-degree burns are characterized by reddened, painful skin but can be treated effectively with natural remedies (assuming you don't have an open wound).

WHEN TO CONSULT A DOCTOR More serious burns (blisters start forming with second-degree burns), large or deep burns and all chemical and electrical burns require medical attention. People who may be at greater risk from the effects of burns—such as children, pregnant women or anyone over age 60—should also see a healthcare professional immediately. Second- and third-degree burns that cause blistering and tissue damage are serious, with a high risk of infection caused by germs entering the body through the damaged skin.

HOME remedies

- To cool skin, reduce the pain and clean the wound, hold the affected part under cold running water (not ice water) for at least 30 minutes.
- Apply calendula salve to the burn if the skin is unbroken. It soothes and can help damaged skin to heal more quickly.
- Take vitamin C to build and maintain new skin.
- Squeeze a few drops of the juice from a cut piece of an aloe vera plant on the burn. It will help soothe it and prevent infection.
- Apply fresh sauerkraut, a traditional German burn remedy rich in vitamin C, directly to the burn.
- For healing without scars, pour 6 cups (1.5 L) water over 1 tablespoon (15 ml) flaxseeds. Boil until scum forms on the surface, strain and let cool. Soak a linen cloth in the liquid, wring out and apply.

CABBAGE poultice

Check the burn with a healthcare professional before trying this traditional remedy.

1 Rinse white cabbage leaves and remove the central vein.
2 Roll the leaves with a rolling pin until soft.
3 Place them on burned skin and secure with a gauze bandage. Change the bandage after several hours and replace twice a day.

GOOD TO KNOW

An outdated recommendation

You can't heed every home remedy from your grandmother's time—some of them can actually be harmful. For example, never treat burns or scalds with butter, which can be a breeding ground for bacteria. Also, under no circumstances should you pierce or burst blisters, as there's a danger of infection.

Colds

Blocked noses, sore throats, aching limbs and fever are symptoms we have to contend with each winter, with antibiotics powerless to help us fight off the season's viral invaders. However, most colds can be treated effectively with traditional home remedies.

In the past, people often used the terms cold and flu interchangeably. Today, doctors distinguish between the two. If symptoms come on gradually and include a sore throat, headache, achy limbs, coughing, a runny nose, elevated temperature or slight fever, you probably have a cold. By contrast, flu comes on fast and hits hard, accompanied by a high fever and chills—you will feel too ill to get up. But drink plenty of fluids to flush out your system and prevent dehydration.

Chicken soup

1 chicken
1 large onion, quartered
Salt and pepper to taste
3 carrots
3 celery stalks
1 kohlrabi (if available) *or*
1 medium-sized cabbage
1 bunch of parsley

Simmer the chicken, onion, salt and pepper in 2 quarts (2 L) water for 1 hour. Add the chopped vegetables and cook for 1 hour more. Remove the chicken from the pot, debone and cut into pieces. Pour the soup through a strainer before returning the chicken to the pot. Stir in the parsley and serve.

TO reduce fever

Fever is the body's response to illness and actually serves to fight infection. But a temperature higher than 103°F (39.5°C) will make you miserable. While the local pharmacy offers a wide range of often expensive relief, you may find the following traditional remedies equally effective.

- Drink plenty of fluids. Good choices include: fruit juices rich in vitamin C and antioxidants, such as orange, black currant and cranberry; noncarbonated mineral water with a dash of fruit juice; or herbal or fruit teas, especially vitamin C-rich rosehip tea. Another classic: Mix the juice of a lemon with 1 teaspoon (5 ml) honey in 1 cup (250 ml) hot water.
- Lime flower and elderflower teas, which are often referred to in traditional medicine as "fever teas," can assist in bringing on sweating—the body's natural way of cooling itself—to help reduce a fever. To get the maximum benefit, sip a few cups, then have a hot bath before snuggling up under a pile of blankets. When you begin to sweat, wait 2 hours and dry off. Change your clothes and, if necessary, the bedclothes. Drink some fluids and return to bed.

TO relieve aches and pains

Traditional wisdom has it that a hot water bottle can relieve pain, promote circulation and help you feel relaxed. Scientists have discovered why: Heat can physically shut down the normal pain response that triggers aches and pains. "It deactivates the pain at a molecular level in much the same way as pharmaceutical painkillers," says one senior researcher in physiology.

But heat brings only temporary relief, so frequent applications may be necessary.

• Evidence dating back to 4500 BC reveals that the ancients favored warm compresses of peat, mud and fuller's earth. Today, we have the luxury of a hot bath or a heating pad to ease pain.

• Apply a mustard plaster, a traditional congestion remedy. Crush 1–2 tablespoons (15–30 ml) mustard seeds (or mustard powder), add the powder to 7 tablespoons (100 g) flour; add water to form a paste. Apply to the chest and leave on for 15 minutes.

TREATING a head cold

Few things will make you as miserable as a head cold, and nothing soothes the misery better than a helping of chicken soup. US researchers from the Nebraska Medical Center recently found that chicken soup contains "a number of substances with beneficial medicinal activity," including an anti-inflammatory mechanism that may ease upper respiratory tract infections. For a healing chicken soup recipe that has stood the test of time, see the box on page 19. Here are some other home remedies.

• In the past, people sometimes placed hot or warm moist compresses with fuller's earth (clay), mashed potato or flaxseeds on the sinuses—an effective and economical remedy. If you have an infrared lamp, direct it onto your sinuses. Or simply warm a wet cloth in the microwave (don't make it too hot) and drape it across your face for 10 minutes at a time.

• To relieve nasal congestion, pour boiling water into a bowl, cover your head and the bowl with a towel, and inhale deeply. To make it even more effective, add 6 drops of eucalyptus or chamomile essential oil to the boiling water.

• Spice it up. Foods that contain chile peppers, hot mustard or horseradish can remedy congestion. If it makes your eyes water, it'll make your nose run.

• Try a nasal rinse. Irrigate your nose with a saltwater solution (from any pharmacy) to soothe stressed nasal mucous membranes.

• Make your own nasal rinse. Dissolve 1 teaspoon (5 ml) salt in 2 cups (500 ml) water. Use a nasal dropper or eye dropper to drip it into your nostrils, then blow your nose gently.

PREVENTION

As yet, there is no permanent cure for the common cold, but you can reduce susceptibility significantly by boosting your immune system.

• Get plenty of exercise in the fresh air and increase your intake of vitamin C—eat fruits and vegetables.

• Avoid stress, nicotine and alcohol.

• Eat lots of pungent onion, garlic, radish or horseradish, which have an antibacterial effect and cleanse the blood.

• Take echinacea (purple coneflower), a traditional remedy, available in tincture, tea or tablet form from pharmacies and health food stores. Recent studies support its ability to cut cold risk by as much as half.

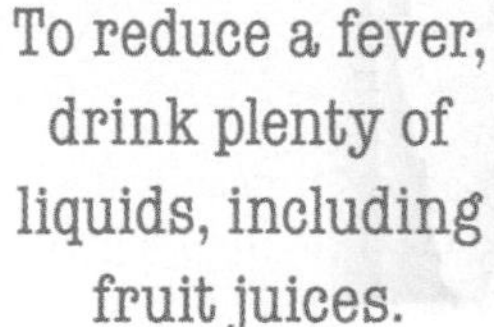

Constipation

Lack of exercise, not eating enough fiber or being overweight or underweight are just some of the causes of irregular bowel movements and hard, painful stools. However, harsh laxatives shouldn't be necessary to get things moving again.

HOME remedies

- Drink a glass of prune or elderberry juice, diluted apple cider vinegar or warm water with honey in the morning on an empty stomach.
- Alternatively, first thing each morning drink a large glass of warm water mixed with the juice of a lemon.
- Dissolve 1 teaspoon (5 ml) sea salt in 2 cups (500 ml) warm water and drink to soften stools.
- Before each meal take 1 teaspoon (5 ml) herbal bitters in water to improve general digestive function and stimulate the production of bile, the body's laxative.

Prunes and other dried fruit relieve constipation naturally.

- Try a tried-and-trusted German cure. For centuries, Germans have touted the curative effects of the pickled cabbage dish, sauerkraut. In fact, sauerkraut is rich in *Lactobacillus* bacteria, which help to soften stools and keep intestinal flora healthy.
- Give yourself a daily stomach massage with a cold washcloth (working in a clockwise direction) to stimulate a sluggish intestine.
- Slippery elm and psyllium are bulking laxatives, substances that have the capacity to swell in the bowel, making the stool softer and easier to pass. Add 1–2 teaspoons (5–10 ml) of either or both to your morning cereal or to a smoothie.

PREVENTION

- Consume only moderate amounts of fat and sugar, which slow the operation of the intestines.
- Make room in your daily diet for additional digestion-regulating fiber, such as wheat or oat bran and flaxseed. Sprinkle them on cereal.
- Combine a high-fiber diet with ample fluid intake.
- Avoid the tannins contained in dark chocolate, cocoa, black tea and red wine, as they disable digestive muscles. Stay away from these foods if you are prone to constipation.
- Exercise, such as a bike ride or a regular walk, is often all it takes to get a sluggish intestine going.
- Take a probiotic. Good bacteria keep things moving along nicely. Yogurt containing acidophilus may help or opt for a supplement.
- Relax and take your time. Being pressed for time on the toilet doesn't help.

Laxative tea

These herbs regulate digestion.

¼ cup (50 g) dried peppermint leaves
1 tablespoon (15 g) fennel seeds, ground
1 tablespoon (15 g) dried elderflowers
2 teaspoons (10 g) dried chamomile flowers

Mix the ingredients together and pour 1 cup (250 ml) boiling water over 1 teaspoon (5 ml) of the mixture. Let steep for 5 minutes, then strain. Drink a freshly prepared cup three times a day.

Diarrhea

Whether the cause of your discomfort is yesterday's lunch special or a viral infection, "Montezuma's revenge" can be most unpleasant. But it is also extremely effective at expelling whatever it is that ails you. Rather than trying to halt the condition immediately, it is now considered better to allow it to run its course. Start eating—plain food, little and often—when your appetite returns.

When diarrhea strikes, drink plenty of clear liquid (including rehydration fluids) to replace the lost water and the salts essential for retaining water in the body.

Thyme tea

This traditional remedy can ease the unpleasant stomach cramps that often accompany diarrhea.

½ teaspoon (2 ml) dried thyme
1 cup (250 ml) boiling water

Infuse the dried plant for 5 minutes and strain. Drink three cups a day.

FIRST aid

- Sip noncarbonated mineral water or black tea flavored with sugar and a pinch of salt.
- Buy a pack of special glucose–electrolyte mixtures from a pharmacy to offset salt loss. These solutions are especially important for children, pregnant women and older people for whom major fluid loss is particularly dangerous.
- Make your own electrolyte solution: Mix 2 cups (500 ml) noncarbonated mineral water with 7 teaspoons (35 ml) sugar, 1 teaspoon (5 ml) salt and 2 cups (500 ml) orange juice or fruit tea to provide potassium and flavoring. Drink throughout the day.
- Drink at least 1 cup (250 ml) of tea three times a day. Tea made from catnip or raspberry leaves contain tannins that have a soothing effect on the intestines.

WHEN TO CONSULT A DOCTOR Infants and small children with diarrhea should see a doctor right away. Adults should seek medical treatment if the diarrhea continues for more than 3 days.

HOME remedies

If diarrhea persists for a day or two, it's important to restore a healthy balance to the intestinal flora. There are plenty of long-standing home remedies available for this purpose.

- Slippery elm powder soothes the inflamed lining of the digestive tract. Take 1 teaspoon (5 ml) daily.
- Eat yogurt, which contains "good bacteria," to combat any harmful bacteria that may have caused diarrhea in the first place. Replacing them can help you feel better faster. Look for yogurt that contains live bacterial cultures or probiotics. It must be a product with billions of bacteria in it, as you will need this many to recolonize your intestines.
- Eating 1–2 teaspoons (5–10 ml) dried blueberries is a time-honored Swedish cure for diarrhea. The berries act as an astringent, contracting tissue, reducing inflammation in the intestine and ultimately slowing diarrhea.
- Dark chocolate contains a high percentage of cocoa and flavonoids that ease diarrhea.

Stick to low-fiber foods, such as toast, when recovering from an acute case of diarrhea.

• Apply a little heat. Heat calms the intestine and makes you feel better. A hot water bottle should do the trick.
• Boil two handfuls of fresh calendula flowers in water, strain, place the flowers into a cloth bag and put it on your stomach. Test it with a fingertip first to make sure that it's not too hot.
• Calm your nerves. Nervous diarrhea can be treated with aromatherapy massage. Mix 3–4 drops of chamomile, sandalwood, juniper or lavender oil with 2 teaspoons (10 ml) almond oil and massage your lower abdomen clockwise.

SLOWLY introduce a bland diet

When diarrhea subsides, gradually return to a normal diet. Start with low-fiber foods such as crackers, toast, rice, boiled potatoes and chicken. Doctors will often recommend a diet of bananas, rice, applesauce and toast, also known as the BRAT diet. These binding foods are suggested as the first to try after an episode of diarrhea. Applesauce contains pectin and other nutrients your body needs and because the apples are cooked, they are easier to digest. Bananas are easily digested and contain high levels of potassium, which helps to replace the electrolytes you lose when you have diarrhea.

• Next, treat yourself to a clear vegetable broth or a potato and carrot soup (*see below for the recipe*) and dry toast.
• Try some cooked carrots, which are also high in pectin—boil or roast and purée.
• Gradually broaden your menu with a little fat and easily digestible protein.
• Avoid milk and dairy products until symptoms stop. Some of the organisms that cause diarrhea can temporarily impair the ability to digest milk.
• During this time, avoid coffee and alcohol. Instead, treat yourself to a cup of peppermint tea, which can help to soothe the intestines.

Potato and carrot soup

This soup delivers fluid and minerals without further irritating the intestinal mucous membrane.

1 cup (250 ml) water
2 medium potatoes
1 carrot
1 pinch salt

Bring the water to the boil. Add the peeled and chopped vegetables. Cook over low heat until tender, then purée and season with the salt.

ESSENTIAL HOME MEDICINES

Next time you have an ache or pain, try some traditional cures before rushing to the pharmacy. A home medicine cabinet can be equipped relatively cheaply, and nature's simple remedies can treat a wide range of ailments.

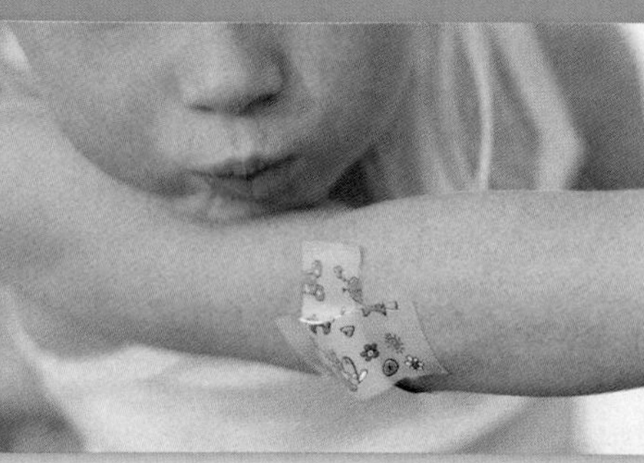

Medicine cabinet must-haves

The following belong in every well-prepared home pharmacy:

- Hot water bottle
- Thermometer
- Disposable gloves
- Tweezers, scissors
- Adhesive bandages in several sizes
- Sterile compresses
- Gauze bandages, elastic bandages
- Bandage clips, safety pins
- Triangular bandage
- Eye patch

Emergency numbers

Keep a list of the most important emergency numbers handy or on speed dial: emergency services (police, fire and ambulance), family doctor, nearest hospital with an emergency room and your local pharmacy.

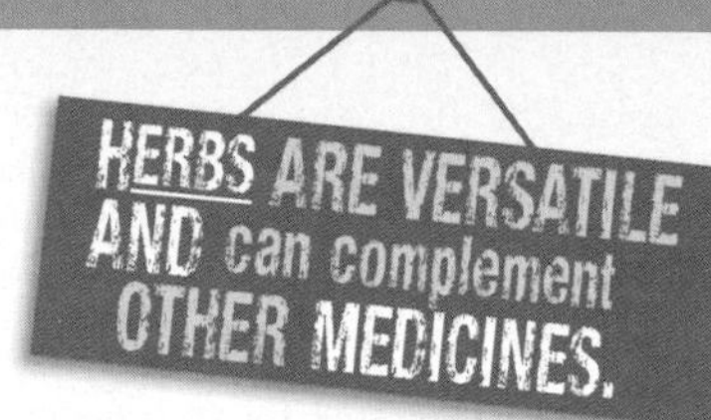

Recommended commercial preparations

For ailments that require quick intervention, have the following medications on hand:

- Antihistamines in case of allergic reactions
- Antiseptics for minor injuries
- Pills to control pain and fever
- Medications for constipation and diarrhea
- Gel for burns and cuts
- Hydrocortisone cream to soothe itchy insect bites

Scissors plus bandages in several sizes are essential.

At the pharmacy, always ask for less expensive generic medicines.

A soothing cup of herbal tea can help with a wide range of ailments, from fever to nausea.

Proper storage

Store your essential home medicines in a dry, dark, cool place in a lockable cabinet—preferably out of the reach of small children. Check the contents regularly to be sure that the expiration dates of the remedies have not passed and that there is enough on hand should you need them.

Natural remedies

When it comes to stocking a home medicine chest, add to your basic equipment with these natural solutions.

- Two essential oils have a place in every medicine cabinet: tea tree oil (healing of wounds) and eucalyptus oil (respiratory passages). Use 3–5 drops of each for wraps, as additives to bathwater or for inhaling. Essential oils are available from pharmacies or health food stores (*see also pages 62–63 for more about essential oils and safe use*).
- The most important tinctures come from calendula flowers and chamomile. Use them externally or internally. Chamomile soothes ailments such as stomachaches and colds. A rule of thumb: For internal applications, use 10 drops 3 times a day in water or juice; for external treatment of things such as skin injuries, dilute the tincture in a 1:4 ratio and use with compresses or add to bathwater (for example, chamomile for insomnia or stress). Tinctures can be pricey but you can make your own. Combine 1 tablespoon (15 g) herbs per 7 tablespoons (100 ml) rubbing alcohol and store in a dark, sealable glass bottles. Kept cool, they will last for about a year.
- Prepare teas from 1 teaspoon (5 g) dried flowers and leaves of various herbs (*see below*) and 1 cup (250 ml) hot water.

Herbal teas

Chamomile • Stomach and digestive ailments

Lime flowers • Feverish cold and illnesses, stomach and intestinal cramps, nervousness, headaches (particularly migraines), infections

Lemon balm • Sleep disturbances, queasy stomach and intestinal problems, nervousness

Peppermint • Nausea, vomiting, inflammation of the stomach lining, flatulence

Dandelion • Blood cleanser, liver tonic, constipation, digestion, fluid retention

Eye problems

Of our five senses, sight is the one people fear losing the most. So it's important that we take care of our eyes, especially as they are exposed to numerous environmental factors that can affect vision. Fortunately, traditional rinses and compresses will help with a range of problems, from simple eyestrain to a stye.

Eyes are buffeted by countless irritants, including wind, smoke, dust, sun and even bacteria and viruses, which can lead to eye strain or eye ailments. Here are some ways that you can protect them.

- Wear glasses to protect your eyes against direct sunlight, wind or dust.
- Reduce or avoid drafts and don't spend long periods in indoor areas with high humidity. Dampness and mold can cause eye irritation.
- Use an adjustable reading lamp with a wide emission angle for reading.
- Get plenty of sleep at night, and strengthen your body's defenses with relaxation, exercise and nutritious food.

Refreshing eye compresses

2 teaspoons (10 g) cornstarch
4 teaspoons (20 g) dried chamomile flowers
4 teaspoons (20 g) dried cornflower

Pour about 1¼ cups (300 ml) boiling water over the herbs and strain after 10 minutes. Apply gauze pads soaked in the cooled solution to tired, closed eyes.

WHEN TO CONSULT A DOCTOR When the layer between the eyelid and eyeball, the conjunctiva, becomes inflamed, the result is itchy, red and watery eyes. If the cause of the irritation is a viral or bacterial infection, the ailment is highly contagious, so it is important to consult a doctor or pharmacist immediately.

LONG HOURS AT the computer CAN CAUSE EYE STRAIN.

RELIEVING conjunctivitis

- You can help by keeping your eyes clean. Carefully remove the discharge caused by the inflammation several times a day with a cotton ball soaked in distilled water.

SOOTHE with compresses

After cleansing, soothe inflamed eyes with eyebright (*Euphrasia*) compresses. Check with your healthcare professional first.

1 Pour 1 cup (250 ml) boiling water over 1 teaspoon (5 ml) dried eyebright flowers.
2 Let the mixture steep for 2 minutes before straining the liquid.
3 When the liquid is just lukewarm, soak two sterile gauze pads in it and apply them to your eyes for several minutes.

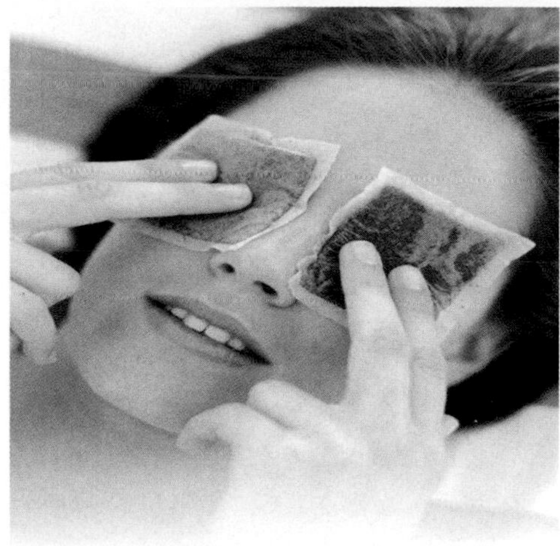

Wring out black or green tea bags and cool them in the refrigerator. They work wonders for swollen eyelids.

RED eyes

Windburn or barbecuing can leave you with red, burning eyes. But don't rub irritated eyes—you might make them worse.

- Apply cucumber slices. They not only help with swollen eyelids, but also with reddened eyes.

SWOLLEN eyelids

Since swelling results from a buildup of tissue fluid in the eyelid, anything cold can help soothe the inflammation by contracting the blood vessels and stimulating circulation.

- Spoon a little cold, plain yogurt on a cloth to make a poultice and place it over closed eyes for 15 minutes. Try not to get any in your eyes.
- Apply slices of cold cucumber to your eyelids for 10 minutes.
- Apply a cold pack to swollen eyelids. Crushed ice in a cloth works just as well, as does a metal spoon cooled in the refrigerator (not in the freezer) and laid carefully on your eyelids.

TIRED, strained eyes

Long hours at the computer, poor lighting, lack of sleep—all of these things can result in eye strain, the symptoms of which include burning, itching and watery eyes.

- For relief, rub your hands together until they are warm and place them gently over closed eyes.
- Make sure that you blink frequently—this should happen unconsciously about 13 times a minute but people tend to blink less when using a computer. Blinking spreads a tear film over the eyes that clears away dust and dirt particles. It also keeps eyes moist.
- Try this natural remedy: Dampen a clean cloth with freshly boiled, warm water. Place the cloth over your eyes and leave for 15 minutes.

STYE

The most common cause of that angry-looking pustule on the edge of your eyelid is bacteria. You should never squeeze a stye, as you risk causing a severe infection. However, with a little help from heat and a compress you may be able to bring it to a head so that the pustule opens on its own.

- Use infrared light to hasten the ripening of a stye.
- Dampen a clean cloth with freshly boiled warm water. Leave the cloth over your eye for 15 minutes. Throw the cloth away after using.

DRY eyes

As people get older, their eyes tend to produce less moisturizing tear fluid and even the fluid itself is less rich in oils so they can't lubricate the eye as well. Eyes may feel itchy and gritty at times.

- One over-the-counter solution is artificial tears but your eyes will also benefit from a healthy diet that contains walnuts, oily fish and other sources of omega-3 fats.
- If you suffer from dry eyes, it is also best to avoid smoky atmospheres, air conditioned rooms and too much sunlight or wind. Blink frequently and take regular breaks from close-up work such as reading, sewing or working at a computer.

Fatigue

It is normal to feel tired after a long, strenuous day at work. But if exhaustion is a constant companion, sapping your energy and your zest for life, it's time to do something about it.

Many people don't feel fully awake in the morning until they've had their first coffee. Unfortunately, coffee has only a short-term effect. Instead, rediscover some traditional techniques to get you moving. Open the window wide and breathe in the fresh air. Get your circulation going with a couple of deep knee bends and move your arms in a circle. Follow this up with a healthy breakfast. If you are still not feeling energized, here are a few other things you can try.

Cold arm shower

one Direct a cold stream of water along the outside of your arm, moving slowly from the fingers of your right hand up to the shoulder.

two Go back down with the water, this time on the inside of your arm.

three Do the same with the left arm.

HOME remedies

- Alternate hot and cold water in your morning shower. A cold arm shower (*see box, right*) will give you a kick start, especially if low blood pressure is causing your fatigue. If you're in a hurry, take a cold arm bath for a few seconds: Just dip your arms up to the elbows in a sink filled with cold water.
- Need a siesta after a big meal? Eat more frequent, smaller meals. High blood sugar levels can switch off the brain cells that keep you alert, making you feel sluggish after a big meal.
- If fatigue is a result of stress, get moving and take a walk. Exercise releases "feel-good" endorphins, leaving you revitalized and more positive.
- Drink 2–3 cups (500–750 ml) of stimulating nettle leaf or ginger root tea a day.
- As the Chinese will tell you, ginseng tea can reduce feelings of stress and anxiety and combat fatigue. Pour 1 cup (250 ml) boiling water over 1½ teaspoons (7 ml) finely chopped dried ginseng. Steep for 10 minutes then strain. Drink 2 cups (500 ml) a day.
- Go herbal. For thousands of years, rosemary has been treasured for both its aroma and its medicinal effects. It is thought to help blood circulation and improve memory and concentration. When added to a cool, brief bath, rosemary can provide an effective remedy for fatigue and exhaustion. Or try 5 drops peppermint or juniper essential oil in your bath.

Open the window wide and breathe in some fresh air.

GOOD TO KNOW

Take a power nap

In addition to a good night's sleep, a power nap may be just the thing you need to stay sharp throughout the day. Recent research found that sleeping for 30 minutes to an hour during the day can boost your brain power and increase your ability to learn new facts and skills. The theory is that having a nap during the day allows your brain to file away memories and new information. Aim to take your nap about 8 hours after getting up in the morning so that it doesn't disrupt your nighttime sleep.

DRINK an energy potion

A trusted home remedy is molasses mixed with apple cider vinegar.

1 In a cup, stir together 2 teaspoons (10 ml) molasses and 4 teaspoons (20 ml) apple cider vinegar.

2 Fill the cup with honey and mix.

3 Take 2 teaspoons (10 ml) when you get up, before bed, and 1 teaspoon (5 ml) before lunch and dinner.

NUTRITION to combat fatigue

- Increase your iron levels. If your diet is low in iron, blood cells aren't able to carry their usual load of oxygen around the body and your energy level plummets. Eat iron-rich foods such as red meat, liver, whole grains and green, leafy vegetables.
- Iodine deficiency can also cause chronic fatigue. You can counter it by eating oily fish and sprinkling food with iodized table salt.
- Buy whole-grain products. Whole grains break down slowly in the body, releasing sugars into the bloodstream evenly. This means your body gets a constant energy supply and blood glucose levels won't fluctuate dramatically, causing fatigue.
- Fresh vegetables, plus milk and milk products, contain a wide spectrum of vitamins and minerals crucial to well-being. They can boost the body's performance capacity, so include them in your diet.
- Enjoy a tasty, healthy vitamin and mineral boost. Spread a slice of whole-grain bread with cream cheese and add avocado, alfalfa sprouts and chives.
- Avoid coffee, tea, cola and any other caffeinated drinks. They are often promoted as pick-me-ups, but the boost doesn't last long and frequently has a boomerang effect.
- Avoid sweets such as chocolate and candy. They contain "simple sugars" that quickly elevate blood sugar levels and performance capability—but this high is followed just as quickly by a crash, sending you into an energy slump.
- Snack better. Instead of sweets or fast food, have a yogurt cup or a piece of fresh fruit.

WHEN TO CONSULT A DOCTOR If fatigue persists, see a doctor. A blood test can determine if you are suffering from a condition such as anemia (low iron levels) or hypothyroidism (low thyroid levels) that can cause extreme tiredness.

Flatulence

Everyone has it, but gas can cause bloating and discomfort, and passing it in public is embarrassing. Diet, lack of exercise and stress can all contribute to these unpleasant feelings of abdominal pressure.

If it's any consolation, Hippocrates—the father of medicine—proclaimed that passing gas "is necessary to well-being." But even the ancients sometimes turned to nature to restore the health of their intestines and eliminate gas. A distressed intestine needs soothing. When the stomach is distended, it's wise to consume less and try one of the following natural ways to reduce flatulence, using medicinal plants or heat applied to the abdomen.

GOOD TO KNOW

Gas in babies and small children

Tiny clenched fists, a scrunched up face and an earth-shattering wail are the telltale signs that a baby has colic. Fortunately, there are some gentle, time-honored remedies that may help. Even babies can benefit from the digestive properties of fennel tea. Mix 1 teaspoon (5 ml) of the tea into formula for bottle-fed babies. For breast-fed infants, use an eyedropper to administer the tea three times a day. Alternatively, place a warm hot water bottle on the child's stomach or gently massage his or her tummy in a circular motion to provide a little relief.

HOME remedies

- Mix together 1 tablespoon (15 g) each caraway, fennel and anise seeds. Pour 1 cup (250 ml) boiling water over 2 teaspoons (10 ml) of the mixture. Steep for 10 minutes, strain and drink unsweetened.
- Finely grind caraway and coriander seeds; take ½ teaspoon (2 ml) with water before every meal.
- Use licorice root to help with bloating: Steep 1 tablespoon (15 ml) licorice root from a health food store in 1 cup (250 ml) chamomile tea. Drink a cup a day.
- Let heat soothe the discomfort. Heat a wheat pack to about 104°F (40°C) in the oven or microwave, and place it on your tummy.

NUTRITION

Flatulence can be aggravated by certain foods that are difficult to digest, while the problem can be aided by others. Also, people will react differently to certain foods so there are no hard and fast rules, but here are some things to try.

- Season food with spices that aid digestion, such as caraway seeds, anise, marjoram and ginger—they can reduce flatulence and bloating.
- Eat slowly and chew thoroughly—swallowing air is a major cause of gas.
- Avoid gassy foods such as carbonated drinks and beans.
- Cook legumes, leeks and cabbage thoroughly so that they will be easier to digest.
- If you suffer from lactose intolerance or have difficulty digesting other foods, this could trigger a gas attack. Avoid the foods in question.
- Avoid sweets, diet products and chewing gum sweetened with sorbitol, xylitol or mannitol. They are difficult to digest.

Use a mortar and pestle to prepare stomach-friendly spice mixtures.

Gallstones

Your gallbladder acts as a kind of storage tank for bile—a substance the body needs to break down fatty food into digestible bits. But when there is too much cholesterol present, gallstones begin to form in tiny, hard globules that can grow to the size of an egg. A diet packed with rich, high-fat foods is a big contributor, as are alcohol and nicotine.

Bile fluid contains high levels of cholesterol and the pigment bilirubin, both of which precipitate as crystals and form stones. These may be as fine as beach sand or as coarse as gravel. Gallstones can develop in both sexes but are most common in overweight, middle-aged women.

HOME remedies

When your gallbladder goes on strike, it is a signal that your liver needs strengthening and the flow of bile must be restored.

- The herb boldo (*Peumus boldo*) is a valuable remedy for gallstones. Ask a qualified herbalist to make up a tincture for you and take as directed.
- Eating bowls of boiled dandelions to counteract the effects of fatty meat is one ancient remedy for gallstones. Today, dandelion tablets or capsules can be bought at a health food store. Alternatively, drink several cups of dandelion tea daily. Add 1 teaspoon (15 ml) of the leaves to 2 cups (500 ml) water, boil and strain.
- Chew several caraway seeds every day or use them to flavor foods and aid digestion.
- Heat can ease the pain of a gallbladder attack. Apply a small, warmed wheat bag to the liver area. Cover with a cloth and top with a blanket.
- Turmeric tea can help keep a gallbladder in good health. Pour 1 cup (250 ml) boiling water over ½ teaspoon (2 ml) powdered turmeric, let steep for 5 minutes, strain and drink. Try to drink 2–3 cups (500–750 ml) a day.
- Avoid fatty processed and fast foods. These generally contain plenty of "bad" saturated and trans fats (hydrogenated fat) that can lead to gallstones. If in doubt, read the ingredients label.

WHEN TO CONSULT A DOCTOR Frequent, severe distension, a feeling of fullness in the upper abdomen and pain in the liver area are early warning signs of gallbladder ailments. Gallstones can form with time, interfering with bile flow and causing a great deal of pain. Get yourself to the doctor early and have the problem treated as quickly as possible.

Dandelion tea helps to counteract the effects of eating fatty meat.

Hair loss

Hormones or genes can be responsible for hair loss in both women and men. This can be difficult to combat. But to keep your hair in a generally healthy condition, there is no need to turn to expensive "wonder cures." Nature offers an array of effective remedies and applications that are much easier on your wallet.

Many hair problems respond well to home remedies. Hair loss that is not genetic could be a result of poor nutrition, ongoing stress, illness or incorrect or harsh treatment. In some cases, it may also be a side effect of medication.

HOME remedies

Anything that stimulates circulation to the scalp will aid hair growth and help you to avoid hair loss.

- Rub your head with an onion. It may sound quirky, but rubbing your scalp for 10 minutes with the surface of a freshly cut onion is a tried-and-true home remedy. The odorous vegetable contains plenty of sulfur that aids the formation of collagen, a substance that makes hair fuller and stronger. Follow up by washing your hair.
- To guard against hair loss, try a tonic consisting of about ¼ cup (50 g) each fresh nasturtiums and thyme plus 1 quart (1 L) vodka. Let the ingredients steep in a closed container for 10 days before straining. Massage the tonic vigorously into your scalp twice a day.
- Another traditional hair loss tonic mixes 1 cup (200 g) dried nettle leaves, 2 cups (500 ml) white wine vinegar and 1 quart (1 L) water. Boil the ingredients together for 30 minutes and strain the liquid. Once it has cooled, pour it into a bottle. Use the tonic three times a week.
- Massage a few drops of pure rosemary oil into your scalp to stimulate hair growth.
- Try alternating hot and cold water while shampooing every morning and evening. Always end with cold water, then carefully towel the scalp dry.

THE SULFUR in nasturtiums HELPS TO FORTIFY HAIR.

PREVENTION

- To encourage blood circulation to your hair roots, massage your scalp with your fingertips for 5 minutes three times a day.
- Avoid overstyling. Washing with very hot water, extensive blow drying, curling irons and curlers can damage hair. Avoid perms and hair dyes, too.
- An unhealthy diet can contribute to hair loss. Avoid saturated fats and opt for foods high in hair-friendly vitamins and minerals, such as iron, zinc, protein and B vitamins.

Hay fever

Springtime is greeted with mixed emotions by people with pollen allergies. The reawakening of nature is heralded by sneezing fits, red and watery eyes and, in severe cases, allergic asthma. The good news: There are many time-tested home remedies that offer relief.

Allergy symptoms are signs that your immune system is on the rampage, reacting to normally harmless substances such as pollen from grasses or plants. Here's how to wage war on the microscopic menaces that send your immune system into overdrive.

HOME remedies

- Black cumin, used for centuries to promote health and fight disease, can help to support an overly sensitive immune system. Make an herbal tea by steeping 1 tablespoon (15 g) crushed seeds in 1 cup (250 ml) boiling water for 10 minutes. Drink 4 cups (1 L) a day for 3 months.
- Watch what you eat. Nutrition plays an important role, especially in the lead-up to hay fever season. Vitamin C (fresh fruit, salad greens and vegetables) and magnesium (nuts, milk and grain products) strengthen your immune system. It may also help if you eliminate meat from your diet.
- A nasal rinse with table salt may help clear a congested nose and remove trapped irritants. Dissolve 1 teaspoon (5 ml) salt in 1 cup (250 ml) of warm water. Put the salt solution into a container with a long, thin spout or a shallow bowl. Lean over the sink and sniff the liquid up into one nostril at a time, allowing it to drain out through your nose or your mouth. Nasal rinses are best used before going to bed.
- Cider vinegar is a proven treatment for hay fever. Put 1 teaspoon (5 ml) cider vinegar in ½ cup (125 ml) water and sip the mixture slowly, preferably in the morning.
- Apply a moist cloth to itching eyes for fast relief. Use cold or warm water, whichever feels better, but make sure it has been freshly boiled and cooled.

BEHAVIOR tips

The following tips will keep your exposure to allergy-causing pollen to a minimum.

- Keep windows closed during the day. That inviting breeze is bad news for an allergy sufferer, as it could potentially be carrying a load of pollen.
- Don't hang laundry outdoors to dry. Pollen clings to moist surfaces.
- Change your clothes as soon as possible after outdoor activity.
- The middle of the day is peak pollen time, so stay indoors.
- Vacuum rugs frequently. Opt for a vacuum cleaner with an allergy filter and mop the floors regularly.
- Avoid having flowering plants and cut flowers in the house—regrettably, they spread pollen, too.
- Wash your hair before going to bed to avoid getting pollen on the pillow.
- Take shelter inside before a thunderstorm and for up to 3 hours afterwards. Storms are preceded by high humidity that makes pollen grains swell, burst and release their irritating starch.
- Wear wraparound sunglasses to shield your face when you go out.

Headaches

Headaches are a symptom, not an illness in themselves. There are a number of possible causes and most of these can be treated without reaching for the painkillers. Resourceful home remedies can provide gentle, quick and lasting relief.

Stress, overexertion, sensitivity to weather, low blood sugar, colds, dental problems and psychological issues can all trigger a headache. Tension headaches involve a cramping of the neck and shoulder muscles, and respond well to acupressure treatments. Migraines, a specific type of headache, take the form of pulsating pain on one side of the head, often accompanied by sensitivity to light and noise, nausea, vision abnormalities and neurological problems. Possible triggers include alcohol, caffeine, cheese and the flavor enhancer monosodium glutamate (MSG), plus a lack of sleep, stress and hormonal influences.

HOME remedies

- Rest for a few minutes on the sofa and place some ice cubes wrapped in a cloth on your forehead.
- Rub a few drops of lemon balm, lavender, peppermint, or rosemary essential oil on your temples, forehead and neck (not suitable for people with neurodermatitis or children under two years).
- After removing the white inner skin, place the inside of a lemon peel on your temples for a few minutes.
- Sprinkle cooled, strained lime flower tea on a cotton cloth and place the cloth on your forehead like a headband.
- For a relaxing neck compress, wrap flaxseeds, chopped onions (warmed in a pan of hot water or microwave) or hot mashed potatoes in a cotton cloth and hold on your neck until the compress cools.
- Eat your greens. Studies suggest that migraine sufferers may have low blood levels of magnesium and could benefit from magnesium therapy. Dark-green, leafy vegetables, nuts and fruits are good sources of this mineral.
- Posture plays an important role in tension headaches, so pull those shoulders back and stand up straight.
- If a migraine strikes, head for a quiet, dark room for a little rest to help relieve the pain.
- Freshly boiled tea made from white willow bark contains salicin, a natural relative of the acetylsalicylic acid used in many common pain medications. To prepare the tea: Heat 1 teaspoon (5 ml) dried white willow bark in 1 cup (250 ml) cold water and boil briefly. Let steep for 5 minutes, strain and sip a cup at a time, several times a day.
- If a headache is caused by nasal or sinus congestion, perhaps from a cold or hay fever, try a little bathwater aromatherapy. Put some eucalyptus or peppermint oil in the hot bathwater for inhalation and relaxation.
- Caffeine makes pain medications 40 percent more efficient, so drinking small amounts may help hasten and increase relief, unless you are sensitive to it.

WHEN TO CONSULT A DOCTOR If unexplained headaches persist, make an appointment with a doctor as soon as possible.

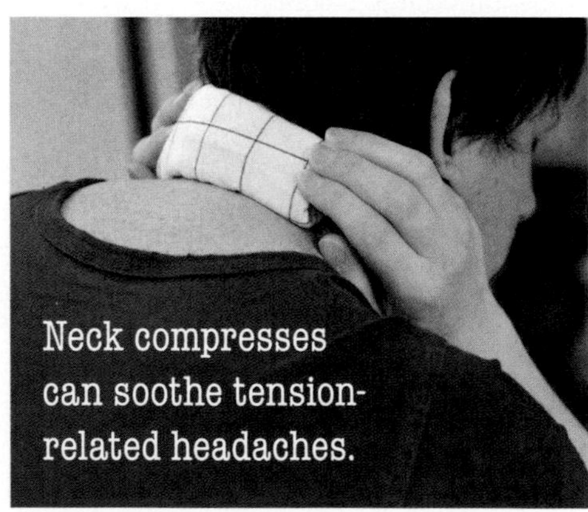
Neck compresses can soothe tension-related headaches.

PREVENTION

- If you take aspirin or ibuprofen frequently, stop. These drugs can cause "rebound headaches" that start when a dose of medication begins to wear off.
- Avoid any form of nicotine as it constricts blood vessels.
- Limit alcohol consumption. Its toxic metabolic products increase the risk of a headache.
- Red wine and chocolate can trigger headaches in those with sensitivities.
- Get enough sleep and rest.
- Exercise such as jogging, walking and swimming encourages circulation and reduces stress.
- Feverfew doesn't just prevent fever, it reduces the frequency and intensity of migraines in those who take it regularly. Used for thousands of years by healers around the world, the herb can be grown in your garden, in a balcony pot or picked up in supplement form from a pharmacy or health food store.

Espresso flavored with the juice from half a lemon can be a balm for headaches.

Acupressure

1 Use your index fingers to massage the depression just under the outer end of your eyebrows gently for 1 minute in a clockwise direction.

2 Massage the middle joint of the fourth finger on your right hand, on the side next to your little finger, for 1 minute in a clockwise direction.

Heart and circulation problems

The heart and circulatory systems are the body's lifeline, so it's essential they run smoothly. A healthy diet, regular exercise and a smoke-free environment are all vital. But look to nature, too, as there are many natural ways to stimulate circulation and fortify your heart.

Symptoms of circulatory disorders include tingling in the fingers or toes, pale skin and cold hands and feet. Don't ignore these signs. The first line of defense should be a visit to the doctor for a medical diagnosis and appropriate treatment. But cardiovascular disease is nothing new and the following traditional ideas may help. Just be sure to consult a doctor first before using a herbal remedy if you are taking prescription medicines.

HOME remedies

- Enjoy a gentle massage. Gentle, whole-body massages encourage circulation, particularly when a few drops of pine, eucalyptus or rosemary oil are added to the massage oil.
- To promote blood flow, sip tea made from equal parts of dried calendula flowers, daisies and chopped fresh ginger. Pour 1 cup (250 ml) boiling water over 1 teaspoon (5 ml) of the mixture. Strain after 5 minutes and drink slowly.
- Encourage blood flow to your skin by rubbing it forcefully in the shower with a massage brush or a coarse washcloth.
- A mustard bath will increase circulation, open pores and stimulate sweat glands. Mix 1 cup (200 g) mustard powder with 2 quarts (2 L) cold water. After a few minutes, strain the mustard water and pour it into a hot bath.
- Take contrasting footbaths to boost circulation, especially in your legs. Soak your feet in hot water 100–108°F (38–42°C) for 5 minutes, then in cold water 64–68°F (18–20°C) for 5 minutes. Repeat. Dry your feet thoroughly and rest for an hour. The procedure is particularly effective when practiced twice a week.
- Quite rightly, Chinese physicians have long recommended drinking green tea for health. Several clinical studies indicate the antioxidant-rich tea can reduce bad cholesterol and increase circulation.
- Health experts recommend 2,000 mg of blood pressure-lowering potassium per day. Good sources include bananas, oranges and apricots.
- Reduce salt intake. The more salt blood contains the higher blood volume will be because sodium attracts and retains water. Spice up home-cooked meals with herbs instead, and stay away from packaged food.
- Eat celery. The crunchy vegetable is effective for controlling circulatory problems. Four stalks a day should do it.
- Eat chocolate. Dark chocolate is not just good for the soul, it has a proven ability to lower blood pressure. Just ¼ ounce (6 g) of chocolate a day will do the trick—and the darker the better.

WEAK heart

The following suggestions are some of the many home remedies that were recommended for a weak heart in days gone by. To avoid any adverse effects, be

The sulfur in raw garlic helps to protect the heart. Cooked garlic is far less effective.

sure to speak to your doctor before you try any of these herbal cures—especially if you are taking other medication.

- Peppermint milk provides an economical drink that can help stimulate blood circulation. Pour boiling milk over some dried peppermint leaves and let it steep for 5 minutes. Strain and drink the milk in small sips.
- The hawthorn shrub has been a stalwart of both European and Chinese herbal medicine since ancient times. In the 1800s, it became particularly renowned as a heart tonic, and now some clinical trials support this claim. A qualified herbalist can make up a tincture for you, but it should be taken only under professional supervision.
- Sprinkle cinnamon on cereal and include it in cookie and cake recipes. Cinnamon may help to strengthen the cardiovascular system, shielding the heart from disorders. The spice also acts as a blood-thinning agent that increases circulation.
- Eat nuts. Nuts have many healthy effects on the heart. They help to lower the levels of LDL (low-density lipoprotein, or "bad" cholesterol) in the blood—high LDL is one of the primary causes of heart disease. In addition, nut consumption reduces the risk of developing blood clots that can cause a fatal heart attack and improves the health of the lining of the arteries.

Fortifying heart tea

1/4 cup (40 g) dried lime flowers
1/4 cup (30 g) dried lemon balm leaves
A good pinch of cayenne

Pour 1 cup (250 ml) of boiling water over 1 tablespoon (15 ml) of the herbal mixture. Wait 10 minutes, then strain. Drink a cup three times a day.

Menthol in peppermint and B vitamins in milk can help the heart.

NERVOUS heart ailments

Anxious people have about a 25 percent higher risk of developing coronary heart disease than their calmer counterparts, and are almost twice as likely as more relaxed people to die of a heart attack over about 10 years, according to researchers at Tilburg University in the Netherlands.

- Indulge in a daily cup of calming valerian tea, preferably in the evening: Pour 1 cup (250 ml) cold water over 2 teaspoons (10 ml) dried valerian root; let stand for a couple of hours, then strain. Warm the tea and sip slowly.
- Caraway or lemon balm tea soothes nervous heart ailments, and they are quick and easy to prepare from fresh ingredients or tea bags.
- Add essential oils (anise, lavender, peppermint, orange, rose) to bathwater or use in fragrant oil burners for a calming, relaxing effect.
- Get more rest. Lack of sleep has been linked to high blood pressure, heart attack, atherosclerosis and stroke. One theory is that poor sleep causes inflammation, infection, irritation or disease. That in turn revs up the sympathetic nervous system, which is activated by fright or stress.

WHEN TO CONSULT A DOCTOR If you feel exhausted at the slightest physical exertion, are constantly short of breath and retaining fluid in your legs, make an appointment to see your doctor.

Insect bites

Insects such as ticks, wasps and mosquitoes have plagued human beings for centuries. As a result, some highly effective home remedies have evolved to relieve the pain and swelling and to soothe that maddening itch.

Stings from bees, wasps and fire ants can be painful but are usually harmless. Some people have a more serious allergic reaction and emergency treatment is vital. While most spiders are harmless to humans, some species (black widow and brown recluse spiders) are highly venomous and require antivenom. In regions where mosquitoes are known to transmit diseases such as West Nile virus, take precautions to prevent bites. But usually mosquito bites are just a nuisance and together with other minor stings can be treated with home remedies.

HOME remedies

- If you are stung by a bee or wasp, remove the stinger, scraping it out with a fingernail or hard object. Do not remove it with tweezers, as this can squeeze more venom into the skin.
- To relieve the pain of bee, wasp and ant stings, soak a cloth in very cold water and wring it out, or use an ice pack covered with a damp cloth.
- Cleanse the area. Stinging insects may have undesirable bacteria in their venom. Wash the sting well with soap and water or use an antiseptic wipe.
- To prevent swelling, place fresh slices of onion (a natural anti-inflammatory) or lemon on the sting.
- Stir together 2 drops of peppermint essential oil and 1 teaspoon (5 ml) honey and spread generously on the site of the sting to prevent inflammation.
- Always remove ticks promptly, as in some areas prolonged bites can cause Lyme disease. After removing a tick (*see above right*), disinfect the site with a few drops of tea tree oil, iodine or alcohol.

GOOD TO KNOW

Tick bite

If you get bitten by a tick, it is crucial to remove it quickly, including the head. Grasp it with tweezers as close to the skin as possible and slowly pull it out. If the head remains buried, consult a doctor. Be particularly wary of a circular rash spreading around the site of the bite some days or weeks afterward or if you develop a fever of over 100°F (38°C)—this can be the first indication of Lyme disease, a very serious condition.

WHEN TO CONSULT A DOCTOR A sting on the mouth or throat carries a risk of suffocation and, for people with allergies, a sting anywhere can be life-threatening. In either case, go straight to hospital.

If bitten by a spider, seek medical advice right away (kill the spider or trap it in a jar and take it with you for identification).

If you develop a rash around the bite site or a high temperature within 3 weeks of a tick's removal, seek medical advice.

If you develop fever, joint pains and rash up to 3 weeks after a mosquito bite, see a doctor.

PREVENTION

- Don't swat bees or wasps.
- Use perfumes and hairsprays sparingly—they frequently attract insects.
- When mosquito bites are likely, wear light colors, pants and long sleeves to keep your skin covered.
- Sweat attracts insects. Change sweaty clothes quickly.
- Use a mosquito net when sleeping with open windows and without insect screens.
- Avoid walking through moist, bushy areas, as ticks may be present, especially if deer are in the area.
- Repel insects by adding 5 drops of citronella oil to 1 cup (250 ml) water and dabbing it on exposed skin.

Joint treatments

Rheumatism was once a catch-all term for any ailment involving the joints. Today, we distinguish between rheumatoid arthritis, osteoarthritis and gout, which have different causes but can all result in serious pain and reduced mobility. Thankfully, traditional remedies can be helpful.

Rheumatoid arthritis is an autoimmune disease that results in joint pain and deformity; osteoarthritis is a degenerative joint disease and gout is a metabolic disease that can result in joint damage. Try some of these home remedies to bring relief.

OSTEOARTHRITIS

- Apply fuller's earth poultices (*see page* 63) to the affected joints once a day to soothe discomfort.
- Rub in arnica oil to combat joint inflammation and pain.
- A mud bath no hotter than body temperature 98.6°F (37°C) also eases arthritic pain.
- Drink a cup of nettle tea three times a day to help with pain and inflammation. Use 1 tablespoon (15 ml) dried herb in 1 cup (250 ml) water and let steep for 10 minutes.
- Try borage oil capsules or salves containing arnica, comfrey or capsaicin (the active ingredient in chile peppers). Most health food stores or pharmacies can provide you with a range of compounds containing natural ingredients that will help to reduce inflammation.
- The roots of devil's claw (available as tablets or capsules) contain substances that soothe pain and inflammation. Originally from Africa, it has long been used around the world to treat painful joints.

RHEUMATOID arthritis

Whether you opt for a hot or cold treatment depends on the phase of the malady. If your joints are inflamed, hot and swollen, treat them with ice and cold packs made from mud, fuller's earth or clay (from a health food store or pharmacy). When the condition is less acute, turn to heat to soothe discomfort and promote circulation.

- Relax. When your body is tense, pain is more acute. Relaxation techniques may also ease pain.
- Teas made from dried meadowsweet or white willow bark can help to alleviate symptoms. Use 1–2 teaspoons (5–10 ml) per cup (250 ml) hot water.

Regular, gentle exercise helps to strengthen the joints.

Oil wrap for osteoarthritis

one Soak a cotton cloth in hot water and wring it out.

two Mix rosemary, marjoram and lavender oils in equal proportions, and put 10 drops of the mixture on the cloth.

three Wrap the hot oil pack around your afflicted joints for about 10 minutes once a day.

four Repeat the application several times as needed.

- A celery infusion can be a quick, effective remedy. Mince 1 heaping tablespoon (25 ml) celery and pour 1 cup (250 ml) water over it. Boil, steep briefly and strain. Sweeten with honey; drink 2 cups a day. **Note:** Always prepare the infusion fresh and do not use it if you have a kidney infection.

ARTHRITIS prevention

- Oily fish such as salmon, mackerel and sardines provide omega-3 fatty acids that ease swelling and pain. If you don't like fish, take fish oil supplements instead.
- Vitamin C has a positive influence on the course of the disease. It is abundant in citrus fruits, kiwi fruit and peppers.
- Vitamin E (abundant in plant oils) intercepts free radicals, which form in greater quantities with acute inflammatory joint diseases.
- Avoid coffee, alcohol and nicotine.
- Some studies indicate that a diet rich in fruit, vegetables, salads, whole grains and low-fat milk products can help ease the symptoms of rheumatoid arthritis. Reduce saturated fat intake by cutting down on meat, fatty cheese, butter and cream.
- Slim down. Being overweight can increase joint damage.
- Take up tai chi. When practiced correctly, it relaxes all joints.

GOUT

Gout is a metabolic disease. When the kidneys become less effective at flushing away excess uric acid, the acid begins to crystallize in your joints, tendons and muscles, leading to swelling, pain and tenderness. To guard against gout, eat oily fish twice a week, reduce the amount of meat you eat, and eat lentils, peas and red and white beans only in moderation. It is best to avoid alcohol and sweets entirely—both slow the body's ability to excrete uric acid considerably.

- Drink plenty of water or herbal tea to help kidneys flush out uric acid.
- Cherries have long been a folk remedy for gout. A recommended dose is a handful (about ten cherries) each day.
- Make a charcoal poultice by mixing 1 tablespoon (15 ml) activated charcoal (from pharmacies) with 3 tablespoons (45 ml) flaxseeds, ground to a powder in a blender, and enough hot water to make a paste. Apply the mixture to the affected joint and cover with plastic wrap.
- Try adding mud bath mixtures (available from pharmacies, health food stores or speciality stores) to body-temperature water to alleviate pain. Do this twice a week.
- Rub painful joints with camphor spirits (a solution of camphor and rubbing alcohol).

Muscle pain

Over-use, tension and injury are the common causes of muscle pain, and intense but infrequent physical exertion often wreaks its revenge the following day. But sore, stiff muscles respond well to a bit of traditional wisdom.

Aching muscles are unpleasant but usually harmless and tend to ease after a few days. In the meantime, heat applications are a good way to alleviate the pain. However, muscle cramps can also be due to other causes, such as circulatory disorders or a mineral deficiency. You should consult a doctor if cramps are particularly painful or if the pain persists.

SORE muscles

- If you develop sore muscles, take it easy for the first 12–48 hours. When sore, muscles don't have full function and continued strenuous demands carry a heightened risk of injury.

Warm up and rub muscles with diluted tea tree oil before intensive exercise.

- A hot bath can help you feel better. Add 5–10 drops of chamomile, lavender or eucalyptus essential oil for a soothing effect. The caveat: Avoid heat for 2–3 hours after a tough workout, as it will promote circulation and increase inflammation.
- A warm wrap with a few drops of arnica tincture can ease the pain.
- Massage can help ease sore, stiff muscles.
- Ample fluid intake flushes excess acids from the body and supplies it with important minerals. Opt for herbal teas and vegetable and fruit juices, diluted with mineral water containing little or no sodium.

MUSCLE cramps

- To relax a cramp in the calf, stretch the muscle carefully against the direction of the cramping, then walk back and forth. In stubborn cases, sit on the ground, pull your toes towards you and stretch your leg out fully. Then gently massage the muscle.
- Rubs containing extracts of menthol, camphor or horse chestnut can add extra power to a massage to loosen up cramps. So can essential oils of eucalyptus, spruce or thyme.
- A lack of minerals, such as magnesium, potassium and calcium, is probably the biggest cause of night leg cramps. These minerals are abundant in fennel, broccoli, bananas, dried fruits, oatmeal, nuts, milk, sweet potatoes and melon.
- Cider vinegar provides your body with potassium. Drink 2 teaspoons (10 ml) cider vinegar in 1 cup (250 ml) water every evening for at least 4 weeks.
- If cramps are the result of a magnesium deficiency, taking magnesium tablets is a good idea. Check with a doctor first, however.

Nausea

Tainted food, too much alcohol, a virus, motion sickness, pregnancy or even stress can all trigger nausea and vomiting. Try some of the following suggestions, which can help to alleviate these unpleasant symptoms.

Travel or motion sickness is especially common in children, whose balance mechanisms are much more sensitive than those of adults. A number of home remedies can effectively combat this and other types of nausea. However, as uncomfortable as it feels, a brief bout of vomiting can effectively rid your body of toxins. It is one of the body's most powerful defense mechanisms against harmful substances and, once it's over, nausea and stomach pain should disappear.

HOME remedies

- You can ward off rising nausea effectively by inhaling the aroma of a freshly cut apple. Breathe it in deeply.
- For sudden nausea, dot a few drops of peppermint essential oil on the back of your hand and inhale the aroma.
- In days gone by, people kept scent bottles handy for such a crisis. Today, we are more likely to reach for essential oils. Put 2 drops of lavender oil on a handkerchief and draw the scent into your lungs.
- To help calm your stomach, crush 1 teaspoon (5 ml) fennel seeds in a mortar.

Sucking on a freshly cut slice of lemon can help to nip rising nausea in the bud.

Put the crushed seeds in a pan and pour 1 cup (250 ml) water over them. Bring to a boil and let steep for 10 minutes before drinking.

FOR motion sickness

- This tea will help to prevent motion sickness. Prepare it in advance and take it with you on your trip in a small thermos bottle. Pour boiling water over one piece of cinnamon bark and let it steep for 10 minutes before straining.
- If nausea increases, it sometimes helps to chew slowly on a little piece of fresh ginger.

Chamomile wrap

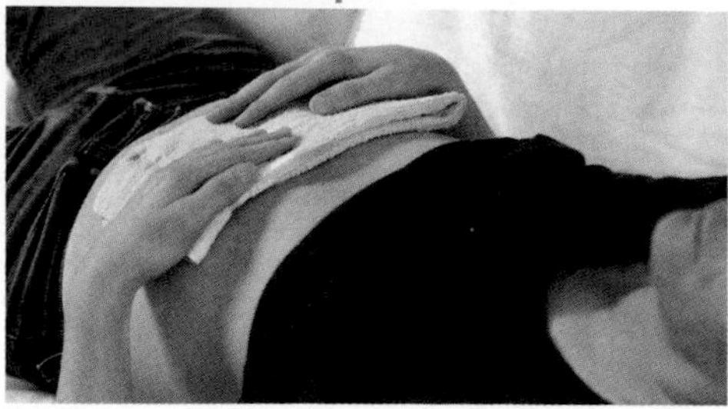

1. Fold a hand towel in two, dip it in warm chamomile tea and wring it out.
2. Place the towel over your stomach area, spread a dry towel over it and hold it in place with a wool scarf.
3. Let the wrap work for 10 minutes and replace it as needed.

Nervous problems

Overstimulation, conflict or a day packed with deadlines can jangle nerves and leave you feeling tense. The result can be anxiety, nervous tension and sleep disorders. When it comes to re-storing your calm, these traditional teas, bath additives and scent mixtures can help.

When you feel overloaded, a little self-indulgence can work wonders—a relaxing bath by candlelight perhaps, or a soothing massage. But if anxiety and nervous tension become overwhelming, you should seek professional advice.

HOME remedies

- Add a few drops of lemon balm and chamomile essential oils to the bathwater to stabilize emotional balance; or try lavender, bergamot, sandalwood or cedar.
- For a fragrant and relaxing herbal bath, boil about ½ cup (100 g) each chamomile, lime and lavender flowers in 2 quarts (2 L) water for 30 minutes. Strain and pour into hot bathwater.
- Sandalwood helps to reduce anxiety and nervous tension. Mix 3 drops of sandalwood oil with 1 teaspoon (5 ml) almond oil and gently massage your shoulders, neck, arms and legs. Better still, ask a partner or friend to do it for you.
- To calm your nerves and for a restful night's sleep, place a sachet of dried hop flowers under the pillow.
- Three drops each of peppermint, basil, sage and lavender oils are a calming mixture for a scent burner.

Breathing relaxation exercises

one Sit erect on a chair with your feet resting near each other on the floor. Let your arms hang down at your sides.

two As you breathe in through your nose, slowly spread your arms straight out to the sides then bring your palms together over your head. Then stand up energetically.

three Rotate your hands so they are back to back. Lower your arms straight to your sides. As you do so, slowly sit back down and expel the air through your mouth.

four Wait a couple of seconds, then repeat the entire exercise. Do the whole exercise a total of 10 times.

PREVENTION

- Relaxation techniques, such as autogenic training, yoga, progressive muscle relaxation and meditation exercises, have a balancing and calming effect.
- Be sure to get plenty of sleep and take rest breaks.
- Structure the day so there is some time for you.
- Take leisurely walks in the fresh air.
- Caffeine and refined sugars in alcohol can make symptoms worse, so avoid them.
- Fish oils (omega-3 fatty acids) may elevate mood and calm anxiety. As some fish can contain high levels of mercury, 2014 recommendations of the U.S. Food and Drug Administration and Environmental Protection Administration state that pregnant or breastfeeding women and young children avoid eating tilefish, swordfish, shark and king mackerel and limit white albacore tuna to 6 ounces (175 g) per week.

Respiratory disorders

Pollution, stress, smoking, smog and office buildings with poor ventilation can all adversely affect your respiratory system. The good news: Nature offers plenty of weapons to combat asthma, bronchitis and chronic coughs or to complement medical treatments.

The health of our lungs and respiratory system is affected by the quality of the air we breathe, and the effects of poor air quality can be far reaching. Thankfully, home remedies can help to alleviate the following conditions.

ASTHMA

Asthma is a serious condition, and without careful monitoring and ongoing treatment can rapidly become dangerous. The condition results in an increase in mucus production that narrows the airways in the lungs, causing a sudden feeling of breathlessness. Infections, allergies, stress, anxiety and stimuli such as dust, smoke and cold can all trigger life-threatening asthma attacks.

Asthma must be treated medically but, as scary as this condition can be, leading a healthy lifestyle can strengthen breathing passages and boost the body's natural defenses. If you do have an attack, anything that breaks up mucus and relaxes your bronchial muscles will help. The caveat: If you have allergies or your asthma is allergy-related, be particularly cautious about using animal or plant-based remedies. These substances can trigger immune reactions and should be used only with medical supervision.

- Try a mixture of honey and freshly grated horseradish in a 1:3 ratio. Take 1 tablespoon (15 ml) three times a day.
- To combat airway spasms and mucus, mix 2 teaspoons (10 ml) cider vinegar and 1 teaspoon (5 ml) honey in 1 cup (250 ml) water and drink three times a day for 3 months.
- A warm chest compress breaks up mucus: Soak a cotton cloth in water about 120°F (50°C), wring it out and lay it over your chest. Cover it with a dry cloth and rest in bed for 30 minutes.
- Excessively dry air irritates breathing passages. You can buy a humidifier, but bowls of water placed strategically around the house are a cheaper alternative. The water will evaporate into the air, providing moisture and some relief.

Thyme and lemon drink

Thyme can help to relieve coughing and make breathing easier.

1 tablespoon (15 g) dried thyme leaves
2 tablespoons (30 g) dried lemon balm leaves
1 quart (1 L) water

Place the herbs in a heatproof bowl. Boil the water and pour it over them. Let brew until cool and strain. Drink 1 cup (250 ml) three times a day.

BRONCHITIS

Bronchitis is an inflammation of the bronchi, the tubes leading from the throat to the lungs, usually as a result of infection or irritation. To encourage healing, drink plenty of fluids. Teas and other hot drinks can soothe irritated airways and liquefy mucus, making it easier to cough up. In addition to traditional herb, clary sage or chamomile teas, home remedies that make use of common ingredients such as onions and sugar can be remarkably effective, and steam inhalations may soothe a persistent cough.

- Grind 1 tablespoon (5 ml) aniseeds in a mortar and mix in a bowl with 1 tablespoon (15 ml) dried thyme. Pour 1 quart (1 L) water over the mixture. Let the tea steep for 5 minutes, strain, sweeten with honey and drink throughout the day.
- Peel and slice a large onion. Sprinkle the slices with a thick coating of brown sugar, layer them inside a glass jar, seal tightly and place in a warm spot overnight. Take 1 teaspoon (5 ml) of the mixture three times a day. Refrigerate the remainder.
- Chamomile soothes irritated respiratory passages. To inhale it, drop a handful of dried chamomile flowers into a bowl of boiling water, cover and let steep for 10 minutes before carefully inhaling the steam. As an alternative to chamomile flowers, add 1–2 drops of eucalyptus, thyme or cypress oil to the hot water before inhaling.

GOOD TO KNOW

A change of air

There are times when you really are "under the weather." A change of climate can have a positive impact on chronic respiratory ailments. The salt content of sea air, for example, can help dissolve tough mucus in your breathing passages. What's more, sea air is largely free from pollutants and allergens. The clean, clear air and sunlight of the mountains can also benefit tortured respiratory passages.

COUGH

Despite the huge sums spent on over-the-counter cough remedies every year, doctors say they are largely ineffective against a nagging cough. To relieve symptoms, gentle, soothing home remedies can work wonders. Teas made from licorice, thyme or marshmallow can relieve a dry cough, and hot baths and cough remedies made from medicinal plants may speed your recovery.

- For homemade cough syrup, combine ¼ cup (50 ml) lemon juice with 1 cup (250 ml) of honey in ¼ cup (50 ml) warm water. Take 1–2 tablespoons (15–30 ml) every 3 hours.

Note: Honey should not be given to children under 2 years of age.

- For adults, warm beer can ease a dry cough and send you off to sleep. Before going to bed, warm about 2 cups (500 ml) beer with 3 tablespoons (45 ml) honey but don't let it boil. Sip slowly.
- Three drops of eucalyptus oil and a bit of water in an oil burner can soothe troubled breathing passages.

Drinking 2–5 cups (500–1,250 ml) fennel tea a day will have a soothing effect on respiratory ailments.

Shingles

About one-third of the U.S. population will develop shingles and the risk increases with age, starting at around age 50. The infection causes a burning, blistering rash and mild to severe pain that can last for several weeks.

Many people had chickenpox in childhood. After the illness has gone, the virus remains dormant in the nervous system. But if the immune system is compromised by age, disease or stress, the virus can be reactivated many years later and cause shingles. This affects the nerves and the area of skin around them. You will need medical care to deal with the condition, but lots of rest and natural remedies can help to speed the healing process.

HOME remedies

- Try various essential oils to alleviate pain. Mix 2 drops each bergamot and eucalyptus oils and 2 tablespoons (30 ml) almond oil. Use a cotton ball to dab the mixture on the blisters.
- A fuller's earth (*see page 63*) poultice can also alleviate pain and dry up blisters.

Healing herbal wrap

1 cup (200 g) finely ground oats
4 teaspoons (20 g) dried chamomile
4 teaspoons (20 g) dried calendula
2 heaping tablespoons (35 g) dried lavender
1 quart (1 L) cold water

Pour the water over the ingredients and bring to a boil. Steep for 5 minutes; strain.
Dab the warm liquid on the affected skin with a cotton ball or soak a cloth in it and cover the area.

Used in an herbal wrap, chamomile can be a useful ally.

Stir the fuller's earth with a little water to form a thick paste, spread it finger-thick on a cloth, cover with gauze and apply, cloth-side down, to the rash. Replace the pack as soon as it warms up. Apply twice daily.

- Apply washcloths soaked in soothing chamomile or yarrow tea to the rash.
- Blisters heal more quickly when they are sprinkled with a little diluted homemade tincture of calendula—one part tincture to four parts water.

PREVENTION

- Strengthen your body's defenses to make sure viruses don't have a chance. Regular exercise, adequate rest and a vitamin-rich diet will help.
- Avoid extended sunbathing, as ultraviolet rays are stressful to the body.

WHEN TO CONSULT A DOCTOR Shingles is the product of the herpes zoster virus. If you have a rash on your forehead or anywhere near your eyes, see a doctor immediately to avoid the risk of damaging your corneas. Although you can expect some pain—unfortunately, it comes with the condition—if the pain is unbearable, it could indicate the presence of nerve damage (post-zoster neuralgia), so seek medical help. Home remedies can support a doctor's treatment, but it is equally important to get plenty of rest. Physical exertion can exacerbate the problem.

Skin treatments

Skin acts as a barrier protecting us from the outside world. Crucial to our survival and well-being, we need to be kind to it—as its health and appearance can play an important role in our sense of identity.

Despite scientific advances in treatments for skin problems, many people still prefer to rely on natural ingredients and home remedies.

ECZEMA

This chronic skin condition, characterized by an itchy, red, scaly rash, can be relieved with natural remedies. Cleansers, salves and plant-based poultices can help to soothe the itching and inflammation, and moisturize dry skin.

BASIC skin care

If you are prone to eczema, your skin needs oil and moisture to restore its natural balance.

Note: If you have allergies, animal and plant ingredients can trigger an allergic reaction, so use them with caution.

- Soap-free cleansers are gentle and are far less irritating to the skin.
- Plant-based salves with jojoba or evening primrose oil are good moisturizers.

TREATING eczema

Check with a doctor before you use a home remedy, as eczema varies from person to person. The remedy you use must be right for you.

- Press raw cabbage leaves with a rolling pin until the juice comes out. Warm the leaves in a strainer held above steam and apply twice daily.
- Pour 1 cup (250 ml) cold water over 2 teaspoons (10 ml) dried chickweed. Boil for 5 minutes, strain and cool to lukewarm. Soak a cloth in the liquid, wring it out and apply to the rash for 15 minutes.
- Stir together 3 tablespoons (45 ml) fuller's earth (*see page 63*) and an equal amount of cold water to form a thick paste. Apply to eczema for 20 minutes. Rinse with cool water then treat your skin with an anti-inflammatory salve containing vitamin E.
- Chamomile or calendula ointments can moisturize skin and soothe the relentless itching: For best results keep products in the refrigerator and use them cold.
- Aromatherapy baths—no longer than 10 minutes, no hotter than 95°F (35°C)—return moisture to the skin: Add 10 drops chamomile or lavender oil with 2 tablespoons (30 ml) sweet almond oil.

Note: Oil baths are slippery, so be careful.

A PASTE OF FULLER'S EARTH AND water aids eczema.

GOOD TO KNOW

Causes of eczema

Contact eczemas are an allergic reaction to specific foodstuffs, metals, cleaning agents or cosmetics. Atopic eczemas are usually inherited. Around 10 percent of the population is affected by them. The most common atopic eczema is neurodermatitis, which requires medical care.

THINGS to avoid if prone to eczema

- Alkaline soaps, cosmetics containing alcohol and synthetic grooming products dry your skin out even more and make it susceptible to secondary infections from bacteria, viruses or funguses.
- Frequent contact with water over 95°F (35°C).
- Intense sunbathing.
- Handling chemicals without protective gloves.

SUNBURN

Sunlight has many beneficial qualities but we must also protect ourselves from health problems caused by its rays, including skin cancer. Since sunburn is a first-degree burn, anything that cools the skin will help to relieve the pain—from a wet T-shirt to a cold cloth soaked in saline solution and placed on the burn. To make the solution, dissolve 1 teaspoon (5 ml) salt in 2 quarts (2 L) distilled water.

HOME REMEDIES for sunburn

You could try one of the following, but never use any remedies on skin that is blistered or open.

- Wraps with milk, yogurt or buttermilk soothe pain and cool the skin. Apply at least twice a day for 30 minutes.
- Rub the burn with the cut surface of a lemon or a tomato—the vitamin C encourages healing.
- Place a wrap soaked in cooled black tea or witch hazel tea—1 tablespoon (15 ml) witch hazel in 1½ cups (375 ml) water—on reddened skin several times a day.
- Mix a equal amounts few drops of evening primrose and lemon oil apply daily.
- Try gels or creams containing aloe vera or arnica.
- Drink plenty of fluids, preferably cool herbal teas, mineral water or fruit juices.

Only expose yourself to midday sunlight for a few minutes.

WHEN TO CONSULT A DOCTOR For severe headaches, sunburn in babies and little children, severe pain and burn blisters, see a doctor. Never pierce or burst the blisters.

PREVENTING sunburn

Check the weather on your smartphone or radio for that day's UV Index level and the time period during which sun protection is needed.

- **0–2 (low) UV Index:** Minimal protection required. Wear sunglasses and use sunscreen with a SPF factor of 15+. Cover up if outside for more than an hour.
- **3–5 (moderate) UV Index:** Wear a hat, sunglasses and a sunscreen with a SPF factor of 30+. Cover up if outside for 30 minutes or more. Reduce time in the sun between 11 a.m. and 4 p.m.
- **6–7 (high) UV Index:** Wear a hat, sunglasses and apply sunscreen with a SPF factor of 45. Avoid direct sunlight between 11 a.m. and 4 p.m.
- **8–10 (very high) UV Index:** Use extra precautions—unprotected skin will burn quickly and could suffer long-term damage. Avoid going outside between 11 a.m. and 4 p.m. If you must, stay in the shade, cover up and apply a sunscreen with a SPF factor of 45+.
- **11+ (extreme) UV Index:** Take exceptional precautions. Stay inside, or remain in the shade. Cover up and apply SPF 60 sunscreen.

CUTS & SCRAPES

Whether it is a finger cut during food preparation or a grazed knee following a fall from a bicycle, there are plenty of traditional remedies that can treat minor skin damage effectively.

FIRST aid

The most crucial aspect of wound care is to clean and disinfect the wound thoroughly.

1 Carefully remove any foreign objects from a cut, scratch or abrasion with disinfected tweezers.

2 Disinfect with an antiseptic solution or cream such as neosporin.

3 To stop bleeding, wrap a clean cloth or towel around the affected area and apply pressure.

HOME remedies

Twenty-four hours after the injury, the wound should have closed and can be treated to aid healing. Only use these remedies on unbroken skin. You will find any number of commercial antibacterial ointments at the pharmacy, but why not try one of Mother Nature's simple, low-cost solutions?

- Tea tree oil compresses have proven their worth to many generations of healers. Add 5–8 drops of oil to a clean cloth and cover the wound for 24 hours. Repeat regularly.
- For a yarrow wrap, add ½ cup (100 ml) boiling water to 1 tablespoon (15 ml) dried yarrow flowers and strain. Moisten a cloth with the solution, gently wring it out and apply to the injured skin.
- To speed healing, scald a lavender tea bag, let it cool and place it on a wound.
- Vitamin C helps wounds heal. Treat yourself to an extra serving of strawberries or a juicy orange.

Bandage with chamomile tincture

one Pour about # cup (100 ml) rubbing alcohol over 1 tablespoon (15 g) chamomile flowers. Let the solution steep for 10 days.

two Carefully strain the solution and thoroughly wring out the juice from the chamomile flowers. Pour the mixture into a clean bottle.

three Dilute the tincture with water in a 1:4 ratio and apply to a piece of muslin. Leave on your injured skin for at least 30 minutes.

CABBAGE wrap

Not only is cabbage packed with important nutrients but its leaves also have many healing properties. A wrap made with cabbage alleviates pain and helps to promotes healing. Use it twice a day.

To prepare:

1 Rinse a few inside leaves from a head of cabbage and remove the central rib.

2 Soften the leaves with a rolling pin, then apply to your wound for several hours at a time using a bandage or plastic wrap to hold them in place.

PREVENTION of cuts and scrapes

- Minor accidents are inevitable, but taking sensible precautions, such as wearing protective gloves, storing knives correctly or wearing kneepads when cycling, will minimize injuries.
- Check that your tetanus shot is up to date.

Try boiling some cabbage, and cleanse your skin with the cooking water.

Sleep

Your body needs at least 7 to 8 hours sleep a night to regenerate itself fully. But anxiety, sleep disturbances or an underlying health problem can all result in insomnia. Here are some proven ways to help you get a good night's sleep.

Stress, worries or hormonal changes during menopause are often the root cause of an inability to fall asleep or a tendency to wake up repeatedly. Sleep disturbances are frequently temporary, but sometimes they drag on for weeks, months or even years and become a nightmare for the sufferer. You may not be able to control all the factors that are interfering with your sleep, but going back to having warm milk before bedtime, as you did in childhood, may help. Sometimes a calming drink and a change in routine can be enough to solve the problem.

HOME remedies

- Slowly sip a cup of calming valerian or hops tea before going to bed. If you wish, you can sweeten it with a little honey.
- Have a little alcohol. Hops produce their calming effect not only in the form of teas and scent bundles, but also in beer. In moderation, alcohol adds to the soporific qualities of hops. A small glass—¾ cup (185 ml) in the evening—can work wonders but drinking more could have the opposite effect.
- An hour before bedtime, sip a glass of warm milk containing 4 teaspoons (20 g) finely ground almonds.
- Take a dip. It is difficult to fall asleep if your feet are cold. Warm socks can help, as can contrasting footbaths before going to bed. Dip your feet into warm 100°F (38°C) water for 5 minutes and then into cold 54–60°F (12–16°C) water for 20 seconds. Repeat, ending with another dip in warm water.
- Try a sleep-inducing mixture in a scent burner of 4 drops chamomile oil and 2 drops each lavender, sandalwood and neroli oils. Place the burner in the bedroom an hour before bedtime or add the drops to a small bowl of warm water to disperse the scent.
- Drip a few drops of lavender oil on your pillow. Your body heat will cause the oil to evaporate gradually, bringing on drowsiness.
- Take a warm, relaxing bath containing a sachet of dried lime flowers about half an hour before going to bed.
- Here's another trick you can use: Lie down on the bed in complete darkness, keep your eyes open and force yourself to stay awake—usually the reverse happens and you will quickly fall asleep.
- Modern methods such as autogenic training help to induce sleep through autosuggestion.

Hang fragrant, dried lavender clippings—cut just before flowering—in the bedroom to aid sleep.

A slumber drink

This tea will make it easy to fall asleep and help you to stay asleep through the night. Use dried ingredients.

3 tablespoons (40 g) valerian root
4 teaspoons (20 g) hops
1 tablespoon (15 g) lemon balm
1 tablespoon (15 g) peppermint leaves
2 teaspoons (10 g) bitter orange peel

Mix the ingredients, and use 1 teaspoon (5 ml) of the mixture for each cup.

TIPS for a good night's sleep

- Keep your bedroom quiet, dark and not too warm—no more than 63°F (17°C).
- Before going to bed, make sure the bedroom has been thoroughly aired.
- There should be no television in a bedroom—it belongs in the living room or family room.
- Going to bed and getting up at regular times provides a healthy sleep rhythm and synchronizes your body's biological clock.
- Make sure the mattress is good quality. Before buying a new one, test it by lying down on it.
- Use sheets made from natural materials (such as cotton or linen) to avoid night sweats.
- Get lots of exercise during the day, preferably in the fresh air, to be sure that you are tired at bedtime. But avoid strenuous exercise within 4 hours of going to bed.
- Take a short walk before going to bed.
- Avoid fatty foods or eating a heavy meal in the evening, as they take a long time for your stomach to digest.
- Don't consume alcohol in excess, or coffee, black tea and cola containing caffeine. They are stimulants and interfere with sleep. Having an excess of any drink in the evening could mean you will have to get up at night.
- Avoid wrestling with problems in the evening—worrying spoils sleep. Make a to-do list of all the things you need to address the following day, and then relax.
- Establish a routine. Children need to be run around during the day to be tired at night, but the hour before bedtime should be low key. Aim for a calm bedtime routine that might include a bath and a story.

Sleep sachets

A sleep sachet provides a pleasant, aromatic route to a refreshing slumber.

1 handful lavender flowers
1 handful hops
1 handful lemon balm
1 small pillowcase

Mix the dried herbs and enclose them in the pillowcase. Use as a pillow or place underneath your pillow.

You may need to make some lifestyle changes in order to sleep well.

Stomach complaints

A frantic lifestyle, poor nutrition, stress and too little exercise can result in an upset stomach. But popping a pill as soon as you start to feel uncomfortable could make things worse. A sensitized stomach is likely to react just as well to nature's much gentler medications.

STOMACH ache

It's an unfortunate fact of life that many of the foods we most enjoy are the ones that our stomachs like the least. And eating too much at once can leave your stomach with too much to handle. However, if you drink plenty of water and unsweetened herbal teas, preferably at least 2 quarts (2 L) a day, eat a healthy diet and don't overindulge too often, your stomach will thank you for it.

- Sip fennel, chamomile, lemon balm or peppermint tea with and between meals to aid digestion.
- Eat a small piece of fresh ginger if you are feeling nauseous. Or, if you prefer, roughly grate 2 teaspoons (10 ml) fresh ginger and let it steep in 1 cup (250 ml) of hot water for about 10 minutes.

GOOD TO KNOW

Bacterial culprit

In the past, most doctors believed that stress and dietary factors caused stomach ulcers (peptic ulcers), with their symptoms of bloating, pain and nausea. The prescription: Get rest, reduce anxiety, eat bland food and eliminate coffee and alcohol. We now know that the culprit in one in every five cases of peptic ulcer is actually a bacterium called *Helicobacter pylori*. A simple test is enough to confirm the diagnosis and, after treatment with a course of antibiotics, only a small proportion of patients relapse.

- Some experts suggest that those cultures that value the after meal burp have been right all along. Sparkling water or soda can help to activate the beneficial gas.
- Prepare an anti-inflammatory tea from 1 teaspoon (5 ml) each licorice root and valerian. Pour 1 cup (250 ml) of boiling water over the ingredients, cover and let steep for 10 minutes. Strain and sip a cup slowly at mealtimes.

Note: Do not use during pregnancy.

- Chamomile tea can help ease cramps.
- Vitamin A helps to rebuild damaged mucous membranes in the stomach lining. Good sources include carrots, green cabbage, spinach, peppers, apricots and honeydew melon.
- The traditional use of licorice dates back several thousand years. There is some evidence to suggest that it can soothe your stomach and help if you have an ulcer.

• Massage your stomach in gentle, circular motions using 1 tablespoon (15 ml) almond oil mixed with 3–4 drops chamomile oil.

HEARTBURN

Sometimes your stomach will rebel against rich, heavily spiced or fried foods, especially if you eat them quickly or shortly before going to bed. The result can be heartburn, which causes a burning sensation just under your rib cage, often accompanied by a feeling of fullness, nausea and stomach pain.

In addition to traditional home remedies such as peppermint and fennel tea, a change in your eating habits and other gentle, natural solutions may help to put out the fire.

- Nux vomica is a homeopathic remedy for relieving heartburn. You will find it at a local health food store.
- Sip a cup of tea made from elderflowers, lime flowers and peppermint (mixed in equal proportions) to relieve cramps and calm your stomach. To prepare, pour 1 cup (250 ml) of boiling water over 1 teaspoon (5 ml) of the mixture.
- Black tea with a pinch of salt and a water cracker can help to calm the stomach.
- A gentle stomach massage in a circular motion with 3–4 drops chamomile or lavender essential oil mixed with 1 tablespoon (15 ml) almond oil will help alleviate pain.
- Coffee, alcohol and spicy or fried foods can upset your digestion. Watch your diet and avoid food triggers.
- Eat small meals more frequently, rather than one or two big feasts a day, and consume your last meal at least 4 hours before bedtime.

IRRITABLE bowel syndrome (IBS)

Doctors don't fully understand the mechanism behind irritable bowel syndrome. What they do know is that it is marked by continuing problems with constipation, bloating, diarrhea, heartburn and nausea. It is likely that stress can exacerbate IBS and certain foods also seem to make it worse. On the positive side, with a little help from age-old wisdom you may be able to regulate and soothe your troubled digestive system.

- Lingering over a meal allows enough time to digest it properly. When you are relaxed, you are less likely to swallow air, which can increase abdominal discomfort.
- Avoid excessively rich foods and divide your total daily food intake into several small meals instead of three full-course meals.
- The aptly named chamomile roll cure—which involves tea and a rolling movement—can provide relief when used in the morning for several days (*see below*).
- Alcohol and cigarettes are poison for a nervous stomach, so avoid them.
- Also avoid coffee and black tea. They will stimulate digestion which is not good if you are prone to diarrhea.
- Avoid strong spices, as well as sweets, smoked foods, doughnuts and fried foods.

Replacing fatty foods with whole grains and fiber is a major step towards calming an unruly stomach.

Chamomile roll cure

one In the morning make a tea using 2–3 teaspoons (10–15 ml) dried chamomile and 1 cup (250 ml) of water.

two Go back to bed and sip the tea on an empty stomach.

three Lie on your back for 5–10 minutes, then for an equal time, lie on your left side, then your stomach then on your right side.

four Keep drinking chamomile tea throughout the day.

STRENGTHEN YOUR DEFENSES

A strong immune system can fight off most viruses, but when it's weakened they can get the upper hand. A healthy diet and lifestyle can strengthen your body's defenses, aiding prevention or assisting if a virus does take hold.

FRUIT, VEGETABLES and whole grains FORTIFY DEFENSES.

Healthy eating

- Vitamin C is essential for your immune system. You'll find it in many fruits and vegetables, but good choices are citrus fruits, kiwi fruit, peppers and fruit juices—especially orange, guava and cranberry.
- Eat a varied diet with plenty of fruit, vegetables, whole grains, plant oils, milk products, fish and lean meats. You will be providing your body with the substances to fortify its defenses: vitamin E, beta-carotene, zinc and selenium.
- Avoid nicotine and alcohol: Both weaken the immune system, and tobacco smoke is a Class A carcinogen.

Reducing stress

Stress, conflict and worry are poison not only for your mental well-being but for your body's defenses. Try to reduce them.

- Build in regular breaks during the day for a little "me time."
- Learn a relaxation technique, such as yoga, progressive muscle relaxation or Qigong.
- Get adequate rest, always going to sleep and rising at the same time each day.

Relaxation techniques such as yoga help to beat stress.

Echinacea tea is a useful ally.

Toughening up

- Even a good, old-fashioned barefoot stroll through the grass can perk up your immune system.
- Start each morning with a contrast shower: Turn on the warm water and after 2 minutes, switch to a cold shower for 15 seconds. Repeat the process three times. End with cold water.
- Avoid car exhaust (it's toxic) and don't spend too much time in poorly ventilated indoor places where chemicals are being used (such as beauty salons and gas stations), or where new materials, such as carpets, have recently been installed.
- Drink at least 6 cups (1.5 L) water every day, which will boost your immune system and lessen feelings of fatigue.

Help from the health food store

Compounds made from echinacea (coneflower; *Echinacea purpurea*) activate your immune system and strengthen the body's defenses. Take it daily for a period of about 8 weeks. If you take it for longer than this, it could have the opposite effect—you may overstimulate and weaken your immune system.

Note: Don't take echinacea if you are allergic to coneflowers.

Plenty of exercise

The fastest way to feel energized is to exercise—you'll feel the effects right away. A simple 10-minute walk will decrease tension, banish fatigue and boost mental alertness for hours afterwards. Make it part of your daily routine and pretty soon you'll be toning muscles, strengthening your heart and improving the functioning of most organs and bodily systems. Exercise immediately lightens the workload of the immune system, speeding up the elimination of germs and other threats by stimulating circulation, making you breathe deeply, accelerating perspiration and increasing muscle activity. Try cycling, swimming or taking a brisk daily walk.

Exercise aids the immune system by stimulating circulation.

Throat problems

A sore throat—also known as pharyngitis—is unpleasant and typically comes with a cold or flu. Most cases are not serious and will pass within a week, but natural remedies can often provide fast relief until they do.

POUR BOILING WATER OVER chamomile flowers AND inhale.

A sore throat is a common complaint normally caused by a viral or bacterial infection, allergy, dry air or by inhaling smoke or another airborne pollutant. It is often the first sign of a cold and can be accompanied by fever and congestion.

SORE throat

Symptoms can vary from a mild scratchiness to severely inflamed mucous membranes in the throat and pharynx. Fortunately, there are a number of proven remedies for this common ailment inside your kitchen pantry.

- Drink lots of fluids to keep mucous membranes moist. Hot herbal or fruit teas (especially anti-inflammatory sage tea) are ideal drinks. Sweeten to taste with honey.
- Honey has a natural antibacterial effect that makes it a particularly effective home remedy. Allow 1 teaspoon (5 ml) honey to run slowly down your throat several times a day to chase the soreness away.
- Heat helps support the body's natural defenses. Wear a scarf when you feel a sore throat coming on and avoid drafts and cold.
- Dry air further irritates mucous membranes. To keep humidity levels in your house high, place bowls of water on the windowsills. Add a couple of drops of an essential oil for a soothing effect.
- Gargling soothes pain and swelling in the throat and pharynx. Mix 1 teaspoon (5 ml) salt with 2 cups (500 ml) water to make a solution for gargling. Or try an old home remedy: Mix 5 teaspoons (25 m) cider vinegar in 1 cup (250 ml) water. Sweeten the solution with honey.

Onion milk with thyme and cloves

Onion milk alleviates pain and helps combat inflammation.

1 quart (1 L) milk
1 onion
1 sprig of thyme
2 cloves

Cut the onion into large pieces and add to a pan with the milk, sprig of thyme and cloves. Bring mixture to the boil, then remove from the heat and let steep for 10 minutes before straining. Drink onion milk three times a day.

GOOD TO KNOW

When to see a doctor

Hoarseness is often the result of a flu-like infection, but it may also be more serious. Visit the doctor if your hoarseness lasts longer than a week or keeps coming back, or if you have become hoarse without any apparent reason. The same is true if the hoarseness gets worse and is accompanied by fever, exhaustion or weight loss, or if you notice a swelling in your throat or enlarged lymph nodes.

- Garlic has antiviral and antifungal properties, so it can be particularly effective at relieving a sore throat caused by a virus. Add it to food or blend a few cloves of garlic, fresh or dried, into a vegetable cocktail.
- An effective home recipe for sore throats is a mixture that tastes better than the ingredients might suggest: Stir ½ teaspoon (2 ml) freshly grated horseradish in a glass of warm water, along with 1 teaspoon (5 ml) honey and a pinch of ground cloves. Drink slowly.
- Get a new toothbrush. Bacteria trapped on a toothbrush may cause a sore throat to linger.

HOARSENESS

There are many possible causes for that frog in your throat: Strained vocal chords, excessively dry ambient air or a viral infection, to name just a few. Resting your vocal chords may be all that is needed, so speak softly and as little as possible. In addition, an array of simple remedies can speed up the healing process. If there is no improvement, you should consult a doctor.

- Hot tea of any kind can soothe a sore throat, especially sage tea, which should ideally be made fresh every time from dried sage leaves. Warm elderberry tea also alleviates discomfort.
- If your mother treated your sore throat with a soothing mug of hot milk and honey, she was spot on. Drinking this beverage several times a day will ease hoarseness quickly.
- A potato wrap speeds healing. Boil, peel and mash 2–3 potatoes. Spread the warm—but not hot—potatoes on a cloth and wrap around your throat with a woolen scarf to hold them in place. Wear the wrap and scarf until the potatoes cool down. Repeat three times a day.
- Make a refreshing throat compress by soaking a tightly woven cloth in warm thyme, sage or meadowsweet tea. Gently wring out the cloth and wrap it around your throat, then cover it with a woolen scarf.
- Add a few drops of either lavender or eucalyptus essential oil to 1 cup (250 ml) boiling water. Lean over the steaming liquid, drape a towel over your head and inhale the vapors to ease hoarseness.
- Ice cream is also a favorite pain relief remedy, and not just for children. Or try a hot drink flavored with lemon and honey.

Honey has natural antibacterial properties that make it a particularly effective home remedy.

Women's reproductive health

While women have the exciting ability to nurture new life, the hormones that control the reproductive cycle can trigger discomfort. Fortunately, there are a number of traditional ways to combat these pains.

From adolescence on, a woman's reproductive system has a major impact on her life. Her complex hormonal balance may be disrupted as she progresses from the onset of periods to childbearing through to menopause. Here are some time-tested remedies.

MENSTRUAL discomfort

Breast pain, bloating, acne, cramps and feelings of intense irritability are a few of the symptoms that may signal the start of your period. It may be preceded by uncomfortable PMS (premenstrual syndrome). More intense cramping and pains in the head, back and stomach are among the problems that can be experienced when the period begins.

- Chasteberry (*Vitex agnus-castus*) has been used for gynecological conditions since the time of Hippocrates. It helps regulate hormonal balance, soothes the discomforts of PMS (such as breast tenderness and itchy skin), and even inhibits severe bleeding. It is available as tablets or capsules from health food stores and pharmacies.
- Warm baths increase comfort and reduce cramping. Additives might include relaxation-inducing lemon balm or lavender, chamomile or yarrow to counter severe bleeding, or thyme to bring on menstruation.
- Massages can help ease pains and cramps: Gently massage your lower abdomen and back with evening primrose or lavender oil.
- A tea made from chamomile, valerian root and peppermint, mixed in equal amounts, may help to soothe severe bleeding accompanied by cramps.
- Tea made from tansy and marigold may help stop cramping.
- A tincture of motherwort (from a herbalist) or tea made from crampbark (available from health food stores) may help to regulate menstruation and eliminate pain.

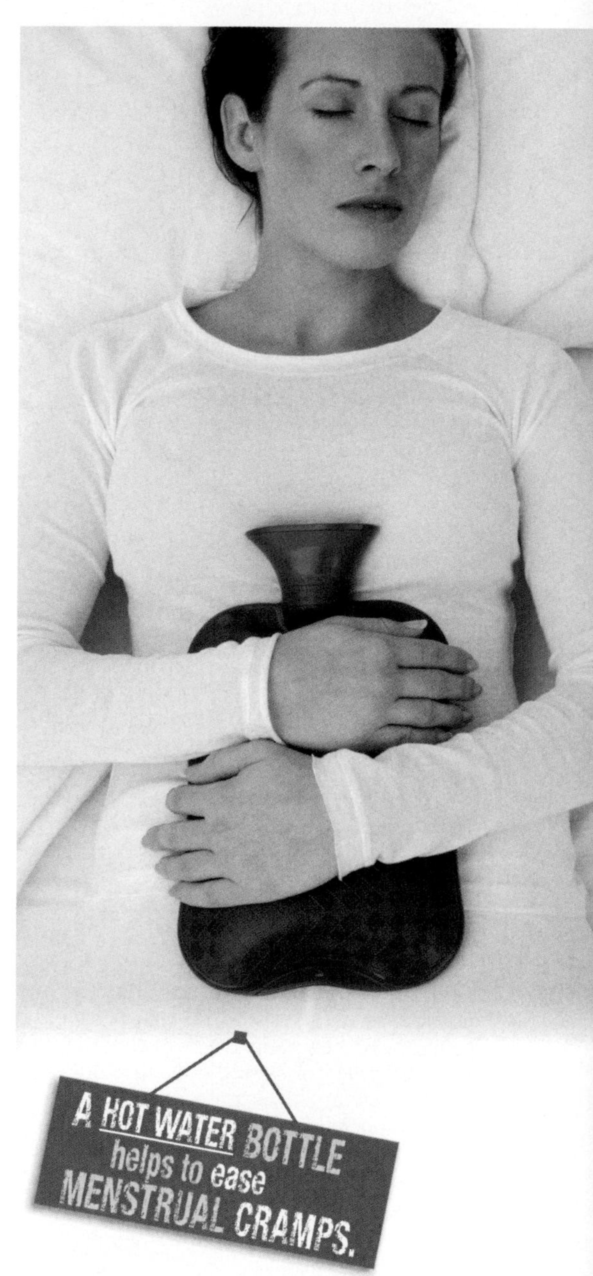

A HOT WATER BOTTLE helps to ease MENSTRUAL CRAMPS.

PREGNANCY

Although a natural condition, pregnancy can be difficult for some women.

- In the first trimester of pregnancy, many women are plagued with morning sickness. This simple trick can help: Take a packet of saltines or water crackers to bed and nibble a few right after waking up in the morning. Then rise, have a leisurely breakfast and sip some peppermint tea.
- Stretch marks may appear on your breasts and expanding belly. Gentle massages with jojoba or evening primrose oil keep your skin moist and elastic.
- A warm wrap with lavender oil helps soothe breast tenderness.
- Swimming or a gentle back massage can alleviate pelvic pain.
- Magnesium, found in whole-grain products and dried fruit, helps eliminate cramping in the calves.

MENOPAUSE

An inevitable part of aging, menopause generally affects women between the ages of 45 and 55. The drop in hormones that is its hallmark can also trigger a series of uncomfortable symptoms, including hot flashes, vaginal dryness, insomnia and mood swings.

- Various tea preparations help women get through menopause. Valerian tea has a calming, balancing effect, sage tea reduces sweating attacks and lemon balm tea can help with sleep disturbances.
- Contrast footbaths may help fend off hot flashes. Fill two foot bowls with hops flowers and water: One 100°F (38°C) hot; the other 50°F (10°C) cold. Alternate placing your feet in warm water for 5 minutes and cold for 10 seconds.
- Nutrition plays a role in hot flashes. Eat plenty of fresh food and abstain from coffee, alcohol and nicotine, which can further lower your estrogen level.
- Soy and red clover contain phyto-estrogens—plant-based compounds that bear a chemical resemblance to estrogen. Asian women have long enjoyed the benefits of soy, making them far less prone to hot flashes. Try incorporating soy milk, soy flour and tofu into your diet.

GOOD TO KNOW

Black cohosh

The roots of black cohosh contain triterpene glycosides, a popular treatment for premenstrual discomfort, menstrual irregularities and painful menstruation, as well as for hot flashes during menopause. Women around the world have been using the herbal supplement for generations and a wealth of modern evidence backs up their choice. In some studies, black cohosh outperformed conventional therapies such as hormone pills and antidepressants in combating menopause symptoms. However, it takes 4–6 weeks from the time you begin taking it for the effects to become apparent.

Ginger tea can help to combat nausea during pregnancy.

Beauty and body care

Keeping your body in good condition is important to help you look better, feel better and stay youthful. Nature can play an important role, with plant-based eye creams, beautiful fragrances, luxurious massage oils, natural shampoos and much more ...

HOMEMADE BEAUTY PRODUCTS

Some cosmetics contain harsh chemicals. Homemade beauty products take advantage of plant-based oils for moisture and essential oils for delightful scents. Here are some of the most popular natural ingredients.

Plant-based oils

- Apricot kernel oil makes an excellent massage oil and has a faint scent of almonds. It is appropriate for all skin types but is particularly good for dry, sensitive skin.
- Avocado oil provides moisture, nourishment and hydration for the skin.
- Jojoba oil, a liquid wax, controls moisture and doesn't leave an oily sheen on your skin. It's suitable for every skin type.
- Macadamia nut oil is rich in fatty acids, making it an ideal ingredient for creams.
- Use almond oil for massages and to care for all skin types.
- Olive oil nurtures every skin type, but is especially suitable for dry, rough skin.
- Wheat germ oil is rich in vitamin E, which combats the aging of dry, mature skin.
- Evening primrose oil stimulates and improves the appearance of skin. It is also sometimes used in conditioners for brittle, overprocessed hair. Use it only in small amounts as it is extremely potent.
- Rosehip oil is rich in essential fatty acids and provides ample moisture for rough skin. Use it only in small amounts—and only for scent, not as a base oil—as it is very strong.

Essential oils

These common oils, found in most pharmacies and health food stores, provide a delightful scent for homemade beauty products. The one you choose depends on personal preference.

Bergamot oil • The finest of all citrus oils with a sweet, citrus-fresh scent

Geranium oil • A soft, flowery, feminine touch

Lavender oil • A pure, fresh, flowery scent used in many products

Neroli oil • A fresh, flowery scent with a touch of bittersweet orange

Rose oil • A sweet, flowery scent with a very feminine oil

Rosemary oil • An intense scent similar to camphor; use sparingly

Sandalwood oil • A warm, heavy and long-lasting scent used by men and women

Jasmine oil • A highly aromatic oil with special softening and smoothing properties

Ylang-ylang oil • An exotic, sensual scent, ideal for perfume, deodorants and bath additives; use sparingly

Lemon oil • A pure, fresh scent with a subtle and sweet touch; ideal for cleansing

Natural beauty products are kind to the environment as well as to your hair and skin.

Useful ingredients

- Beeswax gives creams, salves, lotions and lipsticks a thicker, more solid consistency.
- Fruit or cider vinegar reduces itching, cools and refreshes. It regulates the pH value of skin, acts as a natural antiseptic and promotes blood circulation. The vitamins and minerals that cider and fruit vinegars contain also make them ideal additives for cleansers and baths, but don't use malt, white or distilled vinegar in this way.
- Glycerin is a clear, syrupy alcohol used as a lubricant in creams and lotions.
- Cocoa butter melts at a low temperature and makes a good base for soaps and creams.
- Lanolin—the pure oil from sheep's wool—is a moisturizing skin care all-star, in large part because of its water-repellent properties.

GOOD TO KNOW

Safety first

- Be sure to use pesticide-free fresh plant materials—avoid collecting from roadside locations.
- Try not to get essential oils in your eyes or mouth, and avoid swallowing mouthwashes containing them.
- Some essential oils can cause skin pigmentation in sunlight—avoid applying before exposure.
- If you have allergies, check with your doctor before using any new ingredient.
- Patch-test homemade skin products before use. Apply a small amount to the inner elbow and cover. If there is no reaction after 24 hours, the product is safe for you to use.

Mineral ingredients

- Fuller's earth is a fine-grained soil consisting of white and red clay, loam and aluminium silicates. The sterilized powder is mined from Ice Age loess deposits and can be used both internally and externally to absorb toxins. Use cosmetic-grade fuller's earth in wraps, compresses, face masks, baths and haircare products. It is available from online suppliers or some compounding pharmacists.
- Rhassoul and kaolin, found in some health food stores or online, are natural clay cleansers that provide a gentle, nonsudsy alternative to shampoos and soaps.

Age spots

These little brown marks usually appear on the back of the hands, but sometimes on the arms or face as well. You can lighten and possibly reduce them using natural care products—but these treatments require plenty of patience.

Age spots, which are sometimes referred to as "liver spots," should really be called "sun spots," as they are actually the result of excessive exposure to the sun.

HOME remedies

It's possible to conceal age spots with makeup, or there are costly medical procedures such as laser removal. But home remedies are still worth a try.

Test them first on less noticeable places, such as the hands, before using them on your face. Wait a few days to see if you get a reaction and to get an idea of what effect it has on your skin—we're all different.

- For an easy-to-make paste to lighten age spots, mix 2 teaspoons (10 g) each powdered ginger and rose petals. Stir 2 teaspoons (10 g) of the mix into a small amount of warm water to make a spreadable paste. Apply to the spots, cover with a cloth and leave for about 30 minutes before rinsing your skin clean.

Lemon-based lightening agent

1 egg white
2 teaspoons (10 ml) lemon juice
½ teaspoon (2 ml) vitamin E oil

Beat ingredients together and spread on age spots. Let work for 20 minutes, then rinse thoroughly. This daily regimen should be repeated over the course of a few weeks to lighten age spots.

- Try applying pure lemon juice or buttermilk to age spots twice a day.
- Make a natural lightening agent by mixing together about 1 teaspoon (5 ml) each honey and plain yogurt. Spread the mixture on age spots once a day and leave for 30 minutes before rinsing well.
- Rub age spots several times a day with a piece of papaya, or use gels containing aloe vera, both of which contain substances That stimulate the growth of healthy cells.

PREVENTION

- Free radicals contribute to the occurrence of age spots. Ultraviolet radiation plays a role in this, so it's important to avoid intensive sunlight.
- Add certain vitamins to your diet and avoid alcohol and nicotine, which encourage the formation of free radicals. A well-balanced diet provides the body with nutrients that can combat their effects, such as vitamin C and provitamin A (in fruit and vegetables), vitamin E (in plant oils and grains) and selenium (in nuts, legumes and grains).

Cellulite

Those unattractive dimples on the hips, thighs and buttocks have plagued women for centuries. Consequently, over the years women have found several natural ways to deal with it.

Cellulite appears when a pocket of fat beneath the skin pushes on the connective tissue, creating a cottage-cheese effect. Women are particularly prone to cellulite because their connective tissue is softer than men's.

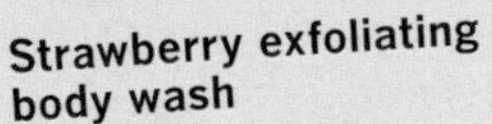

Strawberry exfoliating body wash

An exfoliating body wash has a revitalizing effect on cellulite.

¼ cup (60 g) strawberries
¼ cup (60 g) cucumber, unpeeled
2 tablespoons (30 ml) buttermilk
1 tablespoon (15 ml) yogurt
1 egg yolk
¼ cup (50 g) ground almonds

Purée all the ingredients in a blender or mash them in a mortar. Store in a sealable container and use in the shower. The mixture can be kept in the refrigerator for up to 3 days.

HOME remedies

Methods used to combat cellulite involve a number of effective substances, including potatoes, sea salt and massage oils. But home remedies are not enough. It is also essential to make sure you eat a low-fat diet and exercise regularly.

- To make an effective massage oil, pour 1 cup (200 ml) wheat germ oil over a handful of fresh ivy leaves and let steep for 2 weeks in a sealed container kept in a warm location. Strain the liquid and mix in 2 drops of rosemary oil. Rub into cellulite daily, using circular motions.

- Other oils such as cinnamon, lavender, chamomile, clove, rosemary and sandalwood can be mixed with a base oil (such as almond oil) to create a massage oil for cellulite patches. (*Before using essential oils, read more about them on pages 62–63.*)
- Potatoes possess remarkable healing powers, including the ability to tighten connective tissue. To take advantage of this, peel a potato, slice it thinly and lay the raw slices on the skin affected by cellulite. Cover with a cotton cloth and let the potato work for 15 minutes.
- Create your own mixture to tighten the subcutaneous tissue. Boil about 3 tablespoons (45 g) ivy leaves in 2 quarts (2 L) water for 2 minutes and strain. Moisten cotton cloths with the cooled liquid and apply to the affected areas once a day for about 20 minutes.
- Massaging sea salt into moist skin can also be effective. Do it after taking a shower then rinse the salt off with warm water.

PREVENTION

Diet and exercise are key to preventing cellulite. First and foremost, people carrying excess weight must slim down—being overweight is a risk factor.

- Exercise promotes circulation and keeps skin and connective tissue taut. Weight training is particularly helpful, and specific exercises can target trouble spots.
- Cut back on hydrogenated and saturated fat, sugar and salt, as they encourage fat and water buildup, leading to the dimpled skin effect.
- Drink plenty of fluids to flush out waste and provide the skin with moisture from the inside. Eat a low-fat, high-fiber diet containing plenty of vegetables and fruits.

Eye care

The skin around the eyes is delicate and requires special care. It is also the first part of the face to show signs of aging, so it's important to be sure it's kept properly hydrated. Thankfully, natural eye creams can be used to care for this sensitive area.

Almond oil can help prevent wrinkles.

Eye creams moisturize the delicate skin around the eyes and treat dark circles and wrinkles.

CARE products

- Plant-based eye creams are available in pharmacies and health food stores. These cosmetics contain eyebright, calendula, aloe vera and oils such as wheat germ, avocado and macadamia. Apply eye cream morning and night.
- For a homemade fragrant skin oil that will leave you looking fresh, mix about ½ cup (100 ml) avocado oil and 3 drops rose oil.
- Using easily spreadable plant oils, such as almond, apricot, jojoba and coconut oils, is an excellent way to moisturize the areas around the eyes and keep skin smooth. Apply a few drops directly on the skin or moisten a gauze bandage or two cotton balls with oil and place on closed eyes and the surrounding skin.

CIRCLES under the eyes

Whether the cause is lack of sleep, allergies or just aging, no one looks their best with dark circles under their eyes. These appear when blood vessels show through the delicate skin under the eyes.

- Eye creams or gels containing horse chestnut or cucumber may help to reduce puffy eyes.
- Mix 1 tablespoon (15 ml) egg white with 3 tablespoons (45 ml) plain yogurt to make a refreshing eye mask. Dab on the circles under your eyes, let the mask dry and rinse with warm water.
- To make an invigorating eye compress, pour 1 cup (250 ml) boiling water over 1 teaspoon (5 ml) each dried eyebright and lime flowers. Steep for 5 minutes and strain. Moisten two cotton balls with the cooled liquid and place on closed eyes for a few minutes.
- One easy way to eliminate circles under the eyes is to place fresh, cold cucumber slices on the eyelids. If you are in a hurry, use concealer to cover circles and provide a little visual first aid.

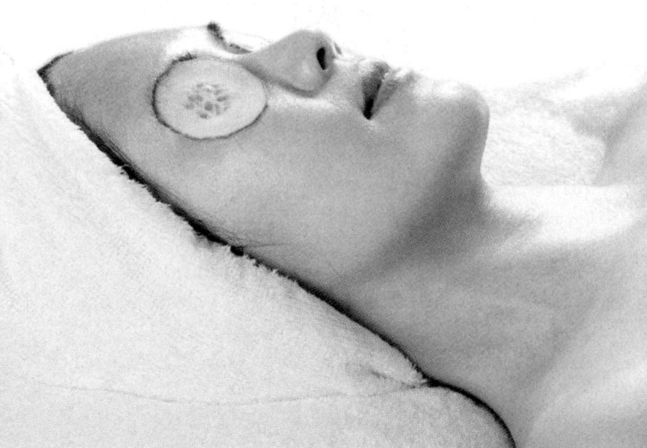

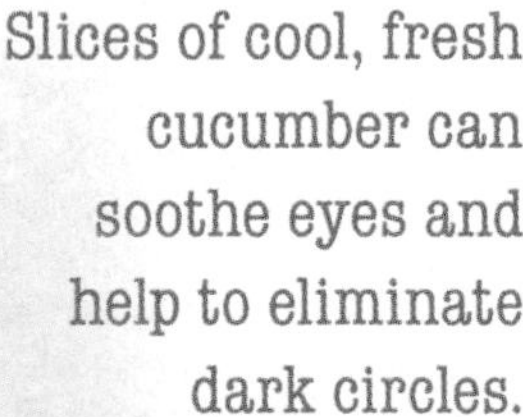

Slices of cool, fresh cucumber can soothe eyes and help to eliminate dark circles.

GOOD TO KNOW

Preparing to moisturize

Before applying an eye moisturizer, cream or oil, clean the area around your eye by dabbing it carefully with a plant-based cleanser on a cotton ball. Since the skin around your eyes is delicate, eye care products should not be rubbed in. Instead, carefully apply them with your fingertip and pat them gently below the eye, working from the outside in.

CROW'S-FEET

As we grow older, our skin becomes drier and wrinkles form around our eyes. It helps to moisturize regularly, but crying, laughing, blinking and winking all leave traces. And don't try to get by without wearing your glasses—continued squinting also produces wrinkles.

- To delay developing crow's-feet for as long as possible, keep your skin smooth with a little daily care. Pure avocado and almond oil and aloe vera gel moisturize and prevent wrinkles.
- For a homemade wrinkle cream, stir together a little almond oil and lanolin and apply under your eyes before bedtime.
- Once a week, treat the skin around your eyes to a nourishing skin-firming mask. Mix together 1 egg yolk, 3 drops of lemon juice and ½ teaspoon (2 ml) olive oil, and apply the mixture with a brush. Leave on for 15 minutes; rinse with warm water and refresh with cold water.

DRINKING WATER KEEPS SKIN MOISTURIZED and LOOKING HEALTHY.

Doing eye exercises twice a day helps to prevent wrinkles.

EYELASH care

Thick, dark, long lashes are easy to achieve by applying mascara.

1 Use mascara with almond oil to strengthen your eyelashes.

2 Carefully remove eye makeup in the evening. Dab a little water on a soft cloth and wipe off makeup by rubbing gently towards your nose.

3 To be sure eyelashes look healthy, carefully apply a little olive or castor oil with a cotton swab for some deep moisturizing—but be careful not to get the oil in your eyes.

Eye exercises

one To prevent wrinkles, close your eyes and then open them after 1 minute and let them circle slowly in a clockwise direction. Stop and relax for a moment.

two With your eyes open, use your fingertips to pull your lower eyelids down slightly. Lift your eyelids against this resistance and close your eyes. Relax for 1 minute with closed eyes.

three Now pull your eyebrows up firmly. Slowly close your eyes against this resistance. Again rest for a full minute with eyes closed. Repeat twice a day.

Foot pampering

During an average lifetime, your feet will carry you around the world three times—or at least an equivalent distance—so it's important that you keep your feet in good shape. Natural footbaths, scrubs and lotions are all part of the foot care program.

Moisturize tired feet after a pedicure.

Corns, calluses, bunions and ingrown toenails are not only unsightly and uncomfortable, but they can also make it difficult to buy shoes that fit. These problems are often preventable and many natural home remedies can ease them. By caring for hard-working feet, walking and other forms of exercise remain pain free and pleasurable.

Herbal spray

Refresh tired feet with this traditional herbal mixture.

2 drops rosemary oil
10 drops peppermint oil
10 drops lemon oil
10 drops cypress oil
½ cup (100 ml) witch hazel

Add all the ingredients to a spray bottle and shake vigorously. Spray the feet several times a day, as needed.

DAILY care

Rub your feet with this nurturing foot lotion morning and evening.

1 To make the lotion, bring 1 cup (250 ml) milk, a handful fresh peppermint leaves and 2 tablespoons (30 ml) fresh rosemary to a boil.
2 Let the mixture steep for 15 minutes, then cool and strain.
3 Mix in 3 drops peppermint oil to the herbal milk and pour into a sealable bottle. It will keep in the refrigerator for 5–7 days.

REGULAR care

- A weekly foot scrub removes scaly skin and makes feet smooth and supple. Mix together 3 teaspoons (15 ml) almond oil, 1 teaspoon (5 ml) sea salt and 3 drops eucalyptus oil. Massage into your feet for a few minutes, then rinse them thoroughly. It's a good idea to have a foot scrub before a pedicure.
- Calluses can be painful. To avoid them, remove hardened skin occasionally with a pumice stone, preferably after a shower or bath. To further soften a callus, tape a cotton ball soaked in vinegar to it overnight. After gently rubbing callused skin, massage with olive oil to keep the skin supple.

TIRED, stressed and sore feet

- A foot massage soothes aching feet. To make a simple massage oil, mix together 2 tablespoons (30 ml) almond oil and 3 drops of lavender oil and massage your feet using gentle, circular motions. Begin with the sole of the foot and proceed from the toes towards the heel. A massage brush or foot roller can also be used.

• To revive tired, swollen feet try an elderflower footbath. Boil two handfuls dried elderflowers in 1 quart (1 L) water with a handful of peppermint leaves. Cool, strain and pour the liquid into a small basin of warm water. Soak feet for 10 minutes.
• Another therapeutic footbath can be made by filling a bowl with warm water and adding a few drops of chamomile or lavender oil. Or add 1 quart (1 L) warm milk to a footbath. This will help to rehydrate cracked skin on your feet.
• To make some stimulating bath salts: Dissolve 2 teaspoons (10 ml) rosemary in 2 tablespoons (30 ml) rubbing alcohol. Add 5 drops of spruce essential oil and 1 cup (250 g) sea salt and mix the ingredients well. Dissolve 2 tablespoons (30 ml) bath salts in about 2 quarts (2 L) warm water and soak the feet for 10 minutes. Store salts in a tightly closed container.
• A sand and sea salt scrub removes callused and scaly skin on the soles. To make it, mix 1 cup (250 g) fine sand, 5 teaspoons (25 ml) sea salt, about ¾ cup (175 ml) olive oil and 2 drops each lemon, rosemary and peppermint oils. Rub into the soles of the feet with circular motions before rinsing with warm water and rubbing dry.

Perfect pedicures

one Take a 10-minute footbath with warm water and a few drops of the essential oil of your choice.

two Using a pumice stone, gently reduce any buildup of thickened skin—pumice has been used for skin care since ancient times. Don't try to pare back calluses with a knife; see a podiatrist for any further treatment and advice.

three If necessary, soften cuticles with olive oil and then push them back with a cuticle stick.

four Trim nails regularly. Always cut or file them straight to keep them from becoming ingrown and painful.

A foot roller provides relief for tired soles.

• Thin, brittle skin can be painful and, if left untreated, can lead to further problems. To make a soothing herbal oil, heat ½ cup (125 ml) olive oil, add 2 teaspoons (10 g) each fresh marigold and lavender flowers, and let steep for 3 minutes over low heat. Strain the cooled oil and wring out the flowers thoroughly. While still warm, apply a thin coat to the feet.
• To help swollen feet, try eating bananas. They are a natural source of potassium, which helps to relieve fluid retention.

FOOT conditioning

Feet are like any other part of the body—they require regular exercise. Walking barefoot is one way to stimulate circulation and toughen them up.
• To strengthen your feet, spread out some marbles on the floor and roll your feet back and forth on them while sitting on a chair. Then try to pick up the marbles with your toes.
• Wearing properly fitting shoes at all times is essential.

Hair coloring

Natural substances such as henna are enjoying renewed popularity as concerns grow over the safety of harsh chemical hair dyes. They are easy on your hair and scalp—and provide a variety of glossy shades.

Always color test a lock of hair first and stick to the exposure time. Protect clothes, wear disposable gloves and use stainless steel or glass bowls to avoid staining.

BRIGHTEN blonde hair

- To lighten and add shine, mix ⅔ cup (150 ml) boiling water with juice and grated peel of a lemon; steep 30 minutes and strain. Stir in 1 teaspoon (5 ml) cider vinegar; apply evenly to washed hair. Rinse with warm water after 10–15 minutes. Repeat weekly.
- Pour a little boiling water over ⅔ cup (150 g) dried chamomile flowers; steep for 30 minutes. Put strained flowers in a bowl with ½ cup (100 g) dried, finely ground rhubarb (from specialty herb suppliers). Mix in 3 teaspoons (15 ml) each olive oil and hot water. Brush on, cover with plastic wrap for 30 minutes, then rinse and wash.

BRUNETTE hair dye

- Blend ½ cup (125 ml) natural henna with 1 cup (250 ml) ground walnut shells (from specialty suppliers). Add boiling water to make a paste. Stir in 1 teaspoon (5 ml) lemon juice and 3 teaspoons (15 ml) olive oil. Brush on. Cover with plastic wrap, leave for 20–30 minutes, then rinse and wash.

A rich, red natural dye

Henna turns dark brown hair a rich, attractive red.

¾ cup (180 g) red henna powder
1 cup (250 ml) black tea
1 tablespoon (15 ml) olive oil

Mix the henna, warm tea and oil and apply immediately. Cover your head with plastic wrap and a large towel and leave on for 2 hours. Rinse hair with warm water and wash.

Henna powder comes from dried ground leaves of the henna bush.

- For a medium brown dye: Mix ½ cup (100 g)crushed onion peel, ¼ cup (50 g) finely ground sandalwood and 1 tablespoon (15 ml) olive oil. Make a paste with boiling water. Apply, rinse and wash.

DYEING hair dark brown or black

- Mix 3 tablespoons (45 ml) black tea, 6 tablespoons (90 g) black henna powder, 1 tablespoon (15 ml) olive oil and 1 teaspoon (5 ml) cider vinegar. Add boiling water to make a paste. Apply as for brunette dye. Rinse after 30–40 minutes.
- For a darker shade, steep 4 tablespoons (60 ml) dried sage, 2 tablespoons (30 ml) dried rosemary and 1 tablespoon (15 ml) lemon juice in 1⅔ cup (400 ml) water over low heat for 30 minutes. Strain, cool and use as a rinse after washing the hair.

COLORING & darkening gray hair

- Mix ½ cup (100 ml) boiling water, 4 tablespoons (60 ml) dried sage and 1 teaspoon (5 ml) black tea. Let steep for 30 minutes and strain. Moisten the hair with the lukewarm solution and rinse after 30 minutes. You will need to repeat this for several weeks for results.

Hand care

We use our hands constantly, so they need protection. Avoid harsh soaps and extremes of temperature, and wear protective gloves for housework and gardening—and take advantage of the range of moisturizers nature provides.

Well-maintained hands remain supple, move gracefully and stay attractive longer, so pamper your hands with these soothing home remedies.

Healing mask

For smooth, soft hands, apply this mask once a week.

½ cucumber
1 egg white
1 tablespoon (15 ml) yogurt
1 tablespoon (15 ml) avocado oil
1 teaspoon (5 ml) lemon juice
2 drops peppermint oil

Peel and purée the cucumber then beat the egg whites until stiff. Mix all the ingredients together and spread on your hands. Leave for 15 minutes before rinsing off with warm water.

TREATING rough hands

- To make chapped hands soft, pour 1¼ cups (300 ml) boiling water over ½ cup (125 ml) fennel seeds, steep for 10 minutes, strain and cool. Soak your hands in this infusion for 2 minutes every time you wash .
- To rejuvenate dry skin, use a yogurt and egg poultice once a week. Mix together 2 tablespoons (30 ml) yogurt, 1 tablespoon (15 ml) cream cheese, 1 egg yolk, 1 tablespoon (15 ml) honey and 2 tablespoons (30 ml) lemon juice. Apply a thick layer to the hands. Wash off with warm water after 15 minutes or so.
- For an exfoliating scrub that will smooth rough skin, stir 1 teaspoon (5 ml) sugar into a little lemon or grapefruit juice and rub your hands with it before rinsing with warm water.
- To make an oil and honey massage that leaves skin softer, mix 1 teaspoon (5 ml) honey and 2 teaspoons (10 ml) almond oil. Massage into dry, chapped hands. Let it work overnight (wear cotton gloves) and rinse with warm water in the morning.
- For a moisturizing emulsion that will cleanse, stir 1 teaspoon (5 ml) honey and the juice of half a lemon into ½ cup (100 ml) warm milk.
- Make a daily hand cream by pouring the juice of 2 lemons through a cheescloth. Mix the clear juice with an equal amount of almond oil. Melt 5 teaspoons (25 ml) beeswax in a pan over warm water, add the lemon–almond oil mixture and stir until the liquid cools. Add 5 drops citrus oil (lemon, neroli, grapefruit or lemongrass). Pour into a clean jar and store in the refrigerator for up to 3 days.
- Soaking hands once a week in warm olive oil will also restore their softness.

To keep hands soft, use a hand cream daily.

Lip care

Our lips have just three layers of skin cells, compared to the 16 layers on most of the face. As they have neither sweat nor oil glands, they dry out easily, it is worth using some natural remedies to keep them soft.

Lips are often exposed to sun, wind and other irritants, but there are a number of easy, natural ways to protect them.

Colored lip gloss

2 tablespoons (30 ml) coconut oil
1 tablespoon (15 ml) almond oil
1 tablespoon (15 ml) beeswax
1 tablespoon (15 ml) cocoa butter
1–2 drops red food coloring

Melt the oils, wax and cocoa butter together in a pan over warm water and stir. Next, stir in the food coloring. Put in a small container to cool. Remember to test the gloss first before applying all over your lips.

CARE and protection

- Massaging your lips carefully with honey on a soft toothbrush every morning will make them softer.
- The active ingredients of papaya also work well. Make a balm by puréeing a quarter of a papaya. Apply generously to the lips and surrounding skin. Rinse with warm water after 10 minutes and apply regular lip balm.
- Make a moisturizing lip balm by melting 2 tablespoons (30 ml) wheat germ oil, 1 tablespoon (15 ml) beeswax and 1 tablespoon (15 ml) honey in a pan over warm water. Add 3 drops peppermint oil and 2 drops chamomile. Stir until thick then cool.
- For an everyday lip balm, melt ½ cup (100 ml) olive oil and 5 teaspoons (25 g) beeswax in a pan over warm water; cool until lukewarm. Mix in 1½ teaspoons (7 ml) honey, 20 drops of chamomile tincture and 1 teaspoon (5 ml) tincture of propolis. Stir until cool and store in a cool place.
- A simple, weekly exfoliating lip scrub made with 1 teaspoon (5 ml) sugar and a little olive oil will remove flaky skin and promote circulation.
- Always protect the lips from ultraviolet rays by using lip balm with a built-in sun protection factor.
- Drink plenty of fluids to keep the sensitive skin of your lips tender and smooth.
- Avoid licking your lips in cold weather—the combination of wet and cold robs them of even more moisture, leaving them dry and rough.

ROUGH, cracked lips

- Smooth chapped lips by applying cocoa butter or carrot juice or by placing slices of cucumber on them.
- Alternatively, mix 1 teaspoon (5 ml) each yogurt and honey. Apply to the lips, wait 10 minutes and rinse with warm water.
- To make a warm compress, mix equal amounts of fresh thyme and dried chamomile flowers. Pour 1 cup (250 ml) boiling water over 1 teaspoon (5 ml) of the mixture, steep for 10 minutes and strain. Dip a soft, sterile cloth into the warm liquid and apply to lips for 20 minutes.

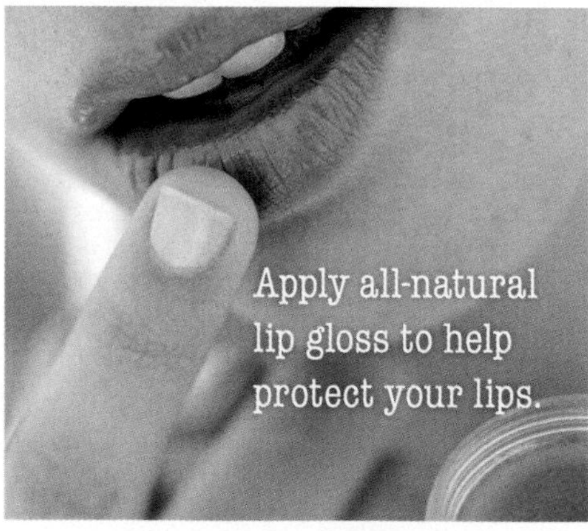

Apply all-natural lip gloss to help protect your lips.

Moisturizers

Advertisements from the cosmetics industry promise consumers a flawless complexion and perpetual youth if they use their (often pricey) products. However, quick, inexpensive and easy-to-prepare natural formulas are often just as effective.

The skin is our largest sensory organ. It excretes sweat and oil, stores fat and moisture and, because it interacts with the environment, helps to protect us from heat, cold and pathogens. There are five basic skin types, and each one needs special care.

NORMAL skin

This type is largely free from blemishes and has adequate moisture. Clean it with a mild, pH-neutral soap or cleansing lotion, apply a moistening floral water such as rose or orange-flower water, and finish with a thin application of a not-too-rich cream or gel.

- For a tried-and-tested skin cream, beat 1 egg white until stiff and add 1 teaspoon (5 ml) honey and 3 drops of almond oil. Beat well to produce a thick, smooth cream that will keep in the refrigerator for 3–4 days.

EGG WHITE, HONEY and ALMOND oil make a good SKIN CREAM.

- Alternatively, melt ¼ cup (50 g) beeswax in a pan over hot water and add ½ cup (100 ml) wheat germ oil and 3 tablespoons (45 ml) elderflower water. Stir the ingredients, put the cream into a small porcelain container and store in the refrigerator.

> **GOOD TO KNOW**
>
> **Day and night cream**
>
> After washing in the morning and evening, treat your skin with a cream appropriate for your skin type. A day cream can help to protect against the environmental effects of cold, wind and sun. A night cream or oil may help your skin to eliminate toxic substances and absorb nutrients. All-purpose creams can be used in the morning or evening.

SENSITIVE skin

This type may be affected by the sun, detergents and some makeup products. Apply:

- Almond or jojoba oil as a moisturizer.
- Orange peel facial scrubs.

OILY skin

This type characterized by large pores, an oily sheen, pimples and blackheads. Despite overactive oil glands, it still needs moisture. A consistent regimen includes pH-neutral cleansing with a soap or lotion, a clarifying, alcohol-free facial toner, an oil, a light cream or a gel with soothing properties, and a weekly exfoliating scrub and follow-up facial mask.

• Make a soothing mask by pouring ½ cup (125 ml) boiling, distilled water over 4 teaspoons (20 g) fresh calendula flowers. Cover, cool and strain through a fine sieve, thoroughly wringing out the flowers. Stir in 4 teaspoons (20 ml) almond oil and blend with rhassoul or kaolin to form a paste. Store in a porcelain jar in the refrigerator for 1–2 weeks.

COMBINATION skin

If you have enlarged pores, an oily sheen and perhaps blemishes on the forehead, nose and chin, but the rest of your skin is often dry, you have combination skin. In addition to using a mild, pH-neutral cleanser, you should:

• Use an exfoliating scrub made from natural ingredients once a week.

• Apply a moisturizing cream on dry skin in the cheek area and a cream for oily skin on the forehead, nose and chin, preferably in combination with astringent herbal waters such as witch hazel or sage water.

DRY skin

This type is characterized by small pores, wrinkles, scaly areas and a feeling of tightness. Gently cleanse skin with moisturizing lotions or plant oils. Use floral water such as orange-flower water and rich facial creams, gels or oils. Try an exfoliating scrub once or twice a month.

• Mix ½ cup (110 g) cocoa butter, 2 teaspoons (10 ml) distilled water, 1½ tablespoons (22 g) grated beeswax, 3 tablespoons (45 ml) sesame oil, 2 tablespoons (30 ml) coconut oil and 3 teaspoons (15 ml) olive oil. Combine beeswax and water and melt over low heat, and add cocoa butter and blend. Gradually add the oils. Pour into a glass jar. The mix will thicken as it cools. Store up to 1 month in a cool, dark, dry place.

• Alternatively, stir together 4 teaspoons (20 g) each lanolin and petroleum jelly, and 2 drops each rose and lavender oils. Stir until smooth. Refrigerate in a porcelain container for up to 2 months.

Oil from orange flowers has long been an ingredient in traditional cosmetics.

GRATED beeswax helps to thicken HOMEMADE SKIN CREAMS.

MATURE skin

• Rose gel may help to plump up mature skin. Warm ⅔ cup (150 ml) distilled water and mix in 1 teaspoon (5 ml) powdered gelatin. Stir in 1 teaspoon (5 ml) rose oil, 4 drops lavender oil, and 3 teaspoons (15 ml) of glycerin. Cool and store in a porcelain jar.

• To preserve skin's elasticity: Melt 2 teaspoons (10 g) grated beeswax in a pan over warm water. Add ¼ cup (50 ml) almond oil, 1 teaspoon (5 ml) jojoba oil, 1 tablespoon (15 g) aloe vera and 5 drops rosewood oil to the wax.

FACIAL oils for night use

Facial oils, when applied sparingly to clean skin, soak in almost completely. All oils are made by combining ingredients in a small, dark bottle and shaking vigorously. When stored in the refrigerator, homemade oils last for about 2 weeks.

- For normal skin: Blend about ¼ cup (50 ml) each jojoba and almond oils with 1–2 drops each rose, geranium, lavender, chamomile and jasmine oils.
- For mature skin: Pour ¼ cup (50 ml) almond oil, 1 teaspoon (5 ml) wheat germ oil and 1–2 drops each jasmine, lavender and chamomile oils into a dark bottle. Shake well.
- For dry skin: Mix ⅓ cup (75 ml) olive oil with 2 teaspoons (10 ml) avocado oil and 5 drops of lemon oil.
- For oily skin: Stir ¼ cup (50 g) powdered aloe into 3 tablespoons (40 ml) distilled water and add 2 teaspoons (10 ml) orange-flower water. Set aside. Mix 1 teaspoon (5 ml) honey and ½ cup (100 ml) apricot kernel oil in a pan over warm water. Combine all the ingredients.
- For sensitive skin: Mix ⅓ cup (75 ml) almond oil and 5 drops neroli oil.

NECKLINE and throat

A woman's décolletage is a symbol of beauty and femininity. Skin on the neck and throat is thinner and more sensitive than other parts of the body, so daily care is required. Try these natural cosmetics, however, they will take time to have an effect.

HOME remedies

- Combat loose skin and aging with an oil wrap. Mix 1 tablespoon (15 ml) almond oil, 1 tablespoon (15 ml) honey, and spread the mixture on a cloth. Apply weekly to your throat for 1 hour.
- For neck wrinkles, use parsley milk. Heat 2 cups (500 ml) whole milk and add a bunch of chopped parsley. Let steep for a few minutes then strain the milk and let it cool to lukewarm. Moisten a soft, clean cloth with the parsley milk, place it on your throat and let it work for 15 minutes.
- To help tighten skin, make a lemon cure by beating an egg white until stiff; stir in the juice of a lemon. Apply and wait 30 minutes. Rinse with warm water and apply moisturizing cream.
- Prepare a balm for nightly skin regeneration: Mix 2 tablespoons (30 ml) apricot kernel oil, 15 drops jojoba oil, 3 drops neroli oil and 1 drop each almond, rose and lavender oils with 2 teaspoons (10 ml) glycerin. Pour into a dark, sealable container. Gently rub in a few drops before bedtime.
- Purée about ½ cup (100 g) raspberries and mix with 2 teaspoons (10 ml) each almond meal and honey, plus an egg yolk. Apply to your neckline as a mask and rinse after 30 minutes with warm water.
- Throat exercises help to keep skin firm. Reach over your head to grasp your left ear with your right hand. Carefully turn your head to the left, hold the tension for a few seconds; relax. Do the same with the other side.

To refresh skin, finish a morning shower with a blast of cold water.

SUN protection

The sensitive skin of the neckline and throat should be protected from the sun. To prevent slackening of the tissue and the formation of wrinkles, always use sunscreen on your face, neck and throat.

Nail care

Attractive nails are a sign of good health and they complement your appearance. When they're well manicured, they make you feel attractive and well groomed. Let your nails shine with regular care and a diet rich in vitamins.

USE AN EMERY BOARD OR glass nail file TO FILE YOUR NAILS.

Nails are made of a hard protein called keratin, which helps to protect fingers and toes from injury. Excessive hand washing and some household cleaners can rob them of vital oil and moisture, sometimes resulting in split or peeling nails. Natural remedies can do much to help keep nails strong and looking healthy, but see a doctor if you suspect you have a nail disease or other nail disorder.

THE essentials of nail care

Ideally, you should give yourself a manicure every other week. Start with a gentle exfoliating scrub to remove scaly skin and dirt, then push your cuticles back. Shape your nails with scissors or a file, filing from the edge of the nail and towards the center. Follow up by massaging your hands and nails with a moisturizing gel, such as aloe vera.

1 To begin with, basic daily cleaning is necessary and simple. Scrub your nails with a soft brush and coat them with a little olive or almond oil.

2 Use a basic hand and nail scrub before a manicure. Heat 2 tablespoons (30 ml) cocoa butter and mix it with 2 tablespoons (30 ml) ground almonds and 5 drops of lemon oil. While it is still warm, massage the scrub into your hands and nails, and rinse with warm water.

3 Soften your cuticles first with a little olive oil. Push them back carefully—don't cut them.

4 Use an emery board or a glass nail file (or even a diamond file for very strong nails) to file your nails; it is a matter of personal preference which you use. Metal files can make nails brittle and fingernail clippers can cause nails to become grooved and frayed.

5 Finish by shining the nails with a chamois nail buffer or a polishing file, or apply clear nail polish.

- An alternative lotion for softening cuticles: Mix together 1 egg yolk, 1 tablespoon (15 ml) fresh pineapple juice, 1 teaspoon (5 ml) lemon juice and 2 drops lemon oil. Apply with a brush or cotton swab. Rinse after 15 minutes.
- Give fingernails a therapeutic oil bath from time to time. Warm ¼ cup (50 ml) macadamia, almond or olive oil and add 1 drop each geranium, sea-buckthorn and lavender oils (from a pharmacy or health food store). Dip your fingers in the oil bath for 2 minutes and massage your hands with the remaining oil.

Nail oil

For flexible, strong nails:

2 tablespoons (30 ml) almond oil
1 teaspoon (5 ml) jojoba oil
5 drops lavender oil
5 drops lemongrass oil

Mix all the ingredients and massage into nails morning and evening.

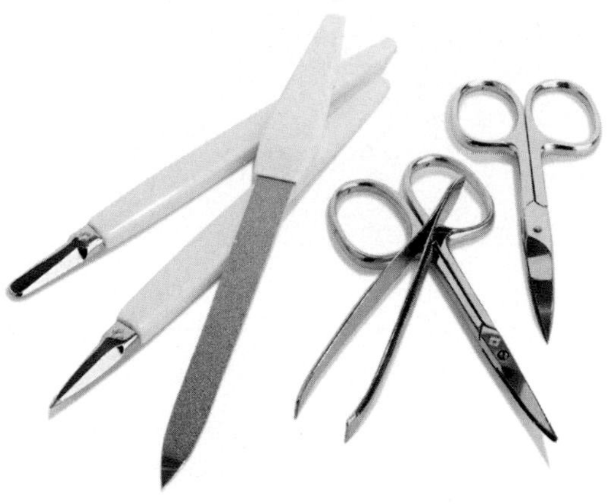

• To make a nourishing poultice: Combine 1 egg yolk and 2 tablespoons (30 ml) wheat germ oil thoroughly; stir in 1 tablespoon (15 ml) each grated carrots and lemon zest. Apply the poultice to nails and the backs of the hands and cover with a cloth. Rinse with warm water after 30 minutes. Apply to nails once a week.

BRITTLE nails and soft nails

Soft or brittle nails that crack or split easily can be frustrating. There are, however, simple ways to strengthen them.

• Coat nails with a little warm olive oil mixed with a couple of drops of lemon juice every evening. Wear soft cotton gloves to bed and let the mixture work overnight.

• Vitamin B_7 (biotin) also strengthens nails. It is abundant in brewer's yeast, soy products, offal and egg yolk.

• Avoid growing long nails, which are naturally weaker, and don't use fast-drying nail polish, as both can make fingernails brittle.

• Soft nails can be toughened up by rubbing them once a day with a mixture of cider vinegar and lemon juice.

When painting your toenails, it helps to use foam separators to keep your toes apart.

Use only high-quality scissors for manicures, or your nails could split.

THE right way to apply nail polish

Look for nail polish that contains as few chemical ingredients as possible. Thousands of years ago, the Chinese painted their nails with a mixture of egg white, gum arabic, gelatin and beeswax.

1 Before applying nail polish, it is a good idea to prime your nails with a protective, nurturing base coat.

2 Apply the nail polish in two coats: Start with a stroke in the center of the nail then do the sides in two or three strokes.

3 Apply a protective top coat so that the nail polish lasts longer.

4 When the time comes to replace it, use nail polish remover that is acetone-free and contains oil to prevent nails from drying out.

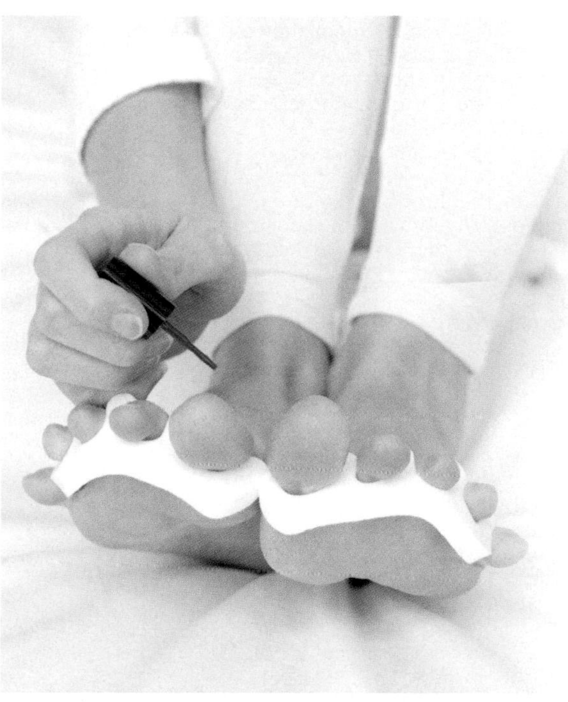

NUTRITION FOR BEAUTY

A healthy, balanced diet is good for more than just keeping off weight. Vitamins and minerals make your skin smooth and supple, strengthen your fingernails, teeth and gums and keep hair shiny and silky.

Vitamins

- A good supply of vitamin A is the basis for healthy skin and a fresh face. Vitamin A keeps skin looking smooth and young by stimulating cell regeneration. You can get it in the form of retinol, which is found in liver, whole eggs, milk and some fortified food products or it's converted from the beta-carotene contained in many orange and green fruits and vegetables. You can make it easier for your body to absorb and convert beta-carotene by boiling or steaming foods containing it and adding a little olive oil or butter.
- B vitamins are key for the growth of skin, hair and nails. Vitamin B_6, in particular, helps to form collagen for firm connective tissue. Biotin, which is often referred to as vitamin B_7, is another of the B-group vitamins that protects skin and hair cells.
- Vitamin C accelerates collagen production in your cells and helps to keep gums healthy. Since vitamin C is quickly destroyed by heat, foods that are high in vitamin C are best eaten raw or lightly steamed.

Minerals

- Iron facilitates oxygen transport in the blood. Pale, brittle fingernails and hair loss can be signs of iron deficiency, one of the most common nutrient deficiencies in the world.
- Potassium helps the body to eliminate harmful substances and plays an important role in keeping skin supple.
- Calcium, which is contained in milk products, makes teeth strong and healthy.
- Magnesium keeps cell walls stable, helping to stop the skin from wrinkling.
- Selenium, found in whole-grain products, may help damaged skin.
- Zinc works with vitamin A in the body to produce and maintain a strong immune system.

Fluids

If your skin is to remain supple, clear and fresh, it needs plenty of fluid. Adequate fluid intake also helps your internal organs filter out harmful substances. A rule of thumb: Drink at least 6 cups (1.5 L) of fluid per day—ideally mostly water, but also moderate amounts of black, green or herbal teas or freshly squeezed fruit and vegetable juices. These are rich in antioxidants to boost your appearance and your health. Drink juices in any combination, but don't underestimate the calorie (kilojoule) content of fruit juices.

Dairy foods are rich in calcium.

Eggs contain a variety of vitamins and minerals.

Sources of vitamins and minerals

Beta-carotene • orange and yellow fruits and vegetables, dark leafy vegetables

Biotin • eggs, legumes, offal

B vitamins • grains, soybeans, nuts, legumes

Iron • meat, whole-grain products

Potassium • dried fruits, legumes, nuts, soy products, vegetables, mushrooms, avocados, bananas

Calcium • milk and milk products

Magnesium • whole-grain products, legumes, mineral water

Selenium • Brazil nuts, brewer's yeast, whole-grain products, seafood, mushrooms, brown rice

Vitamin C • citrus fruits, kiwi fruit, rosehips, blackberries, peppers, papaya, broccoli

Vitamin E • cold-pressed oils, nuts, cereal germ

Zinc • legumes, cereals, nuts, poultry, seafood

Vitamins are classified according to how they are absorbed and stored in the body:

Vitamins A, D, E and K are soluble only in fats.

Vitamin C and the B vitamins are soluble only in water.

Your best source of vitamins and minerals is food, but a multivitamin supplement can offer insurance against gaps in your diet.

Antioxidants

Environmental pollution, cigarette smoke, ultraviolet radiation and stress contribute to the formation of what are known as free radicals in the body. These aggressive oxygen compounds can damage tissue and cause your skin to age prematurely when present in excessive amounts. Natural antioxidants such as vitamin C, vitamin E, beta-carotene and selenium stabilize free radicals and keep them from causing damage in the body. A diet high in antioxidants also reduces your risk of developing many serious diseases. Eating a range of whole foods can help to ward off damaging toxins and free radicals. The following foods are among the top picks for antioxidants.

- Berries are full of healing antioxidants. Blueberries, cranberries and blackberries contain proanthocyanidins that have strong antioxidant properties. Strawberries, raspberries and blackberries contain carcinogen-fighting ellagic acid. Eat them on their own, sprinkle a handful in your morning cereal, make a smoothie or enjoy them for dessert with a little low-fat whipped cream.
- With as much vitamin C and fiber as an orange, gram for gram, broccoli gets a gold star for nutrition. On top of that, it is packed with healthy phytonutrients. Boil it, steam it or use it to make a delicious soup.
- Garlic, also known as "the stinking rose," acts as a natural antibiotic, killing off some strains of harmful bacteria. Roast it whole and spread it on a baguette, or sauté it with a little butter and toss with hot pasta.

Fruit and vegetables should account for about one-third of your diet.

Oral hygiene

Brushing and rinsing, combined with a well-balanced diet, help ensure you have a healthy smile and pleasant breath. They may also improve your long-term health, as many illnesses start in the mouth.

People have believed for centuries that bad teeth signify bad health. It was only comparatively recently that gum inflammation was identified as the problem. The theory is that bacteria from dental plaque seep into the bloodstream via inflamed gums and produce enzymes that make blood platelets stickier and more likely to clot, contributing to the hardening of the arteries. The good news is that this risk factor can easily be controlled.

Healthy teeth and strong gums are the product of conscientious care and good nutrition. Sugar is the number one enemy, as it damages teeth in two ways: by interfering with the absorption of calcium and by causing tooth decay. Milk products, however, contain a healthy amount of calcium, which hardens teeth. To keep gums healthy and strong, eat plenty of fresh fruit and vegetables that contain vitamin C.

Moderately sized heads reach into corners and angles effectively.

TOOTH CARE tips

- Good tooth care does not end with brushing. Cleaning between teeth at least once a day with dental floss is essential. Guide the floss between teeth and wrap it in a "C" shape at the base of the tooth, slightly under the gum line. Slide the floss up to the top of the tooth several times. Finish by rinsing your mouth.
- Recent findings indicate that there's no difference between a regular or electric toothbrush when it comes to thorough cleaning. Because of their rapid, rotating motion, electric toothbrushes clean your teeth effectively in a shorter time, but brushing carefully by hand for 2–3 minutes is equally effective. In either case, replace your toothbrush every 2–3 months.
- Halitosis is often caused by a coating on the tongue, but this is simple to remedy. Just slide a tongue scraper over the tongue several times, twice a day.

Rose flower mouthwash

4 tablespoons (60 g) rose flowers
3 tablespoons (45 g) sage leaves
1 tablespoon (15 g) strawberry leaves
2/3 cup (150 ml) cider vinegar
1/2 cup (100 ml) rosewater

Mix herbs in a sealable container and pour the heated cider vinegar over the top. Steep for 10 days, strain, then wring out herbs well. Mix the remaining liquid with rosewater and pour through a filter. Add a dash to a glass of water and rinse.

MOUTHWASHES

Using mouthwash after brushing leaves your mouth fresh and clean.

- To make a pleasant smelling, refreshing mouthwash mix ¼ cup (50 ml) each water and vodka and 3 drops each of eucalyptus, anise and clove oils in a small bottle. Add 1 teaspoon (5 ml) mouthwash to a glass of water and gargle.
- For another refreshing rinse, mix 2 cups (500 ml) vodka, 2 teaspoons (10 ml) peppermint oil, ½ teaspoon (2 ml) cinnamon oil and ¼ teaspoon (1 ml) anise oil. Add a dash to a glass of water; rinse.
- To make a mouthwash that will help to keep gums healthy, mix 2 teaspoons (10 ml) each arnica, propolis and sage tinctures. Add 10 drops of the mixture to a glass of water and rinse.

HOME remedies for brushing teeth

- For a gum-refreshing tooth powder, finely grate 8 teaspoons (40 g) dried orange peel and mix with about 2 tablespoons (30 g) dried peppermint leaves and 2 teaspoons (10 g) sea salt. Store in a screw-top container. When brushing your teeth, just sprinkle a little powder on a moistened toothbrush.
- For a whitening tooth powder, mix a small container of baking soda with 2–3 drops caraway oil. Don't use it too often as the abrasive action may damage weak tooth enamel.
- To make a tooth powder for sensitive teeth and gums, mix together ¼ cup (50 g) powdered arrowroot, 1 tablespoon (15 ml) cornstarch, 1 tablespoon (15 ml) fine kitchen salt and 5 drops each cinnamon, myrrh and clove essential oils. Sift to remove lumps; store in a china or glass jar with a tight-fitting lid. To use, press a moistened toothbrush into the mixture.
- You can also keep your gums healthy by rubbing them with the inside of a lemon skin. Alternatively, brush your teeth occasionally with warm sage tea.

Flossing will clean your gums and the spaces between your teeth.

Relaxing baths

Take advantage of the power of a long soak to soothe, moisturize and heal your skin. Once you have stepped out of the bath, be sure to apply a moisturizer.

First, determine your skin type (*see pages 73–74 for more on skin types*). Dry and oily skin require different treatments and even normal skin needs special care.

NORMAL skin

- Open your pores with a yogurt-based bath additive. Purée a single-size serving plain yogurt, 1 tablespoon (15 ml) honey, 2 tablespoons (30 ml) almond oil and 1 vanilla bean puréed in a blender. Add 10 drops of orange oil and swirl in bathwater.
- Invigorate skin with a rosemary bath additive. Fill a small jar two-thirds full with fresh rosemary leaves, add enough sea salt to fill the jar then fill with water. Let steep in a warm place for 2 weeks, shaking vigorously every day. Put 2 tablespoons (30 ml) of the mixture in a cloth bag and add it to the bathwater.
- Pamper yourself with a vanilla shower gel. Mix ½ cup (100 ml) neutral, unscented shampoo, ¼ cup (50 ml) warm water, pinch of salt and 15 drops vanilla oil.

OILY skin

- Make a buttermilk bath by adding a purée made from 1 quart (1 L) buttermilk, juice of 4 lemons and 4 generous handfuls of peppermint leaves.
- Soothe your skin with an oatmeal bath. Combine 1 cup (250 g) oats, a handful each of fresh sage and peppermint leaves, and 10 drops of lemon oil in a cloth bag or old pair of clean tights. Drop the bag in your bathwater, squeezing it out occasionally while you soak.
- Stimulate your body with a firming shower gel. Stir together 1 cup (250 ml) shower gel base (available from beauty supply stores or online) with 10 drops each geranium and lemon oils and 5 drops each rosemary, juniper and sage oils.

MATURE and dry skin

- Make skin silky-soft with a bath oil made from ¼ cup (50 ml) almond oil, 10 drops grapefruit oil and 5 drops each lemon and orange oils.
- Soak in a lavender bath. Cover a handful of dried lavender flowers with water, boil for 5 minutes and strain. Add 2 tablespoons (30 ml) honey and 1 tablespoon (15 ml) each cream, buttermilk and olive oil and add to your bathwater.

Skin care

Cleopatra, legend has it, indulged in daily milk and honey baths. Natural ingredients certainly provide nutrients, moisture and subtle fragrances to soothe and refresh skin, and protect it from the sun's harmful ultraviolet rays.

Much time and attention is given to facial moisturizing, but our skin from the neck down requires attention, too. There are many traditional treatments to help keep skin in good condition—just choose those best suited to your skin type (*see pages 73–74 for information on skin types*).

NORMAL skin

- Make a body-nurturing cream by mixing ½ teaspoon (2 ml) lanolin and 1 teaspoon (5 ml) cocoa butter melted in a pan over hot water. Add ¼ cup (50 ml) almond oil and stir frequently until cool. Add fragrance by blending in 5 drops of rose oil (for women) or sandalwood oil (for men).
- Make your skin soft and silky with a poultice of ½ cup (100 g) Dead Sea mud (available at health food stores or online). Mix with 2 teaspoons (10 ml) aloe vera gel and apply to clean, dry skin. Wrap your body in a large towel and let the poultice work for 30 minutes before showering. Use weekly.
- Refresh your skin with body powder. Mix ⅓ cup (75 g) each arrowroot and finely ground polenta. Stir in 5 drops each ylang-ylang and neroli oils. Store the powder in an opaque, sealable container and apply with a powder puff to clean, dry skin.

OILY skin

- Moisturize skin with a nurturing body oil of ⅓ cup (75 ml) jojoba oil with 3 teaspoons (15 ml) almond oil and 5 drops each of lavender and geranium oils. Apply sparingly to skin after bathing.

Squash poultice

Provides moisture appropriate for every skin type.

½ cup (100 g) peeled squash
1 peach
¼ cup (50 g) cucumber, unpeeled
1 tablespoon (15 ml) cocoa butter
1 tablespoon (15 ml) honey
1 egg white

Purée ingredients in a blender. Apply to the skin, wrap your body in a linen cloth or large towel and let the poultice work for 20 minutes before showering.

Body lotions made from plant ingredients can help to refresh and regenerate the skin.

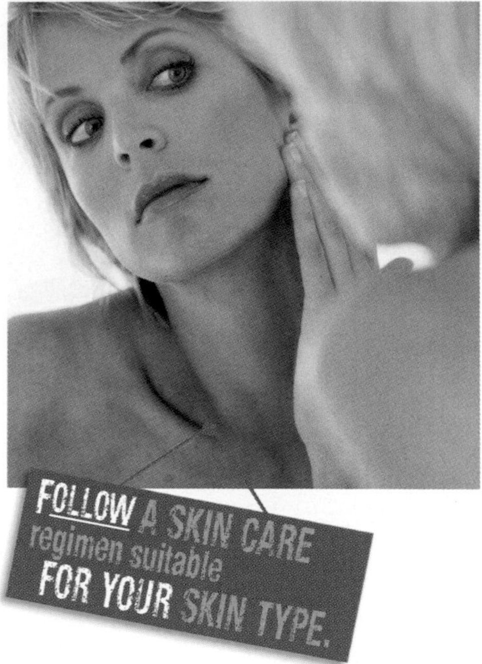

• Fight blemishes on your back and neckline. In a pan over warm water, stir together 2 tablespoons (30 g) whole-wheat flour, 1 tablespoon (15 ml) honey and 2 tablespoons (30 ml) orange-flower water to form a paste. Add 5 drops of lavender oil and spread on problem areas. Shower off after 20 minutes. Apply the mask once or twice a week.
• Remove shine from skin with body powder. Mix 1 tablespoon (15 g) talcum powder, a pinch of cornstarch and 2 drops of lemon oil.

MATURE and dry skin

• Moisturize skin after bathing or showering with a fragrant oil mix. Combine ¼ cup (50 ml) jojoba oil and 10 drops of an essential oil. Good choices include patchouli, mandarin, neroli, lemon, myrrh, rose and lavender oils.
• Treat skin with a body oil that has a floral fragrance. Mix 3 tablespoons (45 ml) each avocado, almond and apricot kernel oils, 15 drops rose oil and 5 drops of lavender oil. Rub in sparingly after a bath or shower.
• Moisturize dry skin with a body cream. Melt 1 tablespoon (15 ml) each cocoa butter and beeswax in a pan over hot water; stir in 1 tablespoon (15 ml) each sesame, avocado and coconut oils. Place in a container and refrigerate for up to two months.
• Soak up the moisture from an exotic poultice. Purée a banana and mix with 2 tablespoons (30 ml) buttermilk, 1¼ cups (300 ml) coconut milk, 2 tablespoons (30 ml) yogurt and 1 tablespoon (15 ml) honey. Massage gently into skin and cover with a large towel. Rinse off after 30 minutes.

ELBOW care

Elbows may be hidden from view for much of the time, but that doesn't mean they should be ignored.
• Treat rough elbows to a poultice. Apply a mixture of 2 tablespoons (30 ml) warmed honey and 1 tablespoon (15 ml) lemon juice. Leave on for 30 minutes, rinse and apply moisturizing cream.
• Alternatively, rub elbows with warm almond oil, wait 5 minutes and wipe off with a clean cloth. Then treat your skin with a mixture of equal parts lemon juice and glycerin.

SUN protection

Sunlight may brighten our lives, but its ultra-violet rays can damage skin and cause premature aging.

Skin test

one Cleanse your face with a mild soap. Apply no other skin care products; wait roughly 2 hours.

two Press a sheet of tissue paper against your face.

three Check the imprint. Oily skin shows imprints of your forehead, nose, chin and cheeks. Normal skin should leave just a glimmer of oil. Combination skin leaves imprints of only the forehead, nose and chin. No imprint will be visible with dry skin.

UVA rays, which have the longest wavelength, are dangerous because they penetrate deeply into the skin, causing damage to collagen and cells. UVB rays are shorter but more powerful, and are most intense during the summer months. They cause sunburn, aging and wrinkling. Research shows repeated exposure to UVB rays can affect the immune system and lead to skin cancer. (*For more information on treating and preventing sunburn, see page 47.*)

GOOD TO KNOW

Sun protection factor (SPF)

Without protection, you can stay in the sun for only a short time before skin begins to burn. The SPF factor is a laboratory measurement of the effectiveness of a sunscreen. Use sunscreen with an SPF of 30, for example, and it will take 30 times as long for skin exposed to the sun to burn. But how long it takes to burn is dependent on many factors, including skin tone, time of day, geographic location and weather conditions.

BEHAVIORAL tips

To protect against sunburn:

- Drink lots of fluids, especially water, to keep the skin from drying out.
- Introduce your skin to the sun gradually—it's best to begin in the spring.
- Opt for the shade (or stay indoors) during the hottest parts of the day.
- Use sunscreen even on cloudy summer days—even though the weather appears dull, ultraviolet rays still pass through the clouds.
- Wear lip balm with built-in sun protection.
- Protect children with sunglasses and a sun hat, as well as keeping their skin protected.
- Wear clothing that is made from natural fibers—ultraviolet rays can penetrate artificial fabrics.
- The closer you get to the Equator, the higher the SPF you need. The same applies to altitudes: The sun's rays are stronger in thinner air. Reflective surfaces (water, snow) also produce intense radiation.

PROPER application of sunscreen

- Apply sunscreen protection several times a day. Be sure to apply plenty to your nose, cheeks, ears, neckline and shoulders.
- Apply sunscreen 15 to 20 minutes before going outdoors and let it dry thoroughly before getting dressed. Use creams if you have normal skin and gels for sensitive skin or if you have an allergy to the sun.
- Reapply cream immediately after swimming, showering or drying off, even when using so-called waterproof sunscreens.

Note: Natural oils, such as avocado or sesame oil, and lemon juice do not provide any protection at all from the sun and are not suitable for use as sunscreens.

Choose a sun hat with a wide brim to protect your neck and ears as well as your head.

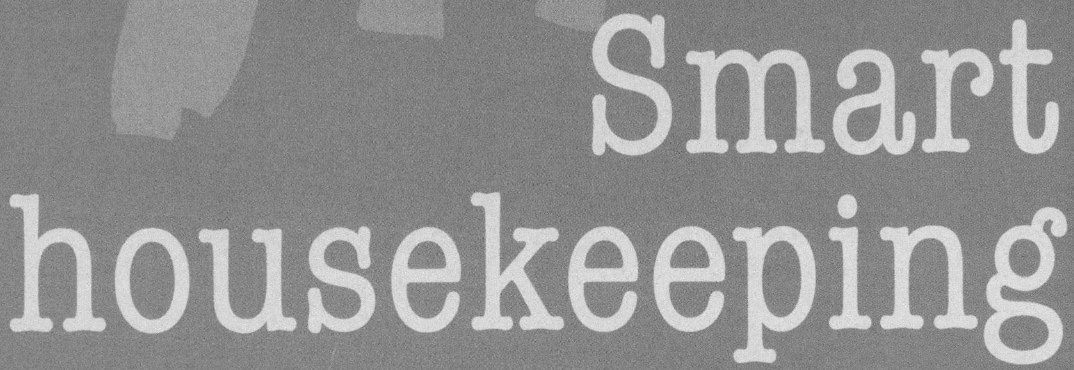

Smart housekeeping

In today's hectic world, we are often so busy with the challenges of work and family that there's little time left for household chores. The good news? There are many easy, traditional ways to clean and care for your home that still produce amazing results.

Bathrooms

Keeping a bathroom clean is essential, but you don't need harsh chemical products to do it. Try these traditional cleaners and cleaning methods to keep your sinks, tiles and fixtures spotless.

For hygiene as well as appearance, your bathroom needs to be cleaned regularly. Bacteria and mold can build up in mineral deposits and soap scum left in the bathtub and sink. Use these sure-fire tricks and keep things sparkling clean.

BASINS, baths and showers

- Clean basins daily with a mild bathroom cleaner then rub them down with a fabric softener sheet—the water will run off easily, leaving no residue.
- Rub off stubborn dirt or mineral deposits with a slice of lemon peel dipped in salt.
- Scrub bathtubs, sinks and tiles with a paste made from salt and mineral spirits to renew their luster.
- Wipe fiberglass bathtubs with a damp cloth and a little baking soda.
- Acrylic bathtubs, which are more delicate than steel tubs, have a reputation for being hard to clean. But as long as you shine them up regularly, all you should need is a little dishwashing liquid and water.
- Help keep shower areas crystal clear with a solution of dishwashing liquid and a soft cloth. Minor soap scum buildup can be rubbed off with vinegar, while serious buildup should be treated with a paste of salt and vinegar applied in a circular motion with a bathtub cleaning brush. Rinse and dry when you're finished. Use a squeegee daily to prevent spots and rub off chalky streaks with vinegar.
- If mold appears anywhere in the shower or bathtub, treat it with vinegar, lemon juice or baking soda.
- Make old tiles gleam by rubbing them with a piece of newspaper or a chamois moistened with ammonia solution. Use 1 teaspoon (5 ml) ammonia in about 2 cups (500 ml) water. Polish with a little cooking oil to add shine and protect against moisture, but avoid getting oil on the grout as this will attract unwanted dirt.

Use an old toothbrush to clean hard-to-reach places.

- Rub away stubborn stains using a cloth with some plain household ammonia.
- Remove rust spots by rubbing them with a mixture of water and vinegar.
- Scour discolored grout between tiles with a solution of household ammonia or baking soda. Dab it on with a moist cloth or use an old toothbrush, let it work and rinse it off.
- Whiten grout by scrubbing it with a little toothpaste on an old, soft-bristled toothbrush.
- Use very fine sandpaper to rub severely discolored grout. Be very careful not to damage the glaze on the tiles.

DRAIN

- Use a small, flat strainer to prevent hair from going down the drain hole and clogging the drain.
- Release any blockages with the suction of an old-fashioned rubber plunger.
- Sprinkle baking soda in the drain and rinse it down with white vinegar followed by boiling water to unclog blocked pipes.
- Eliminate unpleasant smells by sprinkling baking soda directly into the drain and letting it work overnight.

FAUCETS and other fixtures

- Achieve a scent-free shine by rubbing faucets with a mixture of 1–2 teaspoons (5–10 ml) lemon juice and about 2 cups (500 ml) water.
- To remove mineral deposits on fixtures, wrap an old rag moistened with vinegar or lemon juice around the fixture and let it work for a couple of hours or overnight. Remove the softened deposits with a toothbrush.
- Remove scale buildup in faucet aerators and showerheads by letting them soak in a solution of vinegar and salt. Then clean the holes in the showerhead with a nailbrush or toothbrush.

TOILET

- Remove toilet bowl scale by leaving a layer of toilet paper soaked in vinegar on the mineral deposits overnight and rubbing them off the morning.
- Avoid urine scale by putting a dash of vinegar in the bottom of the toilet bowl once a week and leaving it overnight.

Citrus cleanser for the bathroom

This fragrant cleanser is also kind to the environment.

2 teaspoons (10 ml) dishwashing liquid
5 drops lemon oil
5 teaspoons (25 g) citric acid
1 cup (250 ml) water

Mix together the dishwashing liquid and lemon oil. Next, mix the water and citric acid to produce a clear fluid. Add the lemon oil solution to the clear fluid and store in a bottle for up to 3 months.

Beds and bedding

We spend about a third of our lives in bed, so it's worth investing in a good-quality mattress and keeping blankets, pillows and other bedding clean and aired.

A good night's sleep gives the body an opportunity to rejuvenate. It gives muscles and soft tissue time to recover and repair, and the mind a chance to process memories. Poor bedding can disturb sleep, adversely affecting health, mood and quality of life.

BLANKETS, pillows and sheets

- Air and shake out your bedding regularly. This distributes the filling evenly and combats dust mites and other pests that like warm, dark places.
- Hang quilts, blankets and pillows outside on a clothesline on a dry day. However, don't hang out anything with a feather filling in intense sunlight, as this can make it brittle and porous.
- Wash bedding in a washing machine only if the drum is big enough to handle it. If not, have it cleaned commercially.
- Use a gentle detergent or hair shampoo to wash feather or down pillows then put them in the dryer at a low temperature along with a clean tennis ball, which prevents the filling from clumping. Do not vacuum down or feather quilts, or you risk thinning out the filling.
- If you suffer from allergies, wash your bedding frequently and use pillows, quilts and blankets made from synthetic materials or rayon and with synthetic filling, not feathers. These are easier to wash and dry to get rid of mites.

Make sure that sheets and blankets are clean and aired.

GOOD TO KNOW

Mattresses

Good mattresses come in many varieties. They may have a core of synthetic material, such as foam, latex or interior springs, or the core may be made from natural materials such as coconut, horsehair, straw or seaweed. The covering usually consists of linen, cotton or raw silk. Mattresses with a natural core should be refurbished after about five years, as they wear out more quickly than latex or spring mattresses. If you're plagued by allergies, opt for a dust-free, antibacterial mattress of foam or latex.

MATTRESSES

- Prevent lumps from forming by turning a mattress every 3 months and flipping it twice a year. However, a memory foam mattress should never be turned.
- A mattress must be aired and cleaned regularly. Take it out of the bedroom and let it breathe. Then, place a damp sheet on the mattress and beat it. The cloth will pick up the dust and can be laundered.
- Dust a mattress using the upholstery nozzle on the vacuum cleaner whenever you change the sheets.
- Buy a special mattress protector if you have severe dust mite allergies. It will protect the mattress against mites and can be washed at a high temperature.
- Consider mattress covers made of cotton with a polyurethane backing. They are easy to remove and wash, and protect mattresses against stains.

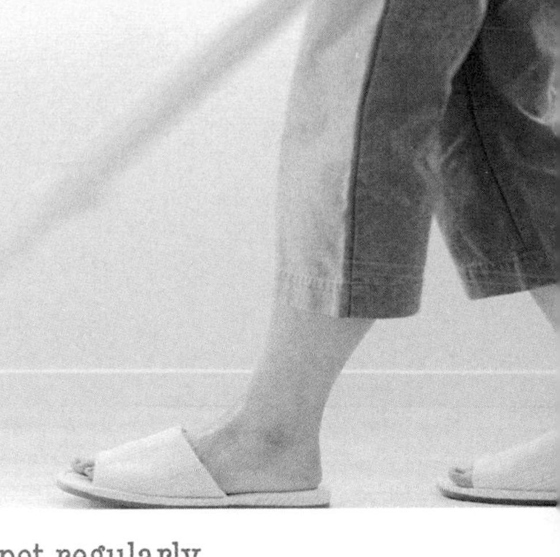

Carpeting

Rugs and carpets in the main areas of the home tend to get a lot of wear. Maintain them on a regular basis so they feel soft under foot, add warmth to a room, look good and last a long time.

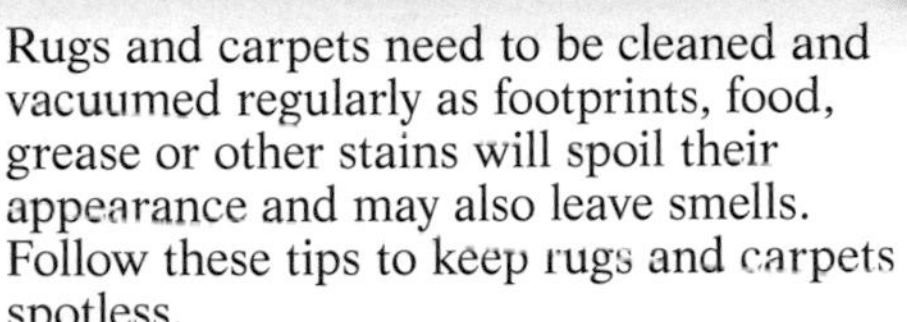

Rugs and carpets need to be cleaned and vacuumed regularly as footprints, food, grease or other stains will spoil their appearance and may also leave smells. Follow these tips to keep rugs and carpets spotless.

DUSTING

- Vacuum a carpet regularly and thoroughly to keep it in good condition, rather than waiting until the dirt becomes visible.
- For the first 6 months, gently brush new rugs to loosen and pick up material.
- Authentic Oriental rugs should be vacuumed only occasionally. Keep the suction level low to avoid damaging the fine fibers.

RUG cleaning

- Wet-clean every rug or carpet from time to time. Put small, washable rugs in the washing machine and clean larger ones by hand with a mild detergent, using a soft-bristled brush or sponge to release the dirt and grime. Rinse afterwards with water and, whenever possible, hang rugs outdoors to dry.
- Use a homemade cleaning powder for rugs. Mix 3 tablespoons (45 ml) soap flakes with 2 cups (500 g) cornstarch. Sprinkle on the rug, work it in with a scrub brush and vacuum.
- Clean and freshen a rug by sprinkling it with moist salt. Let the salt work for a few minutes and vacuum.
- Grate fresh potatoes and scald them with boiling water. After 3 hours, strain them and brush the rug with the potato water. Let it dry and vacuum.
- Freshen a rug's colors by rubbing it with vinegar and water.

Vacuum a carpet regularly to keep it in good condition.

TREATING stains

The occasional accident is unavoidable, but prompt action will help to prevent a permanent stain.

- Soak up rug spills immediately with clean, dry cloths. Weigh them down and leave them for a few hours before treating the stain. When removing stains, work from the edge towards the center.
- Soften dried stains with glycerin to help to loosen them before further treatment.
- Treat coffee stains by dabbing the soiled spots with a solution of 2 tablespoons (30 ml) vinegar and 4 tablespoons (60 ml) water, or a solution of mild detergent. Coffee stains should always be treated as quickly as possible.
- Use cold mineral water on bloodstains, blotting with a clean towel as you go.
- A minor burn spot that hasn't destroyed the pile of a carpet or rug can be removed with an onion-based mix. Boil 1 cup (250 ml) vinegar, ¼ cup (50 ml) talcum powder and two coarsely chopped onions. Allow to cool, then apply and let dry. Once dry, brush off the residue and rub the fibers gently until the burned bits disappear.
- To repair burn holes, use a razor blade to cut some fibers from a section of the carpet that's hidden. Put some all-purpose glue into the burn hole and arrange the fibers in it. Weigh down until the glue dries.
- Treat grass stains with a solution of 1 cup (250 ml) water with 1 tablespoon (15 ml) ammonia, then dab the spot with plain water.

• Soak up grease or oil stains by sprinkling them with plain flour or cornstarch. Let sit for an hour, brush off and remove the residue with water.
• Blot wine stains with paper towels and treat with a solution made from ¼ teaspoon (1 ml) mild detergent and 1 quart (1 L) water. Blot any excess liquid.
• Never put salt on fresh red wine spills because it will set the stain and could leave an indelible blue mark on the pile. Also, it will cause the carpet to remain damp.
• Remove hardened chocolate with a knife, and dab away the residue with cold water, followed by warm water.
• Horrified to find a big wad of chewing gum stuck to the rug? Don't worry. Place a plastic bag filled with ice cubes over it. This will make the chewing gum brittle and it can then be chipped away with a spatula or spoon.

WHAT else you need to know

• To prevent furniture from leaving imprints in a carpet, buy little round plastic coasters just slightly larger in diameter than the feet of the furniture to place underneath them.
• Remove imprints by placing a damp cloth on them and ironing it carefully. Then brush the fibers in the opposite direction.
• Don't let rugs slide. Place rubber rings from canning jars under each corner of a rug to keep it in place and use an anti-slip underlay to stop larger rugs from moving.
• Avoid electric shocks by spraying synthetic fiber carpets with a mixture of 1 cup (250 ml) liquid fabric softener and about 10 cups (2.5 L) water.
• To straighten rug fringes, spray them with laundry starch and smooth them with a comb.
• Spray straw rugs occasionally with a little salt water to keep them flexible.
• Use baking soda to remove bad smells from rugs. Simply sprinkle it on the surface, let it work for half an hour and vacuum it up. For stubborn odors, rub the carpet first with vinegar and water, then apply the baking soda.

Removing furniture impression

1 Move the item of furniture to one side so you can reach the impression.

2 Place an ice cube on the compressed fibers to make them swell up then vacuum to make the pile stand up again.

Curtains

Nets, curtains and blinds shield your family from prying eyes, keep out the cold on winter nights and protect you from summer's heat. By maintaining them carefully, you can extend their life and keep them looking great.

There is a tendency to ignore curtains but, like every other item in your house, they will collect dust, hair and pollution. Regular maintenance will keep them clean so they remain an attractive feature of your interior decor.

DUSTING

- Dust curtains regularly with the upholstery nozzle on the vacuum cleaner so they don't have to be washed or cleaned quite so often.
- Curtains made from synthetic fabrics attract dust. Use cold salt water to dissolve it.

WASHING

- Soak colored curtains in salt water to prevent fading and to help to dissolve dirt.
- Wash delicate curtains by hand in the bathtub with plenty of hand soap or use the detergent recipe given on this page (*see box*).
- Protect sheer curtains in the washing machine by putting them in a pillowcase.
- Always wash curtains using the machine's delicate cycle with plenty of water. That should help to reduce the amount of creasing.
- Allow hand-washed curtains to drip dry; never wring them out. To be sure that they hang properly, weight the bottom edges with clothes pins before hanging them.
- To prevent shrinking, stretch out cotton curtains while they are still wet.
- Stiffen sheer curtains with a 1:3 sugar–water solution added to the last rinse, or put them in water that has been used for boiling rice.

Hang newly washed fine fabric curtains while still damp so they don't have to be ironed.

- Give your curtains a wonderful fragrance by adding a few drops of perfume or essential oil to the wash cycle.

COMBATING yellowing

- Yellowed sheer curtains recover their gleaming white color even without chemical bleaches if you soak them in a baking soda solution of ¾ cup (175 g) baking soda in 10 quarts (10 L) water before washing them. You can get the same effect by adding a glass of cola or 2–3 denture cleaning tablets to the curtains' wash cycle. Dry in the sun.
- Salt, the cure-all, also helps with this. Simply soak smoke-yellowed curtains overnight in a salt solution of 2 cups (500 g) salt in 10 quarts (10 L) water and wash as usual.
- If older sheers lose their whiteness, give them an attractive cream color instead. Just add an infusion of weak tea to the rinse cycle. The intensity of the color depends on how long you let the tea steep.

Detergent for curtains

¼ cup (50 g) soap
10 quarts (10 L) water
4 tablespoons (60 ml) ammonia
4 tablespoons (60 ml) mineral spirits
Dissolve the soap in hot water and stir in the ammonia or mineral spirits. Pour the solution over the curtains laid flat in the bathtub and leave for an hour before rinsing. This works particularly well on delicate curtains.

Dishes

Always hand wash valuable silverware, fragile glassware and pieces of delicate porcelain, which might be damaged by a dishwasher. To remove stubborn stains and baked-on residue from other dishes, pans and utensils, old-fashioned elbow grease and a bit of traditional ingenuity are often more efficient than modern appliances.

Making soft soap

Soap making is an age-old tradition and this recipe has been used for generations. A teaspoonful of the gel will clean the dishes—but don't use it in the dishwasher.

6 tablespoons (90 g) unscented bar soap
1 quart (1 L) cold water
A heatproof jar with tight-fitting lid

Using a fine grater, grate the soap and put it into an old saucepan.

Add the water and place the saucepan over low heat. Bring just to a boil, stirring occasionally, then simmer gently for 15 minutes.

Pour into the jar, let cool, then seal and leave for a day to form a gel.

If you are using a dishwasher, check that the dishes you are putting in are designated "dishwasher safe" by the manufacturer. Wooden chopping boards and plates should not be machine washed, as they can't stand the heat and will lose their luster or even crack and split. You're also better off washing dirty pots and pans by hand. They take up too much space in the dishwasher and require a special, less energy-efficient wash cycle to get them clean.

BEFORE washing

- Soak dried-on food remains to soften them before rinsing. You'll find that grease rinses off better with hot water, but carbohydrates and proteins are best removed with cold.
- Protect delicate porcelain by lining your sink with a towel.
- Rubbing lipstick marks with salt makes them much easier to wash off.

WASHING by hand

- Make some soft soap (*for recipe, see above right*) from odds and ends of old soap. As well as being a proven cleaner, it avoids waste.
- To kill germs, use water heated to at least 140°F (60°C) when washing by hand and change your dishwashing sponge and dish towels frequently.

- As a general rule of thumb, wash nongreasy items first. The proper sequence should be: glasses, cutlery; plates, bowls and other dishes; and finally, pots, pans and baking pans. If possible, fill a second sink or basin with hot, clear water for rinsing.
- Wash glazed and unglazed earthenware pottery by hand, without detergent if possible. Remember that the glaze on earthenware pottery is heat sensitive.
- Take special care when cleaning cutlery with wood, bone and ivory handles. Rinse the metal parts with a damp sponge but don't soak or dip the handles into water. Place the cutlery into the drainer basket with the handles up.

• Remove hairline cracks in fine china by soaking it overnight in a large bowl of warm milk (no warmer than milk you would give to a baby). Gently hand-wash as usual—the tiny lines should disappear.

REMOVING stains from porcelain

• Remove tea stains or residue from porcelain cups by mixing hot water with 1 teaspoon (5 ml) baking soda in the cup, let it soak, then wash it out thoroughly. Or, mix 2 tablespoons (30 ml) chlorine bleach in 1 quart (1 L) water. Soak the cup in the solution for no more than 2 minutes and rinse immediately.
• Light mineral deposits are easy to wipe off with a damp sponge and vinegar.
• Wash off stubborn mineral deposits by pouring a dash of citric acid and hot water into the container to be cleaned and let it sit for 1 hour. Repeat as needed until the residue is dissolved, then wash and rinse thoroughly.
• Wipe brown stains from a teapot with a paste of vinegar and salt.
• Scrub away stains with a mixture of salt and vinegar or lemon juice.

CLEANING teapots and coffeepots

• Never wash teapots with dishwashing liquid or in the dishwasher; just use hot water. A layer of tannin residue actually enhances the aroma of the tea.
• However, if you don't like the look of the tannin, remove it gently by adding vinegar to the teapot and let it steep before rinsing it out. Another option is to dip a damp cloth in baking soda and use this to wipe out the pot before rinsing it.

Gluing porcelain

one Lay out the broken porcelain, quick-drying glue and dressmakers' pins or reusable tape and protect the work surface with newspaper or an old towel.

two Clean the broken pieces of porcelain and the areas to be glued with a lint-free rag. Let dry.

three Apply a very thin layer of glue to the broken pieces.

four Carefully fit the pieces together and let them dry. If necessary, hold them in place with pins or tape. Immediately wipe off any glue that squeezes out from the joints.

• Clean a glass coffeepot by adding a handful of uncooked rice and filling it with dishwater. Put the lid on and shake until the stains are gone.
• Dissolve denture cleaning tablets in warm water to remove stubborn mineral deposits.

AFTER washing

• Air dry dishes for best results. Place them vertically in a dish drainer. Make sure the handles of stainless steel cutlery and silverware all point down.
• Dry dishes while they are still warm to prevent watermarks and bring out the shine. Use dish towels made from an absorbent material, such as cotton or linen, and wash them several times before use.
• Protect porcelain by placing paper towels between each plate before storing them in the cabinet.
• Allow thermos bottles to dry thoroughly and store them with the top off so that they don't smell musty.
• Hang cups if possible to save space.
• Turn the tops of tureens, sugar bowls and teapots upside down to protect any protruding parts.

If you are using a dishwasher, check that the dishes you are putting in are designated "dishwasher safe" by the manufacturer.

Floors

How you care for your floors depends on what they are made of. Some, like shiny, sealed floors, take less effort to keep clean than unsealed ones, while delicate materials, such as wood or laminate, require special attention.

Floors are made to walk on, so naturally they need frequent care to keep them clean and in good condition. Tile, wood and stone floors require special treatment to bring out their characteristic highlights and avoid damage.

TILE floors

- Sweep or vacuum the floor before mopping it. Mop in a wavy line, without lifting the mop from the floor, starting at one end and moving towards the door. If the floor is very dirty, you may need to change the cleaning water.
- Choose a sponge mop for cleaning tile floors, as they do a much better job of cleaning seams and small irregularities in the tiles. For extra stubborn dirt, use a scrubbing brush and wash the tiles by hand—sometimes there is no substitute for elbow grease.
- Clean stone floors by adding a small amount of ammonia to the water. This combination also makes dull tile floors shine like new.
- Seal porous terra-cotta and unglazed natural stone tiles with linseed oil as soon as they have been laid (before grouting), and avoid mopping for 2 weeks. You can use this type of waterproofing for areas that are subject to heavy use, such as doorways and the kitchen.
- Remove liquid stains (such as tea, coffee, cola, red wine, fruit juices and ink) from porous tiles by dabbing them with a little regular stain remover, available from supermarkets or hardware stores.

WOOD floors

- Make sure as little moisture as possible is left behind by a wet mop, as this will cause wood floors to swell and warp. Beware of using extremely hot water as it may cause the wood to crack and split.
- Tackle serious stains and streaks on sealed wood floors by adding a shot of ammonia to the water.
- Sweep up sand and small stones at once, as they are abrasive and could scratch and cause damage.
- Remove scratches in a wood floor with a little shoe polish.
- Mop sealed wood floors with black tea to add a matte sheen and an attractive color.

Removing scratches from wood

one Rub out scratches with a mixture of equal parts lemon juice and olive oil, applied on a soft, lint-free cloth.

two Rub in some furniture wax, or mix a little medium-brown shoe polish with basic floor polish.

three Rub the mixture into the wood until the color matches the floor.

• Avoid waxing floors too often. The trick is to add 4 tablespoons (60 ml) furniture polish and 1 cup (250 ml) white vinegar to mop water occasionally.
• Scrub oiled wood floors with a warm soda solution—3 tablespoons (45 ml) baking soda in 1 quart (1 L) warm water—then mop with tap water. Repeat until the solution is mopped up and floors are clear. Occasionally recoat the floor with a thin layer of linseed oil.
• Carefully scrape off ground-in dirt with a knife, working in the direction of the wood grain. Lightly rub the area with a dab of mineral spirits before washing and polishing with a soft cloth.

OTHER materials

• Sweep and damp mop laminated floors. Too much moisture will make the material swell.
• Damp mop sealed cork flooring then rub dry. Apply wax sparingly twice a year and polish occasionally until shiny. You don't have to dry cork flooring that is vinyl coated.
• You can best protect a stone floor by applying a concrete sealer and wax. Clean slate and stone flooring with water and a sparing amount of household cleaner, but be careful—if you use too much cleaner it can remove the color. After mopping and drying, apply some lemon oil to make the floor shine like new. Remove any excess oil with a dry rag.
• Wash polished limestone flooring with a low-pH all-purpose cleaner or it will become dull. Use a cleaner with as little detergent as possible (10–20 percent) and no more than 4 percent phosphate, as both are not biodegradable.
• Do not use vinegar for cleaning or washing natural stone floors, such as limestone or marble. They can dissolve when exposed to acidic cleaners.

• Remove stubborn marks from vinyl floors by rubbing with kerosene and superfine steel wool. Then wash with warm, soapy water, rinse and mop dry.
• Remove scuff marks and dirt from baseboards covered with polyurethane or oil-based paint with a sponge and a grease-cutting, all-purpose dishwashing liquid then wipe with a cloth dampened with water. You can also use a household spray cleaner—spray on a clean cloth, not the baseboard, to prevent streaking and avoid getting it on the floor.
• If you find really tough stains on the baseboard, test an inconspicuous corner with scouring powder on an all-purpose, plastic scrubbing pad. If the test does not cause any damage, apply the method to the entire baseboard.

Before mopping a parquet floor, make sure it is free from dust and debris.

Furniture

As household items are made from different materials, no single cleaning agent will work on all of them. But there are a variety of excellent, gentle everyday ingredients you can use to keep furniture bright and clean.

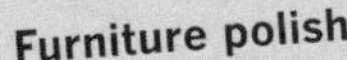

Furniture polish

For light wood:
2 teaspoons (10 g) beeswax granules
½ cup (100 ml) soybean oil

For dark wood:
½ teaspoon (2 g) beeswax granules
1 teaspoon (5 ml) lanolin
4 teaspoons (20 ml) soybean oil
1 teaspoon (5 ml) mineral spirits

Melt the beeswax in a heatproof bowl then beat in the other ingredients. Allow it to cool and pour it into a metal or glass container and seal. Apply sparingly with a soft cloth and buff with a clean one. It can be kept for up to 6 months.

First, clear out all harsh chemical cleaning products stored under the kitchen sink and replace them with the natural, safe cleaning agents now available.

ANTIQUE furnishings

- Never expose antique wood to direct sun or treat with conventional polishes. Because of its age, it's delicate. Rather than using oils that can degrade the finish, polish antique furnishings with beeswax granules (available from a hardware store) made to treat antique wood for long-lasting protection.

WOOD furniture

How you maintain wood furniture depends on the type of wood and how it was manufactured. Veneered furniture should also be treated according to the type of veneer.

- Shine teak or rosewood furniture with a mix of 1¼ cups (300 ml) beer, 1 tablespoon (15 ml) melted beeswax granules and 2 teaspoons (10 ml) sugar. Brush on thinly, let dry and buff with a cotton cloth.

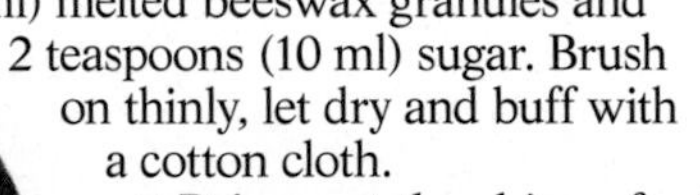

- Bring out the shine of a fine wood veneer:

1 Pour 1 cup (200 ml) olive oil and 4 teaspoons (60 ml) filtered fresh lemon juice in a glass bottle.
2 Seal the bottle with a cork and shake vigorously for a minute.
3 Open and apply the mixture to a 100% pure cotton ball, cover with a linen cloth or dish towel and polish the veneer using a circular motion.
4 Dry it with a clean cloth.

- Maintain oak by applying warm beer then go over it with a cotton rag. Rub remaining stains with mineral spirits and apply another coat of varnish.
- Bring out the grain and color of walnut by rubbing it occasionally with milk. Rubbing scratches with a walnut cut in half work well.
- Grease from your hands or oil can leave stains on untreated or dulled wood, as the wood will absorb it. Press a cheesecloth on it, then apply a warm iron to help loosen and absorb the stain.
- Rub water stains with a mixture of equal parts white toothpaste and baking soda. For light-colored wood, try rubbing a Brazil nut over the spot. For dark wood, dab a mixture of wood ash and vegetable oil on the stains using a cork.

Shine teak or rosewood with a mixture of beer, melted beeswax granules and sugar.

• Remove rings left by glasses by mixing mayonnaise with a little wood ash and rubbed in.
• Remove scratches from light-colored wood with petroleum jelly or a mixture of 1 teaspoon (5 ml) oil and 1 teaspoon (5 ml) white vinegar. For dark wood, use red wine instead of the vinegar.

RATTAN and wicker furniture

• Clean untreated cane, rattan or bamboo by vacuuming the furniture, then cleaning with a cloth dipped in a mild soap solution. (For extra cleaning power, add a dash of ammonia.) For varnished wicker, cane or chairs with raffia or straw seats, soap and water should do the trick. A small, stiff brush is good for cracks.
• Increase the durability of rattan or wicker by brushing it once a year with salt water.
• Lighten the color of wicker by rubbing it with half a lemon or a mixture of salt and vinegar. Rinse thoroughly after treatment and dry naturally.
• Get sagging wicker seats back into shape by dampening them with hot water and letting them dry outdoors for at least 24 hours. As the fibers dry, they tighten and shrink back to their original shape. Make sure they dry in the shade, as direct sunlight could bleach them.
• Treat the underside of furniture with lemon oil to keep it from drying out.

SMOOTH surfaces

• Use a soap and water solution with a dash of vinegar to clean furniture with plastic tops.
• If the glass panes of bookcases or display cases are very dirty, moisten a cotton ball with rubbing alcohol and rub the glass in circles to avoid streaking.
• Marble is extremely porous and must never be cleaned aggressively. Wipe it with a soft cloth moistened with 1 tablespoon (15 ml) liquid soap in 1 quart (1 L) water. If it's not valuable, try a little lemon juice or lemon rind and salt. Let the juice work for just a few seconds or the acids will attack the stone. Apply a mixture of 3 tablespoons (45 ml) baking soda and 1 quart (1 L) warm water to dull marble. Leave it for 15 minutes, rinse and rub dry.

Removing wax from wood

1 Use a hair dryer switched to the lowest fan speed and highest heat setting to melt the wax residue on the wood.

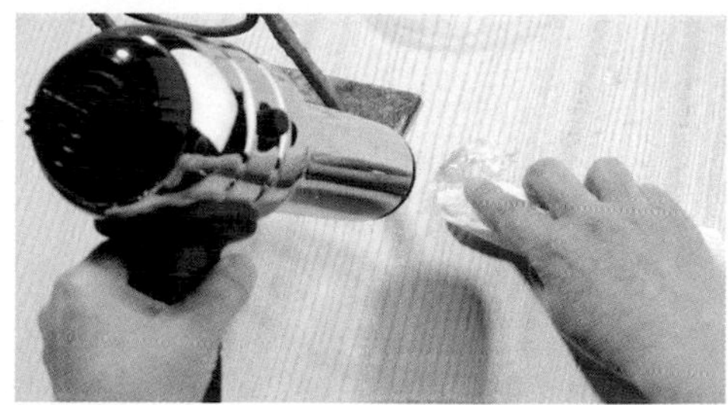

2 Rub the wax off with a piece of paper towel,then wipe with a solution of equal parts white vinegar and water.

Glass and mirrors

They attract dust, dirt and scratches, and every touch leaves a mark. But when mirrors and glass surfaces gleam, the whole house sparkles. Here are some simple methods to keep them looking good.

A few standard household items and a little elbow grease should keep glass surfaces and mirrors clean.

GLASS surfaces

- Wipe tabletops with lemon juice, drying them with paper towels before polishing with newspaper to keep them shining like new.
- Polish away small scratches by smearing on a little toothpaste, then buffing it off with a soft cloth.
- Remove dried-on dirt specks by wiping them with ammonia and water.
- Allow wax to harden before carefully lifting it off with a razor blade. Use rubbing alcohol to remove the remainder.
- Smooth a sharp chip in a glass surface by covering the edge with a thick layer of clear nail polish.
- Clean flat-screen monitors and televisions with a soft, dry microfiber cloth, wiping it gently. Don't scrub. Pushing on the screen can burn out the pixels. Instead, barely dampen your cloth with distilled water.

MIRRORS

- Keep mirrors gleaming with a mixture of warm water and vinegar. Combine 1 cup (250 ml) white vinegar with 1 quart (1 L) warm water and rub on the mirror with a soft cloth. Use crumpled newspaper to wipe the mixture away in slow circles. Presto! No streaks.
- Clean a mirror by rubbing it with a potato cut in half, then rinsing with water and polishing. It will keep bathroom fog at bay, too, which is an added bonus.
- Keep mirrors clean without leaving streaks by wiping them with cool, strong black tea and drying with a chamois.
- Use a little rubbing alcohol to leave a nice luster after polishing. This will also remove the sticky film left by hairspray.
- Defog mirrors with a hair dryer after a shower. A quick blast should clear up the problem.
- Prevent mirrors from fogging up by coating them with shaving cream or toothpaste and wiping them dry with a clean towel before showering.
- Avoid placing a mirror in direct sunlight, as that can dull its surface.

Glassware

People have collected luminous stemware and beautiful crystal drinking vessels for centuries, handing them down from one generation to the next. Being fragile, they need a little special attention and should be handled with care.

By observing a few basic rules, you can banish smudges and water rings on decanters, vases and glasses—without breaking them.

- Hand wash high quality glasses instead of putting them in a dishwasher, which may mark them.
- If you must use a dishwasher, slide stemmed glasses in sideways to be sure they don't break.
- Place a dish towel in the sink when washing delicate glassware to prevent chipping.
- Remove lipstick marks with table salt before washing glasses.
- Clear a cloudy glass by dipping it in an ammonia solution, then wash it thoroughly.
- Add a dash of vinegar or lemon peel to the dishwater to make glasses gleam.
- To keep cold glasses from cracking, wash them in warm water only. Scalding hot water will leach the shine from crystal glasses and dull the gold or silver rims on glassware.
- Wash glasses with painted detail as quickly as possible. If you keep them in the water for too long the decorations may dissolve.
- Rinse beer, wine and champagne glasses with warm, clear water only. Detergent residue can change the taste of a drink as well as take the fizz out of champagne and the head off your beer.
- Dry glasses with a linen dish towel to avoid leaving lint flecks.
- Polish glasses by rubbing on a thin paste of baking soda and water. Rinse thoroughly and buff with a soft cloth.
- Store wine glasses upright. There is a risk that the rims could be damaged if the glasses stick to the cabinet shelf.

Cloudy glass vase remedy

You can combat serious dirt or clouding on glassware with a salt and vinegar paste.

1/3 cup (80 g) salt
2 tablespoons (30 ml) vinegar

Mix the salt and vinegar to form a paste. Spread the paste on the inside of the vase using a finger or a soft brush. Let it sit for 15-20 minutes, then wipe off the paste and rinse the vase with clear water.

SPARKLING clean vases and carafes

- Help crystal maintain its shine by washing it in warm water only, then rinsing and drying it. Or wash it in hot, soapy water, then rinse with hot water and dry.
- Clean narrow-neck glass containers with a bottle brush using vinegar and water.
- Remove hard-to-reach dirt in a decanter or container with crumbled eggshells and lemon juice. Let it stand for 2 days, shake it back and forth a few times then rinse.
- To combat algae in a vase, add a handful of black tea leaves and douse them with vinegar. Tip the vase back and forth until the green coating disappears.
- Buff leaded crystal vases with a chamois after they have been washed.

Store wine glasses upright with the bowls open to the air or they may develop a musty smell.

HOUSECLEANING

The key word when it comes to housework is "organization." Follow a regular schedule that includes daily, weekly and occasional tasks, as well as spring cleaning, and it won't seem so daunting. It will also save you time and energy in the long run.

Daily

Keep your household orderly so that it is easier to keep clean. These daily household tasks can be handled in no time at all.

- Pick up scattered clothing, shoes, toys and papers—you're well on your way to a tidy home.
- Shake out bedding and air your bedroom thoroughly.
- After brushing your teeth in the morning, rinse out the bathroom sink with water to prevent scum buildup.
- Wash all dishes, cutlery, pots and pans used to prepare and eat meals during the day.
- Wipe down the work surfaces in your kitchen to prevent dirt and germs from taking hold.

FROM TOP to BOTTOM, from BACK to FRONT...

Weekly

Make time for these weekly housecleaning chores, and any major spring cleaning will be so much easier than if you had let the work build up.

- Dust, vacuum and mop the floors throughout the house.
- Clean the bathroom thoroughly: Scrub the basins, shower and/or bathtub and toilet; wipe down the tiles in wet areas; and wash the floor.
- Clean the mirrors.
- Wipe out your refrigerator and thoroughly clean the stove and sink.
- Take out garbage regularly and put the bin out every time there's a trash collection.
- Put out recyclables on collection day.
- Change and wash household linens.
- Sweep the deck, porch or patio.

Dust, vacuum and mop the floors throughout the house.

Occasionally

Develop a cleaning schedule to give you an overview of tasks that require less frequent attention. Follow the schedule to be sure that nothing gets overlooked. Include the following:

- Wash windows.
- Wash curtains and blinds.
- Clean doors and door frames.
- Clean upholstered furniture thoroughly.
- Maintain wood furniture.
- Wipe down kitchen cabinets.
- Make sure kitchen appliances are serviced as recommended.
- Clean lamps.
- Clean rugs and carpets.
- Dust walls.
- Take care of all cleaning equipment.

A system for cleaning

Before you start, make sure you have all the cleaning materials you require. You won't need heavy-duty chemicals, even for your annual spring cleaning. A mild, all-purpose cleaner, vinegar, lemon and furniture polish should do the trick.

Set aside adequate time for housecleaning and wear old, comfortable clothing that you don't mind getting sweaty and dirty. You might also want to wear nonslip shoes and gloves, as well as eye protection, depending on the type of work.

If you want a time-honored system for cleaning, follow these three rules:

- from top to bottom
- from back to front
- clean the same items at the same time (for example, clean all the glass, wash all the surfaces, etc.).

Start by clearing the cobwebs from the ceiling, then polish the wood and glass, dust, clean upholstered surfaces, finishing with the floors. Always work from the back corner of a room towards the door. Right-handed people usually work more effectively from right to left, left-handed people from left to right.

Spring cleaning

Take on just one manageable area every day. For example, on the first day clean the bedroom, the next day do the bathroom, and so on.

- Move the furniture and clean neglected corners.
- Clear out your closet and weed out clothes you haven't worn in a long time. A good rule of thumb: If you haven't worn it for a year, get rid of it.
- Check the freezer for out-of-date foods and discard them, then defrost (if necessary) and clean.
- Check stored foods for freshness and throw out any that are past their best.
- Clear out the garage and/or garden sheds, earmarking any reusable items to give to charity or put in a garage sale.

Kitchen care

The kitchen is the heart of the home, where the family gathers and everyone relaxes with a cup of tea or coffee, a mug of hot chocolate or a glass of wine. Guests often congregate in the kitchen, too, so it's a part of the home that needs regular attention.

Generally, you don't need special equipment or chemical cleaners to keep the kitchen looking good if you stick to a routine and deal with spills and other mishaps as soon as they occur.

Cleaning the stovetop

Make sure your stovetop gleams by cleaning it with this mixture. It can be made up in larger quantities and stored as it will keep for up to 4 months.

Boil 1 cup (250 ml) water and add 1 teaspoon (5 ml) soft soap.

Mix 1/2 teaspoon (2 ml) glycerin and 1/4 cup (50 ml) vinegar in a bowl and pour the boiling soapy water in it.

Stir in 6 tablespoons (90 g) whiting (dry, ground calcium carbonate) and transfer to a bottle; seal tightly.

SURFACE care

Countertops and other well-used surfaces in your kitchen require daily attention to keep them clean and free of mold and bacteria.

- Laminate or granite surfaces can be washed off with a sponge and a soap solution, or even with one part vinegar and one part water. Wipe dry immediately to avoid streaks.
- Wipe down large surfaces with a cloth in each hand: one for cleaning, the other for drying.
- To eliminate germs from work surfaces, scrub unsealed wood surfaces regularly with salt or a mixture of 4 tablespoons (60 ml) baking soda and 2 tablespoons (30 ml) lemon juice.
- To make wood surfaces dirt resistant, rub them with a little olive oil or linseed oil after cleaning and removing water stains. (*see "Furniture," page 98*)
- When cleaning cabinets, inside or out, add a little vinegar to the soapy water to cut through grease.

SINKS

- Use a bar of soap to make stainless-steel sinks spotless. Rubbing them with potato peelings, lemon juice or baking soda are also proven methods for removing stains.
- Use a couple dashes of lemon juice on a sponge to rub down a discolored sink.
- Rub out heat marks in the sink by sprinkling on a little baking soda, then rinsing it off.
- Spots from mineral deposits disappear when you treat them with a mixture of vinegar and salt. Place a paper towel over the spot, sprinkle with the solution and let it set. Remove the paper towel and rinse.

STOVETOP

- Wipe up splashes and spills on your stovetop immediately—it will save you a lot of extra work.
- If food gets burned on an electric heating element, dampen a cloth with soapy water, place on the cold element for 2 hours and wipe it clean. Deal with spills in the grooves of the heating element by slightly heating the element and sprinkling it with a little baking soda, then rubbing it in with a sponge. Wipe it off with a damp sponge or cloth.
- Ceramic glass cooktops are especially easy to clean: Simply wipe them with a damp sponge. If food is burned on, sprinkle a little lemon juice on it, let it sit for a few minutes, wipe and, if necessary, remove any residue with a glass scraper. To maintain an attractive shine, polish the cooktop with a little vinegar. And to avoid scratches, lift rather than slide pots and pans from one burner to the next.

• Lightly rub dried-on deposits on a gas stove's nonremovable parts with a moistened dishwasher tablet, then wipe dry. Wear protective gloves.

OVEN and grill

• While the oven is still hot, put a heatproof container of hot water inside; the moisture will make it easier to wipe clean.
• Place foil or a baking tray underneath a baking or roasting pan—it will save you some elbow grease if the pan's contents boil over.
• If your oven is not self-cleaning, while still warm, remove burned-on foods with salt and wipe the surface dry with a piece of newspaper or a paper towel. Use a damp cloth to soften any particles that remain so that they can be scrubbed away easily.
• Loosen baked-on deposits by putting a glass bowl with ½ cup (125 ml) full-strength ammonia, into a cold oven and leaving it overnight.
• Scrub burned-on sugar with newspaper and salt, then wash with soap and water.
• Place food on foil before cooking it to help to keep grill pans clean. Put the foil matte side up to avoid "sparking."

REFRIGERATOR and freezer

• Preserve rubber seals by rubbing them with talcum powder so that they don't become brittle.
• Clean the inside of your refrigerator regularly with vinegar and water, or wipe it down with a solution of baking soda and water.
• If you don't have a frost-free freezer, mini icebergs may form. If this happens, it's time to defrost. Empty the contents of the refrigerator into a cooler or wrap them in old blankets. Then place a pot of boiling water inside the refrigerator and close the door until the ice melts. Wipe with dishwashing liquid, vinegar and water.
• To prevent rapid ice buildup, wipe down the inner freezer walls after you defrost with cooking oil or glycerin. When you defrost next time, the ice will come away from the walls easily.

Keep your kitchen sparkling with the right cleaning techniques.

Kitchen gadgets and utensils

A coffeemaker, toaster, blender or microwave makes life easier, while a good range of utensils makes the preparation and cooking of food easier, faster and more enjoyable. Regular maintenance and a bit of traditional care will keep your kitchen in fine working order.

Most kitchen appliances run on electricity, so special care should be taken when cleaning them. The first step is always to pull out the plug, then detach all removable parts and wash them by hand or put them in the dishwasher.

CLEANING, de-scaling and maintenance

- De-scale the espresso machine or coffeemaker regularly using a mixture of equal parts of vinegar and water. Add the solution to the reservoir and run it through just as if you were making a pot of coffee. Then repeat the process twice using plain water.
- Fill your teakettle with the same solution (equal parts vinegar and water) to remove scale. For significant calcium deposits, bring the mixture to a boil, leave it for 30 minutes, empty it out and rinse thoroughly.
- Before cleaning your microwave, add a slice of lemon to a bowl of water and heat until steam forms. Then simply wipe out the appliance with a cloth. Vinegar and water work just as well.
- Rub a little cooking oil into the rubber seals of kitchen appliances occasionally so they will close tightly.
- Make the hand mixer's beaters easier to insert and remove by putting a tiny drop of olive oil into the installation sockets.
- Empty the crumb tray of the toaster and shake out the crumbs over the garbage can.
- Use a toothpick to remove food particles trapped in the spray arm of your dishwasher. Once a month, clean the filters and run the machine on empty.
- Garbage disposal units are self-cleaning, but they can get smelly. To keep them running smoothly, operate with a full stream of running cold water that will flush

De-scale when water takes a long time to run through or the coffee tastes funny.

GOOD TO KNOW

Vinegar, an all-purpose cleaning agent

White vinegar makes it easy to remove greasy coatings, render surfaces sparkling clean and banish nasty smells. In addition, this versatile cleaner is both safe and inexpensive to use. Its effective ingredient is acetic acid, in a concentration of 5–8 percent. Bear in mind that you shouldn't use vinegar on marble surfaces, and make sure it's properly diluted before using it on grout or it may eat it away.

the ground-up debris away. At the first sign of an unpleasant odor, chop up some orange or lemon peel and run it through the system.

KNIVES

- Invest in stainless steel kitchen knives and sharpen them regularly. If you don't own a knife sharpener, use the unglazed base of a porcelain teacup.
- Knives cut better if you warm the blades up before you use them.
- Use only top quality knives for cutting foods.
- Use either a plastic or a wooden cutting board—glass, metal and stone aren't suitable.
- To protect your knife blades and avoid injury, keep knives in a knife block, on a magnetic knife strip or in a roll.
- Remove stuck-on residue with a dishwashing brush or a cork dipped in salt.

METAL utensils

- Use a toothbrush to clean difficult-to-reach areas in graters and garlic presses.
- Clean metal flour sieves immediately after use in cold water—warm water will make the flour stick like glue.
- If metal gets rusty, sprinkle it with salt and rub with bacon rind.
- Stick metal kebab skewers into a cork; they'll stay together, making them less dangerous.

WOODEN implements

- Don't put wooden spoons in the dishwasher, as heat and cleaners can damage wood.
- It's important to disinfect wooden cutting boards thoroughly after cutting up poultry, meat or fish to avoid cross-contamination of bacteria. Rub boards with a bleach and water solution, then wash as usual and dry.
- Wash wooden handles promptly and allow them to dry naturally. Occasionally rub in some olive oil and wipe off any excess with a clean cloth or paper towel.
- Prevent grease from sticking to cooking spoons by holding them under cold water just before using them.
- Remove dough stuck to a rolling pin by sprinkling a little salt on it, rubbing it off, then washing and drying it.

Ladles, whisks and salad spoons are easily reached when you stand them handles down in a container.

Laundry

Nowadays, the twist of a knob is all it takes to get clean clothes. But back in the days when doing the laundry was an eight-hour ordeal, there were some helpful tricks—some of which are still useful for saving energy and protecting the environment.

We all like to keep our whites clean and bright, but laundry products such as bleach contain harsh ingredients that are tough on lungs and the planet. Traditional methods will let you keep your laundry room bleach-free and provide the special care required for coloreds, wool, lace, velvet and silk.

WHITEN clothes without bleach

- Let your whites soak in a basin of hot water and lemon slices (tied in muslin) for 1–2 hours, then wash as usual. If clothes are particularly dingy, boil the water, turn off the heat, add your clothing and lemon slices and soak overnight.
- White vinegar works well, too. Pour ½–1 cup (125–250 ml) into the wash with the detergent. It will whiten, help to wash away detergent or soap residue and soften the fabric.
- One more idea: The old-fashioned power of sunlight helps to brighten whites and gives them that wonderful fresh outdoor scent.

PROTECT the environment and save

You can get your washing beautifully clean in an environmentally friendly way with an energy-efficient washing machine using the following ground rules.

- Do not add too much detergent and never use more than the manufacturer recommends, as this will result in a soap overflow.
- Take water hardness into account—the softer the water, the less detergent you need.
- Choose the appropriate washing program so the water level matches the laundry load. This protects the machine, especially during the spin cycle.
- Avoid the prewash cycle, which is not necessary for most laundry.

GETTING the laundry ready

- Soak yellowed or graying laundry in a natural bleach (*see left*).
- Put delicate articles into a cloth bag or an old pillowcase before washing.
- Before washing, close zippers and rub them with graphite or a little grease so that they don't jam later on. Also, undo buttons and turn pockets inside out.
- The collars and cuffs of shirts and blouses don't always come out of the wash clean. Before washing them, use a nailbrush to apply a little shampoo formulated for greasy hair or some liquid detergent. Leave for 15 minutes before washing in the washing machine at the hottest possible setting. For a quick treatment, wash the collar only, by hand, rinse well, rub as dry as possible in a thick towel, and iron dry.
- If possible, remove stains before doing the laundry.
- Soak very dirty laundry overnight in soapy water before washing. Make use of oxygen bleach powder and modern stain removers.

FABRIC conditioner

- These can be pricey, so consider a natural softener. Add 1 tablespoon (15 ml) salt to the last rinse, or pour 1 cup (250 ml) vinegar into the last rinse cycle.

WHITES

- Add ½ cup (125 ml) baking soda to the main wash cycle. It will make your white wash whiter and give it a fresh smell.
- Soak discolored white laundry in fresh milk until it turns sour, then rinse and wash as usual.
- Use dishwasher detergent in your laundry loads instead of laundry detergent. However, this can be hard on clothes, so use it only on heavy-duty clothing, sheets and towels.

COLORED FABRICS

Always check the color fastness of new fabrics. To do this, wet the fabric and rub it with white paper. If any dye comes off on the paper, hand wash the item with soft soap. Follow these tips to keep coloreds looking their best.

- Prevent new colored fabrics from running by adding a dash of vinegar to the wash water.
- Add sugar to the rinse water so colored laundry comes out bright.
- Never hang colored laundry to dry in bright sunlight, as the colors will fade.
- Protect jeans from wear by soaking them in a salt solution—1 tablespoon (15 ml) salt in 1 quart (1 L) water before washing them.
- Do not starch colored laundry when it is still hot, or the colors may run.

VELVET and silk

- Hand wash blouses and pillowcases made from natural silk with a special wool or silk detergent, rinse thoroughly and hang up dripping wet to dry.
- Allow black silk to retain its shine by washing it with black tea and a little mild detergent.
- Washable velvet will shine after being laundered if you brush it down with a little salt.
- Wash raw silk by swishing it around in warm, soapy water before rolling the garment in a towel to extract as much of the water as possible. Lay it flat to dry and iron on the reverse side while still damp.

WOOL

- To banish sweat odors, moisten two cloths with a weak water and ammonia solution, place the article of clothing between them and steam it with the iron.
- Woolens stay soft if you add a few drops of vinegar to the next-to-last rinse and a similar quantity of glycerin to the final rinse.
- Shampoo is excellent for cleaning wool and preventing it from becoming matted.
- Soften a scratchy sweater with 1 tablespoon (15 ml) hair conditioner in a sink of water. Swish the item around for 2 minutes, rinse and dry.
- Spinning wool items can cause them to lose their shape. Roll them gently in a dry towel, squeeze out excess water and dry flat.

Odors

Few homes can escape the less desirable smells that occasionally emanate from kitchens, bathrooms, bedrooms or cupboards. But armed with a bit of traditional wisdom, it's easy to control them so that friends and family receive a fragrant greeting.

The kitchen and bathroom tend to produce most of a home's least desirable smells. But tobacco and other fumes may also be brought in from outside. Proper ventilation is the primary weapon against kitchen odors, but there are also a few simple tricks you can use to help during the cooking process.

COOKING

- Mask odors by boiling water with a little cinnamon in a small pot while cooking.
- Stretch a microfiber cloth moistened with vinegar over the pot in which you're cooking fish and other strong-smelling foods.
- Cooking cabbage? Drop a bread crust into the cooking pot to absorb odors. For cauliflower, try half a lemon.
- If milk boils over, sprinkle it with salt to prevent it from boiling over again.
- After cooking, combat food odors by briefly moistening an electric stove's heating elements with a little vinegar, or boil some vinegar in water. You can also try wrapping a few cloves and a cinnamon stick in foil and placing the package on the hot heating elements.

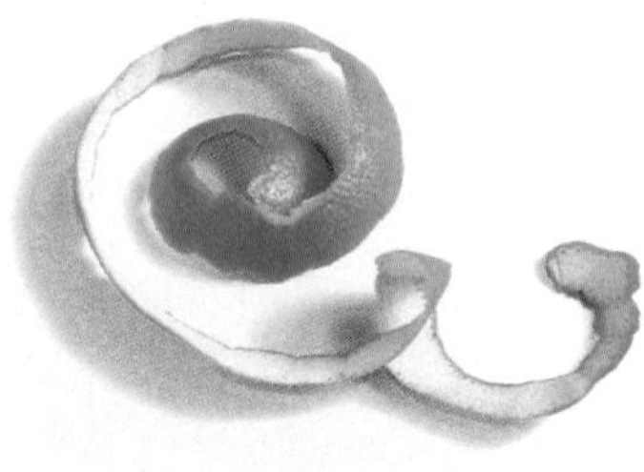

Burning a piece of dried orange peel will spread a pleasant aroma throughout the house.

KITCHEN odors

It's not just the food itself that produces strong odors. Where we store and cook food also contributes to the problem.

- Combat musty smells in kitchen cupboards by washing them with vinegar and water. Bag coffee grounds from the coffeemaker and place them inside cupboards to neutralize any remaining odor.
- Place a bowl of white vinegar on an oven shelf to eliminate odors, or put some orange peel in a warm oven. If you want to eliminate nasty smells in a hurry, try rubbing down the inside of the oven with half a lemon.
- To neutralize microwave smells put half an orange or lemon in water in a microwave-proof dish and heat on high for 2 minutes.
- Avoid stomach-churning odors in the refrigerator by always wrapping foods separately and making sure that containers are tightly covered. If a bad smell does seep through, try placing a bowl of vinegar, half an apple or a little baking soda in an open bag or on a plate or bowl in the fridge.
- Be sure the dishwasher smells fresh and clean by including a little lemon juice with each wash. Lemon is a natural deodorizer and degreaser.
- If unpleasant odors do develop, sprinkle a little baking soda in the bottom of the dishwasher next time you run it. Or, add a few drops of concentrated orange oil during the next wash cycle.
- The smell of onions or garlic can cling to a wooden chopping board. To freshen it up, rub it with half a lemon and rinse. Lemon will work wonders for your hands as well.
- Empty the kitchen garbage can frequently and, if possible, compost all fruit and vegetable peelings (but not meat or cooked foods, as these can attract vermin). If bad odors do develop, add orange or lemon peel or a little baking soda to the can.

BATHROOM smells

• Burn matches or light a candle to help curb stale smells in the bathroom. A potpourri of fragrant herbs and spices—such as cinnamon, rosemary, thyme, cloves or lavender—also does an excellent job.
• Add a dash of toilet cleaner or vinegar and water to the bottom of the brush holder to keep the toilet brush from getting smelly.
• Hang towels and washcloths to dry and launder them frequently so that they don't smell musty.

TOBACCO odors

• Place saucers of baking soda in a room. Ideally, close the door and let them work overnight. Sprinkling fabric with baking soda also works; shake it off outside or vacuum in the morning.
• Rinse ashtrays with a vinegar solution and sprinkle coffee grounds in them to help absorb the smell.

CLOTHING

• A piece of soap or a small sachet of lavender, cedar chips or even coffee grounds will add fragrance to a closet. Also, try to hang coats and jackets outside to air before returning them to the closet.
• Not surprisingly, well-used sports shoes tend to become smelly. One simple remedy is to sprinkle a little baking soda into shoes, let it stand overnight, then vacuum it out in the morning. If you have particularly sweaty feet, put talcum powder inside shoes each time you wear them and change your shoes regularly. When you're not wearing your sneakers, stuff them with a pair of socks filled with cat litter to absorb the odor and any moisture. A final option is to place shoes in a ziplock bag in the freezer overnight to kill odor-causing bacteria.

OTHER odors

Bad smells can occur anywhere in the house. These helpful hints will help keep other parts of your home fresh and fragrant.

• Control musty odors by burning before washing them a bay leaf, placing a piece of citrus fruit peel on a hot heating element, hanging a vanilla bean in the room or using scented candles.
• If exhaust from the vacuum cleaner smells unpleasant, change the bag and vacuum up some lavender flowers or peppermint leaves. Or dab a cotton ball with a little perfume or aromatic oil and vacuum that up.
• Add a piece of charcoal to flower-vase water to keep it from smelling bad.
• You can eliminate smells from plastic containers. After washing and drying them well, fill them with crumpled newspaper or coffee grounds and freeze them overnight.
• Wipe musty-smelling leather suitcases with a vinegar-soaked cloth and leave them open in the fresh air for a few days.
• Eliminate the smell of oil-based paint by placing bowls of peeled, sliced onions around the room.
• Lavender sachets impart a delightful smell. Place one in the linen closet and enjoy its fragrance. An alternative is to fill several cloth bags with a fragrant potpourri mixture.

Absorb the smell of animal litter by adding a little baking soda to the litter box.

Pests

Humans have been sharing their homes with creepy-crawlies for centuries. As a result, a number of simple remedies have been devised to help rid our homes of uninvited visitors. If these don't work, you may need to call in the professionals.

They may be after your food, your blood, the wood that provides the framework of your home or even your clothing. Here are some natural ways to deter or banish those hungry, biting, bacteria-spreading creatures from your property.

ANTS

- Ants follow a scent trail, marching in a straight line one by one. Disrupt the trail by sprinkling dried mint leaves, crushed cloves or chili powder at the point where they enter the house. Once they lose the scent trail they can no longer find their way in.
- Draw a line with a piece of chalk or baby powder through the ants' route. The tiny gatecrashers won't be able to cross it.
- Ants will gobble down baking soda sprinkled on the floor and feed it to their young. This causes their stomachs to rupture, reducing the pest population. They can't resist a solution of sugar, yeast and water, either, which has the same effect.
- Effective baits against ants also include honey, water and syrup. Set them out in a shallow dish; ants get trapped in the sticky solution and die.
- Prevent ants from coming indoors—put tomato leaves and stalks over their nests.

Try driving mice away with chamomile flowers or peppermint.

FLIES

- The best solution is to install screens on your windows and doors and try to keep food covered.
- Set out bowls of vinegar; replace them daily.
- Use blue tablecloths—flies avoid this color.
- The smell of basil, peppermint, lavender or tomato plants also wards off flies.
- Coat meat with lemon balm or basil before grilling it and the flies will stay away.

FLEAS

- If fleas have taken up lodging in the sofa, sprinkle it with borax, leave overnight, then vacuum.
- A dish of lemon slices placed in a cupboard will keep fleas away.
- If a rug is infested, sprinkle it with salt, let it work for a few hours, then vacuum.

WOOD LICE

- Put a bottle of sweet liqueur or leftover wine outside the door. They will climb in and become intoxicated. Discard them and repeat as needed.
- Leave hollowed-out potatoes or turnips as a lure. Crush them together with the wood lice that have crawled inside.

GOOD TO KNOW

How to keep dogs and cats free from pests

After every walk, check your pet for fleas and ticks. If you suspect the presence of pests, put some walnut leaves in the pet's bed. If your dog or cat becomes infested, mix 2 tablespoons (30 ml) vermouth and 1 quart (1 L) water. Let the solution steep for 2–3 hours then rub it on the animal's fur. Lots of brushing and combing also helps keep pests at bay.

MICE

- Peppermint oil, turpentine and camphor are scents that mice find unappetizing. Dab on cotton balls and place them where mice enter.
- If you do decide to set traps, lure mice with peanut butter or chocolate.

MOTHS

- Help to drive away moths with dried citrus peel or cedar chips in small bags—they dislike the smell.
- Moths won't take up residence in fabrics that are clean and used frequently, so shake out and launder linens and clothing regularly.
- Store wool and cashmere clothes in sealed plastic bags immediately after wearing.

WASPS

- Wasps make themselves scarce when they detect the smell of heated vinegar. Lemon slices studded with cloves will keep them away.
- Make a wasp trap by filling a narrow-neck bottle with diluted fruit juice and a little detergent and vinegar. They will fly in but won't be able to get out.

MOSQUITOES

- Window screens will help keep mosquitoes out. A mosquito net will help to prevent them from biting you while you sleep.
- Keep the pests away from patios and balconies by hanging up a cloth sprayed with a few drops of clove or laurel oil. Alternatively, pour the oil into small bowls or an oil lamp.

CARPET beetles

- Vacuum regularly to stop hair and lint from providing food for carpet beetle larvae.
- Seal cracks in parquet flooring and spray neem oil (available from health product suppliers) along baseboards. This makes the larvae stop eating and prevents them from growing and reproducing. Be warned, it will take time.

COCKROACHES and weevils

- For a minor infestation, use a cloth moistened with wine or beer as bait. When the insects have gathered on the cloth, pour boiling water over it.
- Combat cockroaches with a lethal "roach dinner." Mix equal parts of powdered boric acid, white flour and white sugar and place in bowls under the fridge, in the backs of drawers and behind the stove.
- Remove food supplies immediately if they become infested with weevils and wash out kitchen cupboards with vinegar and water.

SILVERFISH

- Sprinkle a little borax on damp cloths and place in the bathroom or kitchen at night. In the morning, shake them outside.
- Grate a potato on a piece of newspaper to attract silverfish, then fold and throw it away.

DUST MITES

- Mites dislike both fresh air and light, so shake out bedding and blankets regularly.
- Vacuum rugs or beat them outside, and wash them frequently.
- Replace carpets with wooden floors or tiles.

BEDBUGS

- Try spraying rubbing alcohol where bedbugs thrive. It will kill some bugs on contact.
- Placing clothing, shoes and boots, toys, stuffed animals, backpacks and other nonwashables in the dryer for 20 minutes on a high temperature may kill bedbugs.
- Wash and dry nightwear and bedclothes at as high a temperature as possible.

Stain removal

We've all been irritated by a stain on a new tablecloth or shirt, but don't despair—milk, fruit, coffee and other common stains may seem disastrous, but with a bit of know-how they can often be remedied quickly and easily.

BASIC rules

Not all stains should be treated the same way. As a general rule, the fresher and damper the spot, the easier it will be to remove.

- Every stain remover—whether store-bought or homemade—should be tested on an inconspicuous part of the fabric first. If it has no adverse effects on the fabric or color, use it directly on the stain. Dab it on undiluted and wash the garment afterwards.
- Always try the gentlest treatment first before resorting to stronger remedies. Take special care with delicate fabrics—some of these remedies are strong, especially those that use ammonia.
- When removing a stain, work from the outside towards the middle. Avoid using hot water as you risk setting the stain, especially if you don't know what it is. Blow dry the wet area to avoid leaving an outline.
- Water-soluble stains are the most common. All you'll need to remove them is tap water, at least when they are fresh. Treat protein-based stains (blood, mayonnaise or egg) with cold water.
- Treat older stains with a mixture of 2 tablespoons (30 ml) water and 3 tablespoons (45 ml) vinegar. Let it dry, then rinse.
- If possible, scrape a dried stain with a spoon or soften it with glycerin before treating it.

THE ABC of stains

Just about any kind of food can stain. The garden and garage are also full of potential hazards.

- Remove beer stains with a dilute soap solution containing a little ammonia and rinse well with water.
- Wash bloodstains on clothing immediately in cold water—hot water will cause the protein in the blood to congeal and attach firmly to the fibers. For stubborn stains, moisten the clothing in cold salt water. Dry bloodstains should be soaked in cold water, then treated with salt water or a solution of baking soda. When cleaning delicate fabrics, use a paste of water and potato flour or cornstarch. Test a hidden section of fabric first. If the color is unaffected, spread it on the stain, let it work for a few minutes, rub it off and rinse thoroughly.
- Gently rinse burn marks on washable fabrics with cold water, sprinkle them with salt and then dry in the sun. Treat burn marks on delicate fabrics carefully with diluted vinegar. However, there is no guarantee that these remedies will work, and you need to be especially careful with these marks because burns will weaken the fabric.

Universal stain remover

1 cup (250 ml) rubbing alcohol
½ cup (100 ml) ammonia
2 teaspoons (10 ml) lighter fuel

Mix the ingredients together in a sealable bottle and test on an inconspicuous area of fabric before dabbing it on the stain undiluted. Be especially careful with delicate fabrics. Wash the garment afterwards.

Keep out of the reach of children.

- Makeup, butter, mayonnaise, cooking oil and engine oil are among the substances that can leave grease stains. Promptly sprinkle them with cornstarch to absorb the grease and brush away the saturated starch. You can also try rubbing off stains using hot water mixed with a little dishwashing liquid to dissolve the grease. For delicate fabrics, place a paper towel on both sides of the stain and iron it. Stains are best removed from wool by rubbing with a little mineral water and a towel.
- Remove tough lipstick stains by dabbing them with eucalyptus oil, letting it soak in before washing. Boil white table napkins, handkerchiefs or washcloths marked by lipstick stains.
- Rub tar stains with lard before washing the item. For an extra boost, add 2 tablespoons (30 ml) baking soda to the laundry detergent. Oil, tar and grass stains can also be treated with a few drops of eucalyptus oil.
- Treat fresh grass stains with ammonia, but first test the sensitivity of the fabric on an inconspicuous spot. Alternatively, apply a halved potato to the grass stain to allow the starch to dissolve the stain, then wash as usual. Soak older grass stains on white fabrics in a mixture of one part egg white and one part glycerin before washing.

For dry, caked-on mud, shake the garment outdoors and rub off as much dirt as possible. Then soak in cold water before washing with detergent and warm water.

- Soak coffee and cocoa stains while fresh in cold salt water and wash with a detergent containing enzymes. Dab older stains with glycerin and wash them out or, for upholstery and rugs, pat them dry.
- Remove chewing gum by putting the affected clothing in a plastic bag in the freezer. Once frozen,the gum is easier to chip off.
- For clear glue spills, try cologne or oil-free nail polish remover; in other cases, mineral spirits, rubbing alcohol or lighter fluid may do the trick.
- Rinse milk spots with cold water before washing. Dab nonwashable fabrics with cold water, then ammonia and finally with warm water.
- Treat fruit stains while fresh by holding the soiled item over a bowl and pouring a little very hot water on it. Alternatively, soak it in buttermilk and wash as usual. For dried fruit stains, sprinkle with lemon juice and rinse after 30 minutes. If the stain doesn't come out, try an ammonia solution—2 tablespoons (30 ml) ammonia in 1 quart (1 L) water—or glycerin solution—equal parts glycerin and water.
- Apply lemon juice, vinegar or carbonated water to red wine stains, or presoak the stained item in a biological detergent for 30 minutes before washing.
- For red dye stains from popsicles or maraschino cherries, mix equal parts hydrogen peroxide and cool water in a spray bottle; spray on the stain and leave for 30 minutes. Rinse with equal parts vinegar and water. Peroxide is a bleach, so test a spot first. Repeat the treatment if it doesn't work the first time.
- Treat sweat stains with a mix of 2 tablespoons (30 ml) vinegar to 3 tablespoons (45 ml) water, or use ammonia solution.
- Scratch off a wax spot, place a paper towel under and over the spot and iron until all excess wax is absorbed. If necessary, replace the paper towel. Remove any remaining stain from colored wax by dabbing it with rubbing alcohol, always working from the outside in.

TRADITIONAL CLEANERS

There's a vast array of synthetic cleaning products available in supermarkets today, some with hefty price tags. Many were originally modeled on existing natural cleaning products, all of which can still be used to help keep your home clean and germ-free.

Most of the cleaning materials mentioned in this book can be bought at the local pharmacy or supermarket, and you can easily mix up the solutions yourself. But wear gloves and a face mask when working with ammonia, talcum powder or turpentine products. Avoid swallowing, breathing or absorbing them through your skin, and store your home-made cleaning materials in labeled containers out of reach of children, just as you would store-bought products. It's always a good idea to check their shelf life regularly.

NATURAL CLEANING SOLUTIONS can also SAVE you MONEY.

Vinegar

The word vinegar comes from the Old French *vin aigre*, or "sour wine." The substance—made by fermenting ethanol—has been used to season food since earliest times. In fact, traces of it have been found in 3,000-year-old Egyptian urns. But vinegar doesn't just liven up your salad; it's an excellent natural cleaning product, disinfectant and deodorizer. To make an all-purpose cleaner for tables, countertops, baths and tiles, simply mix equal parts vinegar and water in a spray bottle, or pour the substance directly into the toilet bowl to remove discoloration. Just be sure to test it on an inconspicuous area before use. Vinegar should never be used on marble and, when improperly diluted, it may eat away at tile grout. But for the most part, vinegar is effective, accessible and cheap.

Glycerin

This colorless, odorless, rather thick nontoxic alcohol is also known as glycerol. Glycerin is commonly used in personal care and pharmaceutical products such as cosmetics, soaps and toothpaste, as well as in certain food products. Glycerin, in its pure form, can be used to treat a number of minor medical conditions, including calluses, bedsores, rashes and cuts. But it is usually used at home to soften up tough, dried-on fabric stains from substances such as coffee, berries and lipstick. It is also used as an antifreeze on windowpanes: Rub windows with glycerin before the temperature drops and they won't freeze over.

Plain white toothpaste makes an easy and economical silver polish.

Use traditional products to keep tennis shoes in match condition.

Ammonia

Ammonia, or ammonium chloride, is the ammonium salt of hydrochloric acid and a crystalline solid. It has been used in everything from fertilizer to rocket fuel. That may make it sound like a dangerous chemical but, in fact, ammonia has also been used for a long time as a household cleaner. Commercially, it's most commonly found as the watery solution ammonia (ammonium hydroxide). Use liquid ammonia at home for stain removal or when cleaning stainless steel, glass and porcelain—it leaves a streak-free shine. It is also used to combat mold and pests. But be careful—don't breathe in the fumes or swallow it as it is caustic.

Turpentine

Turpentine is a mixture of resin and essential oil from various species of pine. Turpentine oil, produced by distilling turpentine, is effective for dissolving grease. The colorless-to-yellowish fluid has numerous applications in the home—for example, as a floor polish, a shoe polish or a solvent for stain removal. Don't dispose of turpentine products by pouring them down the drain, which is damaging to pipes and the environment. Ask your local authority about proper disposal methods.

Warning: Exposure to turpentine through splashes, inhalation of fumes or swallowing can lead to serious health problems. Wear protective clothing, including a face mask, and be sure a room is well ventilated if you are using it. For many applications, it's cheaper and just as effective to use mineral spirits, which is derived from petroleum, to do the same jobs.

Talc

Also known as magnesium silicate hydrate, talc is the softest mineral. It feels soapy, which accounts for its alternative name: soapstone. It is ground up to form talcum powder or a base for makeup. In the home, it can be used as a gentle scrubbing agent and to treat rubber seals or to silence squeaky wooden floorboards and stairs. But be careful not to breathe it in as talc can cause serious inflammation in your breathing passages.

Upholstery

An upholstered sofa in the living room is likely to get slept on, jumped on and have things spilled on it. Given the amount of abuse it takes, maintenance of its upholstery and fabric is important so it looks good and lasts.

It is not surprising that upholstered furniture requires regular care, considering how many hours we spend on the sofa gazing at the television, reading a book or socializing.

USE a CREVICE TOOL to CLEAN BETWEEN the seat and arm of the SOFA.

MAINTAINING upholstery

- Clean upholstered furniture regularly with the vacuum cleaner, but reduce the suction to avoid damaging the underpadding.
- If possible, beat out the dust outdoors to prevent it from spreading through the room and settling on other furniture.
- Before beating large, upholstered furniture, cover it with a damp cloth to catch the dust being released. If you moisten the cloth with vinegar and water, the colors will look fresher afterwards.
- If chairs have sagged or sofas have indentations where people have been sitting, moisten these pressure points with a little hot water, cover with white paper and iron dry. Just be careful not to burn these spots.
- Clean dirty sofa cushions every year with a solution made from one part vinegar and one part water. Apply it with a cloth and wipe it off with tap water.
- Machine-wash or dry-clean removable covers when necessary. Observe the care directions: Brocade, silk, chintz, velvet and wool tweed, for instance, must be dry-cleaned.
- After washing cushion covers, iron them from the inside and put them back on the cushions while still damp; they will stretch better and dry without wrinkling.
- Rub soiled spots on wool or linen covers with a soft rubber eraser.
- Clean dark velvet upholstery covers with a brush moistened in cold coffee. Then moisten a cloth with tap water and pat the velvet to pick up any excess.
- Clean synthetic covers by dipping a cloth dampened with water in a little baking soda and gently rubbing the cushion with it. Go over it again with a water and soap solution. Test this on the reverse side first (or a corner) to make sure that it doesn't leave a mark.
- After using water on fabric upholstery, cover the area with paper towels, weight them down and let them dry overnight.
- Remove lint and pet hair with a damp sponge or a piece of adhesive tape wrapped around your hand with the sticky side out.
- Try to train pets from a young age to keep away from upholstery. Leather is least vulnerable to pet damage. Keep cats from scratching upholstery by providing a scratching post. If that doesn't work, cover vulnerable areas with plastic or attach pieces of old carpet. Cats particularly hate bubble wrap.

REMOVING stains from upholstery

- Remove residue and vacuum up spills at once. Remove stains by working from the outside towards the middle.
- Sprinkle fresh grease and oil stains with talcum powder or cornstarch. Let it set to absorb the grease, then brush it off.

- Dab older grease stains with an ammonia solution, rubbing alcohol or cologne, then carefully rub with water.
- Treat milk spots immediately with cold water or a lather of moisturizing soap and lukewarm water. To finish, pat dry.

MAINTAINING leather upholstery

- Clean washable leather with a soap solution: 1 teaspoon (5 ml) liquid soap in 1 quart (1 L) water. Wring out the cloth thoroughly before wiping the leather. Allow the furniture to dry, then buff.
- Maintain dark leather by rubbing castor oil into it once or twice a year.
- Treat light-colored leather with petroleum jelly. Let it work for about an hour before removing the excess with a soft cloth.
- Restore the shine to scuffed leather upholstery by treating it with a mixture of equal parts beaten egg white and linseed oil.
- For a natural leather polish boil some linseed oil, cool and mix with an equal amount of vinegar. Apply with a soft cloth and buff.
- Special nourishing creams for older leather can be purchased at furniture stores or online. Allow them to work their magic for about 24 hours after application, then buff. But make sure you wipe them well so nothing rubs off on clothing.

REMOVING stains from smooth leather

- Remove water-soluble stains with a damp cloth and moisturizing soap foam; wipe with warm water.
- To treat older grease stains on colorfast leather, dip a cloth into hot water, wring it out, sprinkle on a small amount of baking soda and carefully rub the grease from the edge towards the middle. Go over it with a warm, moist cloth.
- For stubborn dirt or stains, work up a foam with saddle soap and rub it in using a sponge in circular motions. Go over the spot again with tap water and apply leather conditioner after it is dry.
- Pour a little milk on a clean cloth and dab it on leather to help remove marks from a ballpoint pen.

REMOVING stains from full-grain leather

- Sprinkle fresh grease stains with talcum powder. It will absorb the grease and you can simply brush it off. Repeat as needed.
- Use an eraser to remove grease stains. But don't rub for too long or you risk damaging the leather.
- Remove water stains by allowing them to dry, then roughen them with a brush.

Revitalizing upholstery

2 tablespoons (25 g) soap flakes
2 cups (500 ml) water
½ cup (100 ml) glycerin
½ cup (100 ml) rubbing alcohol

Heat the water and dissolve the soap flakes. Let cool and stir in the glycerin and rubbing alcohol. Store in a container. When needed, dissolve 1 tablespoon (15 ml) of the mixture in water, stir with a whisk and apply the foam with a sponge.

Dab a little water on an inconspicuous area first before using it to clean leather. If the water soaks in, then don't use it to clean your furniture.

Walls

Regular maintenance keeps walls and ceilings clean and makes rooms appear light and airy. Whether walls are painted, panelled, brick, plastered or wallpapered, keep them in good condition to avoid unnecessary redecoration and to make sure every room in your home looks inviting.

Keeping walls and ceilings dust and cobweb free should be part of the regular housekeeping routine. However, certain surfaces will require more detailed care. Protect the floor before you embark on any drastic wall cleaning.

MAINTENANCE routine

- Dust walls and ceilings regularly. If you don't have a feather duster, simply tie a dust rag to a broom.
- Suck up cobwebs with the crevice tool on the vacuum cleaner.
- Test all cleaning products on an inconspicuous spot before removing stains. If the product stains the wall, at least it will be hidden from view.

Spray a feather duster with water so cobwebs will stick to it.

- If you plan to put up wallpaper, go for the washable, scuff-resistant variety. This will make cleaning much easier and will cut down on time spent on maintenance.
- Wash walls using a damp, soft sponge and an all-purpose wall cleaner, working in gentle, circular strokes.
- If you have to wet-wash the walls, be extra cautious and switch off the electricity.

BRICK

- Brush brick walls occasionally with a scrubbing brush and sweep up loosened grout.
- Do not wet-wash brick walls—the moisture will soak into the porous masonry and could cause mildew or other damage.

PLASTER

- Dust plaster moldings and decorations regularly, preferably with a feather duster.
- Wet-wash plaster only when necessary. First check that the finish is solid enough, then spray it with a little soap and water so that you're able to reach even the cracks. Finally, spray with a small amount of clean water and dab up all liquid with a dry cloth.

PAINTED surfaces

- Remove dirt or stains on walls painted with oil-based paint with soapy water.
- Wash walls painted with acrylic paint with soapy water containing a couple of dashes of ammonia. Wipe with water and pat dry. A soft scrubbing sponge is helpful around light switches but remember to turn the power off first.
- Never wet-wash whitewashed walls as it will take the color off.
- Use a rubber eraser or a fresh piece of white bread to remove new stains from painted walls.

WALLPAPER

- In heavy traffic areas such as the kitchen or bathroom, choose a washable wallpaper.
- If a section of wallpaper is very dirty, it might be easier simply to remove it and replace it with a new piece. Make sure the remaining wallpaper and the patches abut each other, rather than overlapping at the edges.
- A trick for repairing wallpaper is to tear rather than cut the edge of the patch so that it blends in seamlessly with the "background."
- Dust textured vinyl wallpaper before cleaning then wipe it with a damp cloth, sponge or soft brush and warm detergent solution. Rinse it with water, but don't let it get too moist, and dry thoroughly.
- Dust grease stains on textured wallpaper with talcum powder. Allow it to work, then brush it off. Wipe off any excess powder with a damp cloth or give it a quick vacuum.
- Never soak fabric or cork wallpaper as they will swell. Instead, carefully wipe them off with a damp cloth. If too much water is applied, pat dry with a clean cloth.
- Treat cork wall tiles like washable wallpaper if they are sealed with a matte varnish. This will help to avoid the potential problem of soaking the cork. If the tiles are not sealed, it is worth taking the time to varnish them.
- Carefully vacuum textured wallpaper on low power and avoid wet-washing it.

Removing grease stains from wallpaper

one Place an absorbent paper towel on the grease stain or wax crayon marks.

two Go over it with a not-too-hot iron for as long as it takes for the spot to disappear. Move the paper around occasionally and replace it if necessary.

three Try carefully dabbing any remaining stain with some baking soda on a clean cloth.

PANELING

- Don't ever let waxed surfaces become too wet when you are cleaning them. Treat them as you would waxed floors or furniture.
- Wipe sealed, painted or varnished paneling with soapy water. Avoid using an abrasive powder that could leave scratches.
- Treat wood coated with clear lacquer once a year with furniture polish.
- If minor mold spots appear on wood panels, dry them with a hair dryer and scrub with a soft brush. Finally, polish them with a soft cloth and furniture polish. Note that mold can be dangerous if it grows out of control. Make sure that the room is well ventilated and be sure to wear a protective face mask. If you are ever in doubt about the severity of the mold, call in a professional to deal with what could be a serious problem.
- Remove layers of old polish with a coarse sponge and mineral spirits. Rub with the grain of the wood.

Windows

You don't need special cleaning products to keep your windows clean and streak-free, or your sills and frames looking as if they have just been installed. With the proper technique and correct accessories, this housekeeping chore can be simple and rewarding.

Before window cleaning begins, a little preparation is needed to help make the job easier. First, remove the curtains from the windows and any knick-knacks from the windowsills, then cover sensitive surfaces to protect them from drips.

GOOD TO KNOW

Adverse weather conditions

Avoid washing windows in sunshine as the water dries too quickly and causes streaking. The sun also makes it hard to see if the glass is clean. Extremely cold days aren't ideal either, because the glass is likely to be brittle. If you must wash windows in cold weather, add a dash or two of rubbing alcohol to the wash water. Overcast days are best for window cleaning.

LONG-LASTING chamois

Do yourself a favor: Buy a real chamois. It absorbs water more quickly and is easily squeezed out. With proper care it will last for years.

- Keep your chamois soft and smooth by using it only with water or solutions made with water and vinegar or alcohol. Detergents remove the leather's oils and leave it stiff.
- Rinse out a chamois with warm salt water after every use to keep it soft.
- Never wring a chamois. Instead, squeeze it gently, open it up, shake it out and let it dry slowly in the air.

WINDOWSILLS

- Use a soft soap solution on windowsills to battle everyday dirt.
- Remove water stains with a soft cloth moistened with a solution of equal parts rubbing alcohol and tap water.

WINDOW frames

- Vacuum the window frame joint with the appropriate nozzle on the vacuum cleaner before starting to clean with liquid.
- Wipe wood window frames treated with clear glaze or varnish with a damp cloth. Replace the water frequently and to get them extra clean, rub them with a solution of equal parts rubbing alcohol and tap water.
- Clean painted window frames with a solution of 2 tablespoons (30 ml) ammonia in about 2 cups (500 ml) water.
- Clean wooden window frames with a barely wet cloth, then dry with a clean, soft cloth.
- Rub off specks on wood frames using a rough cloth moistened with water. Another option is to clean them with a mixture of reduced-fat milk and cold water in equal proportions.
- Stick with hot, soapy water for washing aluminium or plastic frames. Scouring powder will scratch them.

WINDOWPANES

- Keep them free of condensation, which attracts mold and can make wooden frames rot easily. Wipe each morning if necessary.
- Clean dirty panes regularly with a vinegar solution of 1 quart (1 L) warm water and 1 cup (250 ml) white vinegar.
- Clean very dirty windowpanes first with warm dishwater, then wipe them down with tap water, making sure you don't leave streaks.
- Add a squirt of glycerin to the water to help windows resist dust and so they don't fog up in winter.
- Mix a few drops of ammonia with the water to keep frost off windows.
- Expel streaks and leftover drips with a lint-free cloth, newspaper or a chamois.
- When squeegeeing windows, moisten the edge of the squeegee to keep it from squeaking and also to improve contact with the glass.
- Polish washed windowpanes with newspaper or an old pair of tights to bring out the shine.
- Clean small windowpanes (skylights, louvre windows, fanlights) with a chamois only. Thoroughly wet the chamois in the wash water, squeeze it out gently and work from the edge towards the center of the glass. Immediately wipe dry to prevent streaking.
- Wash skylights when it's raining hard for maximum effect. Carefully tilt the wet window and lather it with wash water, shut it again and let the rain rinse it off.
- Rub dulled windows or mirrors with olive or linseed oil to get their shine back. Leave the oil on for an hour, wipe dry with tissue paper and clean as you normally do.
- Eliminate grease stains with half an onion. The sulfides are powerful cleaners.
- Remove specks from glass panes with a clean cloth moistened in warm black tea. A couple of squirts of rubbing alcohol will also dissolve them, making it quick and easy to wipe them off.
- If glazing compound has been left on the glass from when it was installed, rub it off with a little ammonia on a cotton ball.
- Scrape stickers off new panes by soaking them with warm water, then removing them using a glass scraper. If any old, brittle stickers remain, rub them with olive oil until the pane is clear.
- Remove fresh paint splashes from panes with mineral spirits or nail polish remover. For dried paint, use a glass scraper, such as those used for cleaning ceramic cooktops.

SPECIAL cases

- Modern stained glass is so strong that it can be cleaned as you would normal glass panes. Take greater care with old stained glass: Simply wipe it carefully with a damp cloth. If the old glass is actually painted, don't wash it at all or you risk removing the color. Instead, dust the panes with a soft brush.
- Clean frosted glass with hot vinegar water to give it a dull sheen and carefully wipe dry.
- Dust etched glass with a soft brush, and clean the textured side of the glass with a chamois. You can simply squeegee the smooth side.

When windowpanes are especially dirty, lather them generously with a water and detergent solution and squeegee them free of streaks.

Home cooking

Traditional ways of preparing foods—such as baking bread or cooking from scratch—have come back into fashion as people discover how economical, delicious and nutritious the results can be. Recreate these rewarding methods in your home kitchen.

Baking, cookies and cakes

If you are wary of attempting your grandma's favorite recipes because of fear of failure, just follow these proven tips. Always read the recipe before you begin and preheat the oven in advance. Measure ingredients exactly and follow directions carefully. With a little effort, you'll turn out delicious baked goodies every time.

Once you master the art of making batter and pastry, and basic cookie and cake-making techniques, there's no limit to what can be prepared in the kitchen.

Shortbread

Butter is an essential ingredient of shortbread. Rice flour or semolina gives it a delicious crunchy texture.

½ cup (100 g) all-purpose flour
¼ cup (50 g) rice flour or semolina
¼ cup (50 g) superfine sugar, plus extra for dusting
½ cup (100 g) salted butter, refrigerated

1 Sift flours into a bowl, add sugar and grate in the butter using a coarse grater. Rub in the butter until the mixture resembles breadcrumbs. Press into a 7 inch (18 cm) cake pan and level the top. Prick all over with a fork.
2 Chill in the refrigerator for 1 hour. Heat oven to 300°F (150°C) and bake for 1 hour or until straw-colored. Cool in the pan for 10 minutes; turn out on a wire rack. While still warm, score into 8 wedges. Dust with the sugar and separate before serving.

TIPS on batter and dough

- Partly replace butter with a vegetable oil, or add 1 tablespoon (15 ml) vinegar to cake batter to make cakes especially light. To obtain the same result, you can substitute mineral water for half of the full-fat milk.
- Before baking, prick shortcrust and puff pastry several times with a fork to prevent bubbles from forming.
- Shortcrust pastry should be smooth after kneading; if it crumbles, it is too dry.
- Don't open the oven door during the first 20 minutes of cooking or the cake may sink.
- To help a cake rise, place a heat-resistant container of water in the oven with it.
- Insert a thin skewer or toothpick to test if a cake is done. If no batter clings to it, the cake is ready.
- To prevent cakes from collapsing, briefly cool them in their pans before turning them out on a wire rack to cool completely.

FAT-FREE sponge cake

When making a fat-free sponge, be sure the sugar is thoroughly dissolved. An electric mixer makes light work of this task.
1 Preheat the oven to 325°F (160°C).
2 Separate four eggs. Beat together ½ cup (125 g) superfine sugar with the egg yolks until light, and add ¼ cup (60 ml) water and 1 teaspoon (5 ml) grated lemon zest.
3 Sift together ½ cup (125 g) all-purpose flour and 3 teaspoons (15 ml) baking powder; add to batter.
4 Beat the egg whites with clean beaters until stiff peaks form, and fold gently into the batter.
5 Put the mix into a cake pan lined with parchment paper and fill it no more than two-thirds full. Bake for 30 minutes.

CLASSIC scones

These simple scones take just minutes to make. Eat them warm from the oven with butter and jam.
1 Preheat the oven to 400°F (200°C).
2 Sift 1 cup (250 g) all-purpose flour. Add 2 teaspoons (10 ml) baking powder and ½ teaspoon (2 ml) salt and sift again.

KEEPING cakes, breads and scones

- Most cakes, scones, muffins and quick breads can be frozen but they should be wrapped well to prevent moisture loss. As many fillings and icings don't freeze well, it is better to freeze a cake plain and fill or frost it after thawing.
- Cookies lose their crispness if frozen after cooking. Most cookie doughs can be frozen raw, rolled and wrapped in plastic wrap or parchment paper, then wrapped in foil. To bake, remove the dough from the freezer and thaw until it can be sliced. It will cook perfectly when just defrosted.

3 Cut in ⅔ cup (150 ml) butter with a pastry cutter (or two knives) until it forms pea-sized crumbs.
4 Gradually add ¾ cup (175 ml) milk, stirring until a loose dough forms.
5 Turn out on a lightly floured board and knead lightly for about 30 seconds.
6 Roll out your dough to about 1 inch (2.5 cm) thick and cut out shapes with a 2 inch (5 cm) cookie cutter.
7 Place shapes on an ungreased cookie sheet and bake for 12–15 minutes.
8 Leave the scones on the cookie sheet for a couple of minutes, then use a spatula to transfer them to a wire rack to cool slightly.

COOKIE basics

- Dough rolled to ¼ inch (5 mm) or slightly thicker makes chewy or soft cookies; thinner dough, ⅛ inch (3 mm) or less, makes crisp cookies.
- Before cutting shapes, dip the edge of the cutter in flour and shake off the excess.
- Always use a cookie sheet, as high-sided pans don't allow heat to flow evenly over the cookies.
- For cookies with little fat, grease the tray—using unsalted butter helps to prevent over-browning. Alternatively, line the tray with parchment paper.
- Check cookies 5 minutes before the recommended baking time is up to avoid scorching or overbaking.

Bread

For thousands of years, humans have prepared and baked bread. There's nothing quite like a warm, fragrant loaf fresh from the oven. And it doesn't take many ingredients or very much effort to create delicious bread.

To make bread dough, in addition to flour or grains you need water, salt and a leavening agent such as yeast, sourdough or baking powder. Generally the more thoroughly you knead the dough, the looser and finer the crumb. Make sure you give dough enough time to rise undisturbed at an even temperature of about 72°F (22°C). The volume of dough determines when the bread is ready to bake: It should roughly double in size.

BASIC bread

Bread dough isn't difficult to make. You can select from a wide range of flours and add seeds, raisins, nuts, sun-dried tomatoes, herbs or other flavorings. This easy-to-follow recipe makes two loaves.

1 Dissolve 1 tablespoon (15 g) fresh or cake yeast, or a 1 packet (7 g) packet active dry yeast, 1 teaspoon (5 ml) sugar in 2 cups (500 ml) lukewarm water; mix well with a fork. Let stand for 10 minutes or until frothy, and stir well.

2 Sift 5 cups (750 g) white bread flour and 1 tablespoon (15 ml) salt into a large mixing bowl. Add the prepared yeast mixture.

3 Mix with one hand, drawing in the flour to make a stiff paste. Add a little more flour if necessary.

4 Turn out on a floured board and knead for 10 minutes, flouring your hands as necessary, until the dough is smooth and elastic and has a slightly blistery surface. Give the dough a quarter turn with each hand movement as you knead, working rhythmically.

5 Lightly grease a bowl with vegetable oil, add the dough and cover with lightly oiled plastic wrap. Leave in a warm place for 1½–2 hours or until the dough has doubled.

6 Punch down and knead well again. Grease two loaf pans. Divide the dough into two and roll each portion into a loaf shape to fit the pan. Put the pan into oiled, sealed plastic bags and let rise (proof) for about 40 minutes at room temperature.

7 Heat the oven to 450°F (230°C). When the bread has risen, brush with egg glaze if wished. Bake the loaves for 35 minutes.

8 When they are baked, the loaves will have shrunk from the sides of the pans and sound hollow when tapped on the bottom. Remove from the pans and place on a wire rack to cool completely.

Note: Yeast dough cannot withstand drafts or cold, so keep doors and windows closed while it rises.

- The dough will keep in the refrigerator for a day. In the freezer, it will keep for up to 5 months.
- For rolls: Divide the dough into 16–20 pieces, shape and place on a greased baking sheet and proof for 15–20 minutes. Brush with egg; bake for 12–18 minutes at 425°F (220°C).

TIME-SAVING tips

- Use a mixer with a dough hook (3 minutes on low speed) or mix the ingredients in a food processor—the ball produced will not require as much kneading.
- Use whole-wheat flour. Because it has less gluten, it requires less kneading.
- Speed rising by using the microwave. After kneading, put the dough in an ungreased bowl and cover with lightly oiled plastic wrap. Heat on high for 10 seconds and let the bowl stand for 20 minutes in the microwave or a warm place. If not doubled in size, heat on high for another 10 seconds and leave for another 10 minutes.

Knead the dough carefully and thoroughly with the heel of your hand for a few minutes.

GOOD TO KNOW

Keep it fresh

Sliced bread stays fresher longer if you wrap it in a cloth. It also helps to put a peeled potato or half an apple in the breadbox to keep bread moist. Before warming up day-old rolls, brush them with water or milk to make them wonderfully crisp again.

SUCCESS with dough

- Avoid mixing salt and yeast as the salt can stunt the activity of the yeast.
- You can add any number of flavorings: Try caraway seeds, some chopped olives or sun-dried tomatoes, or mix in 2 tablespoons (30 ml) sunflower seeds for a tasty change.
- Press a fingertip on the dough. If it leaves an impression, it's risen and ready to bake.
- Prevent air bubbles from forming while the dough rises by punching it down vigorously before shaping it, then knead it again carefully and thoroughly with the heel of your hand for a few minutes more.
- Use baking soda or baking powder for leavening quick breads, which don't need to rise. However, they must be baked in a loaf pan or the dough will spread all over the baking sheet.
- For sourdough bread, buy a premade sourdough starter or make one yourself to use as a leavening agent. To do this, measure out equal quantities of all-purpose flour and warm water, seal the mixture in a jar and let ferment for about a week.
- Bake dough within 3 hours of rising or there is a risk that it will collapse.
- Form rolls by shaping the dough into a fairly thick rope, cutting it into pieces and rolling each one into a smooth ball with your cupped hands.
- Place a bowl of water in the oven during baking so bread comes out crisp but not hard.
- Brush loaves or rolls with a little water or egg yolk for an attractive shine.
- Keep yeast breads for 1–3 days, as they taste best when they are fresh.

Cooking tips

Do you steer clear of cheaper cuts of meat because you are worried they will be tough and dry? As food gets more expensive, it's worth going back to old, more creative ways of turning less popular cuts into delicious dishes.

Whether a meal is fried or roasted, grilled or braised, these helpful hints can make your kitchen experience easier, less time consuming and not as taxing on your wallet.

BRAISING, stewing or frying

Braising is a good way to turn less expensive cuts of meat into an appetizing meal.

1 First, brown the meat on all sides. Whether braising or stewing, searing meat quickly over a high heat before cooking helps to lock in moisture and flavor.

2 Next, add a little simmering liquid such as wine or stock. Use about 1 tablespoon (15 ml) liquid at a time and scrape up the brown bits on the bottom of the pan. Keeping the amount of liquid to a minimum helps to retain the meat's flavor. Cover tightly.

- If you want a thick stew, dredge the meat in flour before browning it.

Steaming is a quick and easy way to prepare seafood and vegetables.

- Before frying or grilling round steak, marinate it for a few hours to add flavor and tenderize the meat, then cut across the grain when serving.
- Bring out the tenderness in ribs by par-boiling the meat before grilling.

THRIFTY fish soup

Fish can be expensive, but a creamy fish soup with plenty of hearty potato chunks is a good way to make it go further.

1 Cut two strips of streaky bacon into ¼ inch (5 mm) cubes and sauté in a large saucepan until the fat is rendered (3–4 minutes).

2 Add half a large onion, chopped, and cook over a medium heat until it is translucent. Add 2½ tablespoons (37 ml) all-purpose flour and stir vigorously until evenly browned but not burned.

3 Slowly whisk in 1 cup (250 ml) fish stock, making sure there are no lumps. Keep stirring until it comes to a boil and add 3 tablespoons (45 ml) white wine.

4 Add ½ pound (250 g) potatoes, scrubbed, peeled and diced, and simmer for 15 minutes, or until you can pierce them easily with a knife.

5 Stir in ¾ cup (175 ml) cream, slightly warmed,and return the chowder to a simmer before stirring in ½ pound (250 g) firm white fish fillets, such as cod or halibut. Heat gently for 5 minutes until the fish is cooked; don't let it boil.

6 Season with salt and pepper and serve with fresh, crusty bread.

FRYING meat, poultry and fish

- Take meat from the refrigerator at least 30 minutes before cooking, whether roasting or frying.
- Sautéing is basically quick cooking in a small amount of fat. Choose oil with a high smoking point, such as canola or peanut oil.

• To prevent the fish from breaking up during frying, slash the skin at an angle in a few places.
• When deep-frying, keep an eye on the temperature. Excessively hot oil gives rise to dangerous toxins, but if the oil is too cool, more is absorbed by the food. After cooking, let deep-fried food drain on a paper towels.

ROASTING and grilling

Tender cuts of meat are better suited to roasting or grilling, which allow them to maintain the maximum amount of flavor.
• For the tastiest roast, always choose meat that is marbled and has a rim of fat. Remove any connective tissue because it becomes tough at high temperatures.
• When turning a roast, avoid poking it too much and losing the juice.
• To seal juices in, brown a roast, add vegetables and a little stock and cook in the oven.
• Use the meat stock and juices from the roast as a base for gravy.
• Insert a meat thermometer to determine if the meat is done.
• You can also use a metal skewer. If it feels warm when you pull it out, the meat is still rare; if it's hot, the meat is well-done.
• Roast on a rack when possible to allow even heat circulation and browning.
• Roast beef or lamb with the fat side up to allow natural basting.

GOOD TO KNOW

Healthy cooking

One of the healthiest ways to cook food is by slowly braising it in a Dutch oven on the stove or in a heavy-botttom casserole in the oven. Cheaper cuts of meat not only stay juicy but will retain their nutrients and flavor.

Bonus: You can pop a meal in the oven for a few hours or, better still, leave it in a slow cooker all day and come home to a finished meal. This is particularly convenient after a busy day at work or whenever you know you'll be home too late to prepare dinner.

• Large roasts continue cooking for up to 10 minutes after removal from the oven. Let the roast sit for at least 10 minutes before carving to allow the meat to relax and become tender and juicy.
• Add seasoning before grilling but salt afterwards to avoid toughness.
• Always baste a chicken with its own juices. A mixture of olive oil, lemon, pepper and garlic gives it a Mediterranean twist.
• The drier the skin of chicken or duck, the crispier it becomes when cooked, so pat the skin dry and, if possible, leave the chicken or duck loosely covered in a cool place for several hours before cooking.

Before grilling, marinate lean meat, fish and vegetables or brush them with oil.

Food safety

Kitchen hygiene is just as important in the home as in a restaurant. With a little established culinary wisdom, you can prevent harmful bacteria from multiplying on work surfaces and equipment, causing food to spoil and endangering health.

Cleanliness in the kitchen begins with you. Wash your hands with soap and water before working or cooking, and between each stage of preparation—especially after handling raw meat or fish.

HAMBURGERS SHOULD be cooked THE SAME DAY the meat is bought.

IMPORTANT rules

- Buy frozen and refrigerated foods last and put them in the refrigerator or freezer as soon as you get home, before putting other groceries away.
- Take out the trash regularly.
- Always wash kitchen utensils in hot, soapy water between each stage of preparation.
- Plastic cutting boards are more hygienic than wooden ones and can be put in the dishwasher.
- Use two different cutting boards: one for raw and one for cooked foods.
- Wash or replace dishcloths, dish towels and sponges frequently because bacteria reproduce explosively in warm, moist environments.
- Don't leave raw foods or leftovers at room temperature for long or germs will multiply.

Check that eggs are clean and not cracked when you buy them.

WHERE special care is required

- Be careful when preparing meat, fish, poultry and eggs to be sure that harmful bacteria don't have a chance to breed.
- When thawing meat, fish or poultry, place on a plate in the refrigerator, unwrapped but covered. Discard the liquid from thawing, as it may contain harmful bacteria.
- Cook minced, rolled or stuffed meats and sausages all the way through. The meat's core temperature must be at least 167°F (75°C) for 10 minutes in order to kill bacteria.
- Cook whole poultry to at least 167°F (75°C). If you don't have a meat thermometer, juices should run clear when the middle of the drumstick is pierced.
- Check that eggs are clean and not cracked when you buy them. Keep them in the refrigerator and use by the best-before date. Wash your hands, utensils and surfaces before and after contact with eggs.

• Shellfish should be cooked on the day of purchase. Wash thoroughly before cooking. Toss out any mussels that are already open or smell unpleasant.
• If you need to keep food warm for some time before serving, put it in the oven at or above 140°F (60°C) to kill bacteria and viruses.
• If cooked food is not going to be eaten almost immediately, cool it rapidly and refrigerate as soon as it stops steaming.
• Reheat cooked food thoroughly until steaming hot, to 140°F (60°C) or hotter.
• Don't store food in its can after opening—contact with tin and iron can affect its flavor.
• Keep dry ingredients in airtight containers to prevent deterioration and deter insects. Clothespins or chip clips are useful for sealing open packets.
• Food past its use-by date may be unsafe to eat, even though it looks fine—its nutrients may become unstable or bacteria may increase to harmful levels.

ALWAYS PLACE meat on a CLEAN PLATE AFTER BARBECUING.

PICNICS and barbecues

When eating outdoors, whether it's a backyard barbecue, a picnic at the beach or a camping trip, you need to take some extra precautions to be sure your food is safe, especially in hot weather.
• Coolers can't keep food cold enough to prevent bacteria from multiplying, so chill all food well before packing it for a picnic.
• Unless wicker baskets are insulated, they are suitable only for nonperishable food, cloths, cutlery, cups and plates.

• Keep a packed lunch cool by placing a frozen drink in the lunchbox or freezing the sandwiches—they'll thaw nicely by lunchtime.
• Take meat out of the refrigerator or cooler only when you are ready to put it on the barbecue. For barbecues away from home, package meat well and place it at the bottom of the cooler, away from ready-to-eat food.
• When the meat is cooked, put it on a clean plate—never use the one that held raw meat.
• Protect food from flies by keeping it covered until you are ready to eat it.
• When at home, don't leave perishable foods such as pâtés, salads, spreads and dips out of the refrigerator for long periods. Instead split these foods into smaller amounts and serve fresh portions on clean plates as needed.
• Put any uneaten cooked meats or perishables back into the refrigerator or cooler as soon as you are finished with them.

Use baskets only for cups, plates, cutlery and nonperishable food.

Freezing

The freezer makes it possible to keep many food items available, ready to whip up a favorite dish. It also allows you to buy food cheaply in bulk or when it's in season, and to bake in batches and save separate portions.

Foods meant for the freezer should be fresh or if they are cooked, they should be packed up and put in the freezer as soon as they have cooled. Never refreeze foods that have already been frozen and thawed.

THE right way to freeze

- Use only freezer bags, plastic containers, foil trays and special freezer containers for freezing. Label all items with the type of food and date.
- Never fill plastic containers right to the top with sauce, soup or other liquids. They will expand and lift the lid or split the container.
- Only partially fill freezer bags so the contents freeze faster and the bags are easier to stack.
- Prevent freezer burn by getting as much air as possible out of the bags before sealing them.
- If cooked food does not fill a container, pack the space with crumpled paper to prevent the food from drying out.
- It's best to freeze many small amounts of food and thaw the packages as needed. This will decrease waste, because once frozen food has been thawed it has to be consumed or thrown out; it can't be frozen again.

WHICH foods to freeze and how to do it

- Individual meat portions should be no more than 4 inches (10 cm) thick, while larger cuts of meat should weigh no more than 5 pounds (2.5 kg). Remove extra fat and bones from meat, if practical. Depending on the fat content, meat can be frozen for 6–12 months. Lean meat lasts longest, as fat gradually becomes rancid at low temperatures.
- When freezing prepacked meats, always remove the packaging and rewrap. Cut out the store label and tape to the new packaging.
- Place pieces of freezer paper between slices of cooked meat or uncooked hamburgers to keep them from sticking together. They will keep for 2 months in the freezer. Chops and steaks will keep for up to 6 months.
- Before freezing uncooked poultry, remove it from its packaging, rewrap in plastic wrap or place in a freezer bag or storage container. Uncooked poultry will keep for up to 12 months in the freezer.
- Freeze only freshly caught raw fish that has been scaled and cleaned in advance. Cook it within 6 months.
- Shortcrust pastry can be frozen raw or baked. Allow yeast dough to rise once before freezing.

Peas are one of the best vegetables for freezing. They taste nearly as good as when fresh.

Blanching vegetables

one Bring 5–10 quarts (5–10 L) water to a boil, and plunge prewashed vegetables in it. Return to a boil.

two Remove vegetables from the boiling water after 2–3 minutes, drain well and plunge into ice water.

three Transfer the vegetables to a colander and let them drip-dry thoroughly before packing.

• Bread and rolls are easy to freeze and will keep for 3 months. If you freeze sliced bread, it can be defrosted as needed.
• Blanch vegetables (*see box*) to reduce the danger of freezer burn. Blanched vegetables will keep in the freezer for up to 10 months.
• Mushrooms, red cabbage and legumes such as peas and beans become even easier to digest after they have been frozen. They lose the substances that lead to flatulence.
• Freeze berries or vegetable pieces on a cookie sheet and drop them in bags. Fruit and vegetables can be kept for up to 12 months in the freezer.

WHAT shouldn't be put in the freezer?

• Whole raw or cooked eggs can't be frozen. Egg yolk and beaten egg white, however, can be frozen in appropriate plastic containers.
• Milk products don't belong in the freezer. The exceptions are cheese and ice cream.
• Keep most exotic fruit away from the freezer. When exposed to extreme cold, bananas turn brown and whole citrus fruit get spots. However, peeled, cubed pineapple freezes exceptionally well.
• Don't freeze water-rich fruit and vegetables such as cucumbers, lettuce and onions, which become soft. Cooked spinach freezes well, and whole tomatoes can be frozen for adding to soups and casseroles.

FREEZER standbys

• For quick meals from the freezer, arrange ready-cooked meals on foil plates, making sure the meat is covered with gravy or sauce. Cover with plastic wrap or foil, seal and freeze.
• When freezing leftovers, store them in portion sizes so that you can take out exactly the number of servings you need.
• Freeze a cooked casserole in a foil-lined casserole dish. When frozen, lift out of the dish and wrap completely in more foil to store in the freezer. To cook, unwrap the frozen casserole and return to the original casserole dish to defrost and cook.
• To save time when entertaining, prepare butter balls or curls in advance, drop into ice water, drain and pack into boxes to freeze. Thaw at room temperature about an hour before needed.
• Before a dinner party, scoop ready-to-serve portions of ice cream or sorbet on wax paper-lined trays and refreeze.
• For instant pie decoration, roll out pastry trimmings and cut into shapes such as leaves or hearts. Freeze in containers and use straight from the freezer to decorate pies before baking.
• Cakes are best frozen without icing. If the cake is decorated, freeze before wrapping so that the top will not get squashed.

Grains

The seven main grain varieties—wheat, rye, barley, rice, corn, millet and oats—are a source of nourishment for people all around the globe. In recent years we've also rediscovered traditional and ancient grains such as bulgur, spelt and quinoa to enhance our diet.

Grains can be eaten either in their whole form (whole grains), crushed or ground. Only the hull or husk is removed from whole grains; with refined grains, the germ layer is removed as well. Whole grains are a healthier choice, because they have a high fiber content and are digested more slowly.

STORING grains

- Protect grains against moisture and insects by storing them in cool, dark places in clean, airtight containers.
- Store whole grains in airtight containers in a cupboard for up to a year.

PREPARING and cooking grains

- Rinse grains thoroughly before cooking to remove dirt and dust particles. Continue to rinse until the water is clear, and throw away any off-color grains.
- Soaking grains such as barley and oats before cooking makes them quicker and easier to cook and digest. Add grains and water to a pot in a 1:2 ratio and soak until they are softer and swollen.
- Strain away any excess liquid that is not absorbed and save it for cooking with later, as it contains many valuable nutrients.
- Grains need to be stirred constantly during cooking—many types will stick to the bottom of the saucepan.
- After cooking, allow grains to sit briefly in the covered saucepan, then fluff them with a fork as you would a pot of rice.
- To separate sticky grains, dump them into a colander and pour a kettle of boiling water over them.
- Cook grains ahead of time and reheat them in the microwave for just a minute or two. Add a little water, cover the bowl with microwave-safe plastic wrap and fluff them when cooking time is up.

OATCAKES

Historically, Scottish oatcakes were toasted on a peat fire. This hot griddle recipe makes about eight.

1 Mix ½ cup (125 g) medium oatmeal, a pinch of salt and a pinch of baking soda in a bowl; make a well in the center.

2 Melt 2 teaspoons (10 ml) butter in 3

A small hand mill lets you to grind as much grain as you want.

Muesli is an easy-to-make healthy breakfast and you can add whatever fresh fruit you like.

tablespoons (45 ml) boiling water and pour it in the well. Mix to form a stiff dough.
3 Turn out on a floured surface and knead lightly. Roll out thinly and cut into eight triangles.
4 Cook on a hot griddle or in a dry, heavy skillet until the edges curl up and the cakes are firm. Store in an airtight container and reheat before eating.

VARIOUS grain types

- Corn, rice, wheat and barley are the most commonly grown grains worldwide.
- Spelt is a protein-rich grain that makes a particularly robust pasta, gives bread a nutty taste and is good as a side dish and in stews. It may also be suitable for wheat-intolerant people, but not for those with celiac disease.
- Whole-wheat kernels should be presoaked and then cooked. They make a tasty rice substitute and can add crunch to a salad and a nutty flavor to chili or stews.
- Rye is high in fiber and low in gluten. It can be made into flour for bread or into flakes that can be cooked as a breakfast cereal like oats.
- Because of its low gluten content, barley flour is unsuitable for baking. But you can make tasty soups, stews and pilafs with whole pearl barley.
- Millet is one of the oldest grain varieties. Use the kernels like rice or incorporate them into a salad. Bread made with millet flour is particularly crispy.
- Nutritionally, oats are one of the most valuable grains, mainly because they contain a protein and fat that are good for you and easy to digest. Oatmeal, oat bran and oat flour are made from oats.
- Bulgur, a form of processed wheat, can replace rice in most recipes, thicken soups and stews, and can be used in salads, breads and even desserts.
- Once called "the gold of the Incas," protein-rich quinoa has a fluffy, somewhat crunchy texture that makes it a wonderful rice substitute or wheat-free alternative to bulgur in tabbouleh and other salads.

BREAKFAST mix

Swiss-style muesli is a healthy breakfast food. It's easy to make and you can modify the ingredients according to your taste.
1 In a large mixing bowl, combine 1 ½ cups (375 g) old-fashioned oats, ¼ cup (50 g) wheat germ, 2 tablespoons (30 g) wheat bran, ¼ cup (50 g) oat bran, ¾ cup (150 g) raisins, ¼ cup (50 g) chopped walnuts, 3 tablespoons (45 ml) soft dark brown sugar and 2 tablespoons (30 g) unsalted sunflower seeds.
2 Mix well and store in an airtight container. It will keep for 2 months at room temperature.

GOOD TO KNOW

Soaking & cooking times

GRAIN	SOAKING TIME	COOKING TIME
Barley	30–60 minutes	30–45 minutes
Bulgur	none	2–5 minutes
Millet	10–20 minutes	5–15 minutes
Quinoa	none	10–15 minutes
Rye	30–60 minutes	30–45 minutes
Spelt	30–45 minutes	30–45 minutes

Herbs

Herbs add a dash of color and flavor to food and are a healthy alternative to salt as a seasoning. They can also make food easier to digest. Use the more pungent varieties sparingly and add tender green herbs to a dish just before serving.

Herbs lose their flavor quickly if not handled correctly. Use them soon after they've been picked or purchased and always chop the tender leaves with care.

HANDLING herbs

- Chop herbs on a moistened wood or plastic chopping board. The flavors can be dulled by the wood of a dry cutting board.
- Harvest herbs at midday, when their essential oils are most intense.
- Wrap herbs in a damp dish towel before putting them in the refrigerator's vegetable drawer, where they'll keep for 1–3 days.
- Dry or freeze herbs for longer storage.

COMMON kitchen herbs

- Parsley is the most popular herb and ubiquitous in most kitchens. It is used to season soups, stews, casseroles, salads, pasta and potato dishes. Just add chopped sprigs near the end of the cooking time, or tear the leaves with your fingers.
- Fragrant basil has a pungent taste that works well in sweet and spicy foods such as stir-fries and spaghetti sauce. Simply tear it apart or cut it into strips to add to salads and marinades, or blend it in a food processor to make pesto.
- Cilantro is one of the most widely used herbs in the world. Its strong flavor adds a boost to Asian, Latin American, Middle Eastern and southwestern U.S. cuisines. Sprinkle the fresh leaves on a finished dish just before serving.
- Rosemary has an astringent, clean scent and tastes great in Mediterranean cooking.

Cut herbs quickly on a moist wooden chopping board to preserve their flavors.

Add the needle-like leaves to lamb and pork, or use the stripped branches as skewers to grill or barbecue meat, poultry or fish.
- Fresh chervil adds a delicious mild aniseed flavor to salads, soups and herb butter, as well as egg and cheese dishes.
- Dill complements fish, shellfish, cucumber salad, vinaigrette and pickles. Sprinkle on before serving.

• Tarragon is native to Siberia and Asia. Introduced to Spain by the Arabs, it was later used in many recipes developed by the French. It adds a distinctive flavor to vinegar, mustard and béarnaise sauce, and goes well with poultry and shellfish. French tarragon has a more delicate flavor than the Russian variety. Its bittersweet and spicy aroma is lost when dried.
• Bay leaves are widely used in soups, stews and spaghetti sauce, but their aromatic flavor is also great with fish and in many Indian dishes like biryani. Bay leaves stimulate the appetite and also act as a preservative. You usually add the leaves whole and remove them before serving.
• Marjoram aids digestion and goes well with meat dishes and summer vegetables such as eggplant, tomatoes and peppers. It can't be frozen but, when dried, it can be added during cooking.
• There are many different varieties of mint but spearmint and peppermint are the most frequently used. Mint highlights the fine taste of spring vegetables, peas, green beans and salads, and adds a fresh, elegant touch to desserts and fruit bowls. It is also a traditional seasoning to lamb.
• Oregano belongs to the same family as marjoram and is regularly served on pizza and in tomato dishes. Use the herb sparingly—it is easy to overdo it.
• Add peppery-tasting sage to roast poultry and pork. It also goes well with tomatoes, beans and pasta.
• Chives taste like mild onions. Use them to dress up salads, vegetable soups, sour cream, potato and leafy salads, and mashed potatoes, as well as scrambled eggs. The younger the shoots, the more tender the consistency and the more intense the taste.
• Use thyme in soups and stews, with vegetables and in casseroles and fish dishes. Fresh lemon thyme goes well with fish and poultry.

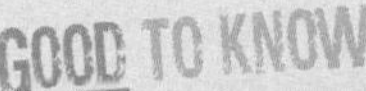

Special collection

A bouquet garni of fresh parsley, thyme, rosemary and bay, tied together with string, will add depth of flavor to a stock, soup or casserole. Remove it before serving.

Freeze fresh herbs in an ice cube tray ready to add to soups or sauces as required.

Kitchen safety

More accidents happen in the kitchen than anywhere else in the home. Cutting yourself with a knife, slipping on a wet floor or burning yourself with a hot pan are among the common dangers. You can minimize the risk of injury by taking a few precautionary measures.

A little care is key to kitchen safety. Learn how to handle sharp kitchen utensils safely and make sure you know what to do in case of emergency. When it comes to stove safety, never leave a pot on the burner unsupervised, especially if you are cooking with gas. Turn off burners immediately after you have finished using them.

PREVENTING burns

- Make sure to position pots and pans carefully on the stove or cooktop so that you can't knock their handles as you move around the kitchen.
- When heating oil, watch the pan carefully because oil is very flammable. Deep frying is a common cause of kitchen fires.
- Step back and let the hot air escape when you open the oven door.
- Be especially careful not to spill hot liquid when removing pots and pans from the oven. Wipe up any spills on the floor at once so you don't slip on them.
- Never place hot foods on the edge of the stove, table or work surface where they may tip over.

Use oven mitts when removing hot food from the oven.

- Keep dish towels well away from the burners which could set them on fire.
- Wash or replace exhaust fan filters regularly. They can easily catch fire when saturated with grease.
- Keep your hands, face and body out of harm's way when using the steam release valve on a pressure cooker.
- For safety's sake, and for peace of mind, it's best to use a kettle that automatically turns itself off after the water boils.
- Never overheat oil in a deep fryer. Also, replace used oil, it is more likely to catch fire.
- Make sure the deep fryer's heating coils are totally immersed in oil or there is a strong risk that the oil will catch fire.
- Run cold water in the sink while draining potatoes or other vegetables so that the rising steam won't scald your hands.

KNIVES, blades and broken glass

- Store knives and other sharp objects in a knife block or on a magnetic wall strip out of the reach of children.
- Don't put knives in dishwater. If they're obscured by suds where you can't see them, you could accidentally grab them by the blade.
- Wash knives with a brush right after use. For dried-on food, let knives soak first in a container of warm water.
- Read the instruction manuals to find out how to safely remove the blades from food processors, shredders, slicers, meat grinders and other kitchen devices with blades.
- Sweep up broken glass immediately and wrap it in newspaper before putting it into the garbage can. Gather up tiny fragments of glass with a piece of sticky tape wound around your hand.
- If a glass breaks in the dishwater, drain the water through a sieve and rinse away any excess soap suds before removing the pieces.

Make sure pans fit well and are stable on the burner.

> **GOOD TO KNOW**
>
> **Don't try to treat poisoning with home remedies**
>
> In the event of someone being poisoned—or if you suspect someone may have been poisoned—call a doctor or poison control center immediately. Don't attempt treatment unless you are advised to do so. Prompt action can save a victim's life, so don't wait to see if the symptoms improve or worsen.

OTHER dangers

- Keep household chemicals well out of the reach of children. Make sure that all such chemicals are clearly labelled and don't store them in food cupboards or in containers that are normally used to store foods.
- Wipe up splattered grease and spills on the floor immediately so no one slips.

WHAT to do in an emergency

- If something does go wrong, remain calm.
- Smother the flames of an oil fire with a thick, damp dish towel or a pot lid, and remove the pan from the heat source. Don't use water or a foam fire extinguisher on the flames, as this has the potential to splatter the oil outside the contained pan and spread the flames.
- Turn off the oven immediately in the event of an oven fire. Keep the oven door closed—the lack of oxygen will suffocate the fire.
- Treat bruises from a fall by applying a cold pack or a bag of ice wrapped in a towel. Never apply ice cubes directly to skin as it will burn.

Note: For severe falls, seek professional advice.

- For a minor burn or scald, run the area under cool water for 10–30 minutes to prevent it from getting worse. Do not use ice, creams or greasy substances.
- Cover the burn with a single layer of plastic wrap; a clean, clear plastic bag is suitable for covering burns on the hand. Do not interfere with the burn or break any blisters.

Note: For severe burns, go to the emergency room immediately.

- Stop bleeding by applying a clean dish towel or wad of paper towels and pressing hard on the spot. Clean it by holding the part of your body that is injured under cold running water. Cover with an adhesive bandage and some antibiotic cream to prevent infection.

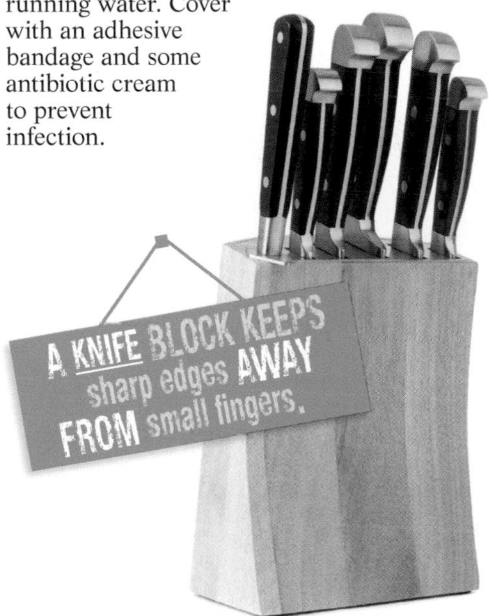
A KNIFE BLOCK KEEPS sharp edges AWAY FROM small fingers.

Leftovers

Around the world, consumers throw away millions of tons of food and drink each year at a cost of hundreds of dollars per household. Spare the environment and your pocketbook by following these simple ideas for banishing waste and turn those leftovers into tasty meals.

Casseroles and salads are the classic way to use up leftover potatoes, pasta and rice. But you can also transform them into delicious soups and puddings.

LEFTOVERS CAN OFTEN be used to CREATE TASTY OMELETS.

USING leftover potatoes, pasta & rice

- Try making potato patties: Mash leftover potatoes and mix them with an egg, salt, pepper, garlic, parsley and a diced onion. Shape the mixture into rounds, coat in breadcrumbs and deep fry in vegetable oil.
- Purée leftover potatoes with stock and season to taste with cream or milk, herbs and/or shredded cheese to make a delicious potato soup.
- Convert a whisked egg and a little cheese, leftover meat and potatoes into a tasty omelet.
- Add a can of black beans and some salsa to leftover chicken or hamburgers to create a tasty topping for tacos or a filling for burritos.
- Add leftover parmesan to breadcrumbs and use to top a pot pie for a great flavor. Because parmesan can burn easily, cover the dish with foil for the first half of the cooking time.
- Add 2 tablespoons (30 ml) capers or sliced olives, a can of tuna and some diced tomatoes to leftover pasta, and season with vinegar, olive oil, salt and pepper to make a light summer pasta salad.
- Pasta salads taste particularly good when you let the flavors develop for a time before eating. The same is true of potato and rice salads.
- Make a hearty rice dish from leftover rice, eggs, pork or chicken, onions and frozen vegetables. For an Asian touch, use sesame oil for stir-frying and season with soy sauce and/or toss in a little curry paste.
- Transform day-old rice into rice pudding: Mix 2 cups (500 ml) milk per 1 cup (250 g) cooked rice. Simmer gently so the milk doesn't burn but the mixture is heated through. In a separate bowl, mix together 2 eggs, ¼ cup (55 g) sugar and ½ teaspoon (2 ml) vanilla. Whisk into the rice and heat through before transferring to a casserole dish. Bake in a preheated oven at 350°F (180°C) for 20 minutes.
- Whip up delicate rice pancakes by mixing leftover rice with flour, milk and eggs, and cook as for regular pancakes. Serve with cinnamon sugar or marmalade.

VEGETABLE variety

- For a simple casserole, layer leftover vegetables with potatoes, pasta or rice in an ovenproof dish and pour cheese sauce over it. Sprinkle with breadcrumbs and bake.

• Make a puréed soup from leftover vegetables: Heat the cubed vegetables in a little stock, purée and stir in milk for a creamy consistency. Season to taste and serve with crunchy croutons made from day-old bread.

VARIATIONS for old bread

• Turn old bread and rolls into croutons for salads or soups. Just cut them into bite-sized cubes and toast in a pan with a little olive oil or butter. Heat until they are crunchy and have browned slightly. Add herbs, crushed nuts or parmesan for extra flavor.
• Dip stale bread into egg whisked with milk and fry to make French toast.
• Soften stale rolls in vegetable or beef stock before using them in meatballs or meatloaf to make the dish especially tasty.
• In summer, when tomatoes are ripe and juicy, try this novel bread salad: Chop stale slices of white bread into bite-sized chunks and mix with diced tomatoes, onions, olive oil and red wine vinegar. Season with salt, pepper and herbs, and let it sit for at least 15 minutes.

OTHER leftovers

• Serve day-old roast chicken or turkey breast on a green salad with additions such as vegetables, chickpeas, walnuts, pine nuts, raisins, cranberries or cheese. Keep it simple—serve with a balsamic vinaigrette.
• Chicken pot pie makes the most of leftover chicken and vegetables. Make a thick sauce with milk, flour, butter, and a dash of salt and pepper. Mix in diced chicken and leftover or sautéed vegetables and pour into a greased baking dish. Top with ready-made pastry, sealing it to the sides. Cut a few vents in the pastry and bake until bubbly and golden brown.
• Cooked grains are a nutritious and filling addition to any soup.

GOOD TO KNOW

Are foods made with mayonnaise prone to spoiling?

Not necessarily. When you turn your leftover chicken into chicken salad, store-bought mayonnaise may actually help to prevent spoilage as the commercial product is slightly acidic. So when you are taking a picnic or setting out a buffet, you don't have to avoid mayonnaise—but you should keep the food cold. And if you know that there will be leftovers, cover the dish and refrigerate it as quickly as possible. But dishes made with homemade mayonnaise that contains raw egg can spoil quickly if left in the open air.

Croutons made from leftover bread add flavor and texture to salads or puréed soups.

Meat, fish and poultry

Cooking meat, fish and poultry successfully involves proper preparation. Use time-honored methods such as marinating overnight and making tasty stuffings so your dishes are tender, moist and appetizing.

Once you have decided what to cook, calculate how much meat or fish you will need, taking into account that it may shrink during the cooking process.

HOW much to serve

- With red meat, allow about ½ pound (200 g) per person, or 2/3 pound (300 g) for a bone-in roast.
- Depending on the size, one 3–4 pound (1.5–2 kg) roasting chicken feeds three to four people. With turkey, allow about 1 pound (500 g) per person, which will allow for you to have leftovers, too.
- With fish fillets, allow about ½ pound (250 g) per person, or 2/3 pound (350 g) if you are buying a whole fish and filleting it yourself.

A GOOD meat and fish marinade

Marinades serve a dual purpose: to tenderize meat and fish and to add a mouthwatering flavor. Most marinades contain an acidic ingredient—such as lemon juice, vinegar or wine—that breaks down muscle fibers. The enzymes in ingredients such as onions, ginger and papaya also act as excellent tenderizers. Marinades have yet another function: You can use them later for making a sauce or gravy.

- For a simple marinade, stir together 4 tablespoons (60 ml) each oil and vinegar, and a pinch each of pepper and sugar. Place the meat or fish you are preparing in a deep container or sturdy freezer bag and cover it with the marinade.
- Use salt sparingly in a marinade to avoid drawing the moisture out of meat.
- Boost flavor by adding extra ingredients such as honey, mustard, wine, lemon, spices, herbs or fruits such as apples and oranges.
- Marinate veal and offal for a maximum of 2 hours, other types of meat for 3–4 hours or overnight, and fish for 2–3 hours in the refrigerator. Game can steep in a marinade for 1–3 days.
- Don't use metal containers or bowls for marinating, as they react with the acids in the marinade, which can be harmful and may leave the meat with an unpleasant flavor.

CUTTING, marinating & stuffing birds

When cutting up poultry, make sure you have a sharp knife and good poultry shears on hand.

1 Lay the bird on its back, cut through the skin between the drumsticks or wings and breast with the knife, then use poultry shears to snip off the bones at the joint.
2 Use the knife to separate the breast meat on both sides of the breastbone.

- Marinate white meat in white wine and herbs, dark meat in red wine.

Garlic and herbs enhance the flavor and aroma of meat.

Filleting fish

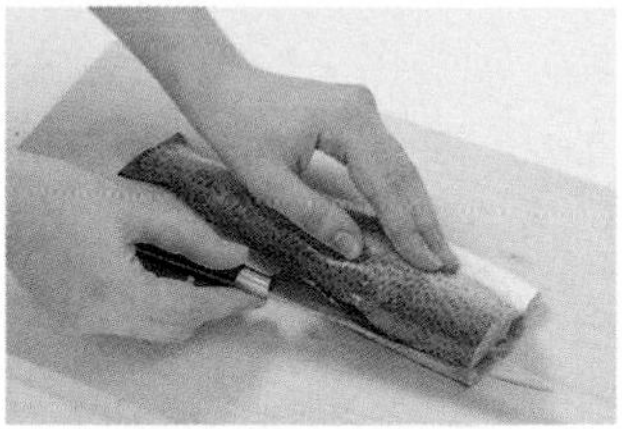

1 Cut off the head just behind the gills. Hold the knife blade horizontal and cut across the body of the fish, using the backbone to guide the knife.

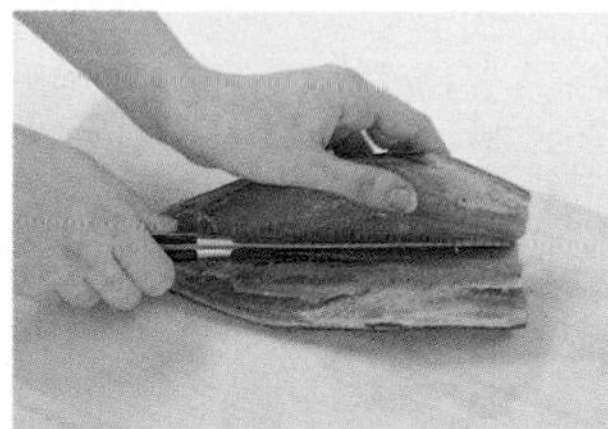

2 Release the upper fillet completely from the bones with a second cut, and set it aside.

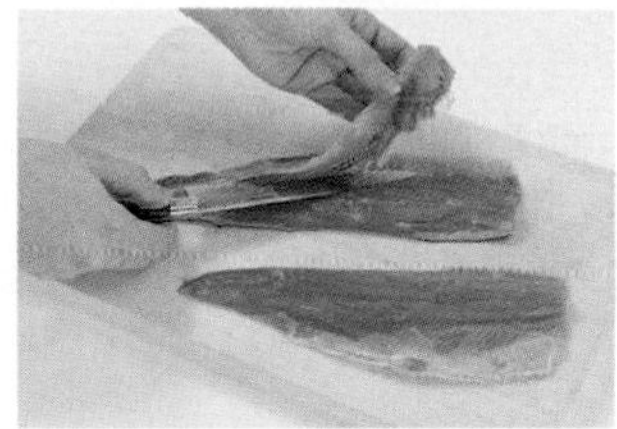

3 With a final cut, guide the knife flat beneath the central bone and free it from the second fillet.

- Give chicken a Mediterranean flavor by rubbing olive oil, lemon, garlic and herbs on and under the skin.
- Good poultry stuffings include savory ingredients such as sausage meat and chestnuts, as well as traditional sage and onion. Or try parsley, onions, almonds and dried apricots.
- Season the abdominal cavity with salt and pepper before you start stuffing.
- When cooking large birds such as turkeys, only stuff the neck end, leaving the body cavity unstuffed so air can circulate as it cooks.

PREPARING fish

- Scale a fish by holding it by the tail while you scrape from the rear towards the head, using a scaler or a knife with a serrated edge.
- Boning is more complicated. Open up the abdominal cavity and cut the perpendicular bones away from the flesh on both sides. Then, separate the central bone from the head and tail and carefully remove it along with the other bones.
- Cut the lateral (side) and dorsal (back) fins off when serving a fish whole.

COOKING fish

Don't overcook fish if you want it to remain tender and juicy.

- To test to see if a fish is done, use a knife to part the flesh a little. It should flake easily.
- Or, stick a toothpick into the fleshiest part of the fish. If it meets little resistance and comes out clean, the fish is done.
- Make it easier to cut fish into chunks by freezing it for 45 minutes first.
- Thaw frozen fish in the refrigerator or cook it frozen; thawing at room temperature increases the likelihood of contamination.
- When roasting a whole fish, wash it thoroughly inside and out, salt and season it with herbs and rub it with olive oil. Bake in a preheated oven at 425°F (220°C). You'll know it's done when the eyes turn opaque and the flesh near the backbone flakes when poked with a skewer.

FRYING fish

- Dredge the fish in seasoned flour, beaten egg and finally breadcrumbs before frying.
- If you have no eggs available for a fish coating, use lemon juice instead. The coating will stick just as well and the fish will have a lovely lemony zest.
- Try chopped hazelnuts, flaked almonds or crushed cornflakes instead of breadcrumbs.
- Always bread fish shortly before cooking or the breadcrumbs will flake off.
- Absorb excess grease by placing the cooked fish briefly on a paper towel.
- If fish portions have skin, fry them skin side down first. Turn them over when nearly cooked through to finish. The skin will be crisp and delicious.

Nonalcoholic beverages

Water is the basic ingredient for all refreshing drinks, as well as being essential for good health. But water alone can be a little dull, so here are some traditional methods to satisfy your taste buds while quenching your thirst.

Drinks should quench your thirst and refresh you without sending your blood sugar soaring. Commercially produced drinks often contain too much sugar, so borrow your grandmother's cookbook and make your own.

STORE COFFEE BEANS in a tightly closed container OR they will get STALE.

WATER, the elixir of life

Advertising by bottled water companies gives consumers the impression their product is safer and healthier than tap water. As a result, world consumption of bottled water has grown enormously in the past 10 years. However, you may be better off drinking the elixir of life straight from the tap. Here are three reasons why.

1 Producing and delivering bottled water creates greenhouse gases, and most discarded plastic bottles end up in landfills.

2 Scientists found that bottled brands contain higher levels of bacteria than tap water.

3 Drinking bottled water can cost up to a thousand times more than tap water.

Lemon and mint add a tangy flavor to tap water.

COFFEE beans

- The amount of coffee you need will depend on personal taste, water quality and the type of coffee maker you are using. Generally, when using a filter coffeemaker, allow about 1 tablespoon (15 ml) coffee per 1 cup (250 ml) water. With hard water, which contains lime, use more coffee.
- Store coffee beans in a dry, cool, dark location and keep them in a tightly closed container or they will get stale.
- Store vacuum-packed ground coffee for several months if unopened. Once opened, keep in an airtight jar in the refrigerator.
- Ground coffee loses its flavor quickly and should be used within 6 months.
- Use a coffee grinder or spice mill to make freshly ground coffee.

TEA

After water, tea is the most widely consumed drink in the world. The term "herbal tea" usually refers to an infusion of leaves, flowers, fruit, herbs or other plant material that doesn't include traditional tea leaves.

- Infuse black tea with boiling water then steep for 3–5 minutes.
- Steep green tea in hot water at 175°F (80°C) for only 2 minutes.
- When water has a high lime content, use strong tea blends or run the water through a filter.
- Store tea in a dry container with a tight-fitting lid. Special metal or porcelain containers and opaque bags are ideal for this.

• Don't keep opened packets of tea in the refrigerator. The sensitive leaves can be damaged by fluctuations in humidity.
• For long-term storage, place unopened tea in the vegetable drawer in the refrigerator.
• Always store the same type of tea in a container, as tea will quickly pick up other flavors, which can ruin its subtle nuances.
• Make delicious herbal teas with rosehips or mint. Depending on the season you can boost their flavor: In summer, use lemon or lime peel with mint tea; in winter, use cinnamon or cloves with rosehip tea.

FOR hot days

Iced tea is a wonderfully thirst quenching drink for hot days and easy to make.
1 Brew 3–4 teaspoons (15–20 g) tea leaves in 1 quart (1 L) water and let it steep for 3 minutes.
2 Stir in the juice of 1½ lemons, sweeten to taste, and strain over about 25 ice cubes.
3 Flavor it according to taste with apple juice, fruit nectar, citrus fruit or mint leaves.

HOMEMADE lemonade

There's nothing quite like the flavor of traditional homemade lemonade, which is refreshing and often healthier than store-bought versions.
1 Boil the zest of 6 organic lemons with 1¼ cups (280 g) sugar and about 2 cups (500 ml) water. Simmer briefly, cool and add the juice of the 6 lemons.
2 Strain the lemonade concentrate and pour it into a glass jug. Fill it up with ice cubes and cold water.
• Honey, ginger or rosewater will add a highly original flavor to lemonade.
• Limes and oranges can be also be used to make equally refreshing drinks.

HEALTHY fruit drinks

Get more vitamins and minerals into your diet by drinking freshly made fruit juices or whipping up thick and frothy smoothies from frozen fruit.
• Make a delicious fruit drink by cutting up your choice of fruits and puréeing them in a blender with the juice of half a lemon, together with ¼–½ cup (55–115 g) sugar. Adjust the amount of sugar according to the fruit used and your taste.
• For a berry punch that will serve about 15 people, put 2 pounds (1 kg) raspberries and strawberries, the juice of a lemon and 6 cups (1.5 L) mixed fruit juice in a punch bowl and cool for several hours. Shortly before serving, add two bottles of mineral water, followed by ice cubes.
• Keep your punch cold by freezing slices of citrus fruits and using in place of ice cubes.
• Blend frozen fruit such as bananas, strawberries, milk and a touch of honey to make a frothy smoothie.

GOOD TO KNOW

Coffee substitute & chicory coffee
In times of crisis, when coffee was too expensive or simply unavailable, people often drank substitutes made from dandelion or chicory roots, or used them to stretch out their real coffee. When people turn to such substitutes now, it's usually for health reasons. Coffee made from chicory is more easily digested, caffeine-free and contains fewer tooth-staining tannins than coffee beans.

Pasta and rice

Noodles and rice have been staples on numerous international menus for centuries. Nourishing and extremely versatile, they come in many forms and can be combined with just about anything.

Nothing beats the taste of fresh, homemade pasta. While it requires some effort, it is not difficult and making food from scratch can be therapeutic.

PASTA dough

Here are some basic recipes for pasta dough. For pasta without egg:

1 Mix about ¾ cup (180 g) durum wheat semolina flour with about ¾ cup (180 g) all-purpose flour and a pinch of salt. Add ¾ cup (180 ml) water and knead into a smooth, elastic dough.

2 Add a little more water if the dough is too dry—it should be solid but not sticky.

3 Let it sit for 1 hour, roll it thinly, cut into your desired shape and let it air-dry.

- Pasta made from durum wheat is particularly good with thick sauces.

For egg noodles:

1 Knead 1 cup (260 g) all-purpose flour, 3 lightly beaten eggs, 1 teaspoon (5 ml) salt and 1 tablespoon (15 ml) olive oil into a smooth dough. (It's ready when shiny and it loosens from the work surface.)

2 Let it rest, roll it out, cut it up and let it dry.

TIPS for making pasta

- Brew coffee when you make pasta—it helps add moist air in the kitchen.
- Turn dough over several times to make the process of rolling it out easier.
- Work on pasta dough in sections. Wrap the rest in aluminium foil to keep it from drying out.
- Egg noodles can be colored and flavored: beet juice turns them dark red; tomato purée, light red; carrot or pumpkin purée, orange; saffron, yellow; spinach, green; mushrooms, brown; and squid ink, black. Mix these ingredients with the eggs, oil and salt, then knead with the flour. You may need more flour for the extra moisture.
- To make tortellini, roll out the dough and cut small squares before adding a dab of filling in the middle. Moisten the edges in so that they stay together and carefully fold the dough over the filling.
- Use a large saucepan for cooking so that the noodles can move freely while they boil.
- Pasta swells to about two-and-a-half times its original volume during cooking. Make sure you add it to water at a full rolling boil.
- Stir pasta around as soon as it is in the water so that it keeps its shape and doesn't stick together.
- Don't add oil to the water. Although it prevents water from boiling over, it won't stop the pasta from sticking together and can prevent the noodles from holding the sauce well.
- Add some stock to the water for a zestier flavor.

TYPES of rice and cooking methods

One of the oldest cultivated plants, rice has shaped the culture, diet and economy of Asia. Without a doubt, it's the world's most important food staple.

- Long-grain and basmati rice both have long, slender grains and a dry, glassy core. For best results, wash them thoroughly before cooking. Then, bring one part rice and two parts salted liquid to a boil, lower the heat and cook, covered, for 15–20 minutes. **Note:** There is no need to soak rice before cooking, but if you do, it will reduce the cooking time; soaked rice should be rinsed to remove additional starch before cooking or the grains will not separate well.
- Before converted or parboiled rice is husked and polished, hot steam is used to force about 80 percent of the vitamins and minerals contained in the outer membrane into the rice grain so that it's high in nutrients. To cook it, bring one part rice and two parts salted liquid to a boil, then lower the heat. Cook, covered, for 20 minutes.
- Short-grain rice is chalk white and soft and sticky at the core. It produces plenty of starch when cooked and can be used for risottos and sweet dishes. Use one part rice to one part water. Bring water to a boil, then reduce heat and cook, covered, for 10 minutes or until done.
- Brown rice is nutrient-dense and high in fiber. Bring one part rice and two parts salted liquid to a boil, then lower the heat. Cook, covered, for 40–45 minutes.

The water-to-rice ratio and cooking times vary for each type and brand of rice; follow the package directions.

TIPS for cooking rice

- Unless you're making risotto, don't stir rice while you're cooking it—the result will be a starchy mess.
- Most rice varieties triple in size when cooked. A side dish of cooked rice is ½ cup (125 g).
- Rice is even tastier when prepared in stock or water and wine, as when making a risotto.
- Reuse cooked rice as fried or baked rice with the help of oil and spices, and additions such as eggs and leftover vegetables.
- If rice is too moist after cooking, let it dry for 10 minutes in a baking pan in the oven.
- If the rice is sticky, drain it in a colander and pour a kettle of boiling water over it to separate the grains.
- Store rice in a dry, well-ventilated place away from strong-smelling foods; it absorbs other flavors easily.

Rice can be husked or unhusked. Wild rice (top right) is actually the seeds of a wild grass.

Rescues and solutions

We all have mishaps in the kitchen, no matter how experienced we are. But all need not be lost. Armed with some home remedies and a little improvisation, a burned roast can be rescued, salty potatoes and watery soup salvaged—even if guests are at the door.

You can't prevent all misfortunes in the kitchen. Luckily, many mishaps can be remedied quickly and easily, and others are easy to avoid altogether.

PREVENTING cooking mishaps

- Milk won't burn as easily if the pan is rinsed out with cold water before heating it up.
- Add a little vegetable oil to the pan to prevent butter from browning.
- Beef stock will stay clear if you boil a clean eggshell with it.
- Boiled eggs won't split their shells if you make a small hole with a pin at the rounded end before you immerse them.
- Keep a roast from becoming tough by basting it regularly with its fat and juices.
- Prevent fried fish from sticking to the pan by dusting it with flour or putting a little salt into the frying oil.
- Fish holds together better during cooking if you pour a little lemon juice over it first and set the fish aside for a moment. The acid in the lemon juice cooks the flesh slightly, creating a thin seal.
- Prevent dishes from burning in the oven by covering them with foil.

GOOD TO KNOW

Stretching a dish

Sometimes you not only have to rescue a dish, you also need to stretch it so that there's enough for everyone. For soups and stews, add lentils or beans, vegetables, rice or pasta. Make salads go further with hard-boiled eggs, fruit, tuna, olives, lentils and nuts.

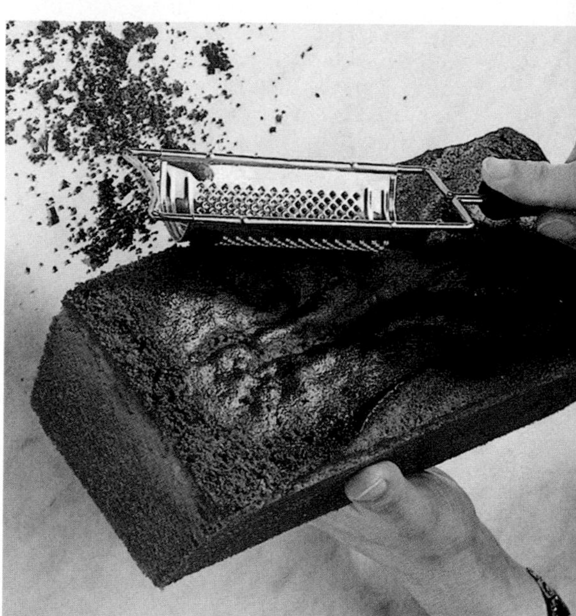

Scrape off burned spots on a cooled cake with a grater, then cover with frosting.

QUICK help

- Add a dash of vinegar or salt to the pan of water if an egg bursts while you are boiling it; the whites will thicken immediately.
- Tough stewing meat becomes tender when you add a dash of vinegar to the cooking liquid.
- To prevent homemade mayonnaise from congealing, beat an egg yolk and a little salt until stiff, then add the oil drop by drop.
- If mayonnaise begins to separate, add 1 tablespoon (15 ml) warm water. Or start again with one egg yolk and gradually add the curdled mixture.
- If noodles stick together, strain them in a colander and set it over a pan of boiling water. The steam will separate them.

- If gelatin clumps together, warm it up carefully while stirring constantly, then add it to a warm mixture.
- When you take a cake out of the oven, place the pan on a warm, damp cloth for 10 seconds so it comes out of the pan more easily when you invert it on a plate or rack.
- To remove the fat quickly from an over-fatty gravy, sauce or soup, skim the top of the liquid with a couple of lettuce leaves or paper towels. The fat will stick to them.

TOO salty, spicy or bland

- In most cases you can neutralize saltiness with a mixture of cider or wine vinegar and sugar in equal proportions.
- Thin oversalted soups or gravies with water, wine, milk or cream.
- Grate a potato into soups or stews to reduce excessive saltiness. This will add thickening as well.
- Add 1–2 raw egg whites to salty soups; they congeal and soak up the salt. Then put the liquid through a strainer or simply skim off the egg white.
- Add a grated carrot or potato to overly spiced meat broth and bring to a boil.
- Add a sprig of parsley to a dish that is too garlicky for 10 minutes, to counter the taste.
- A little sour cream or plain yogurt can often rescue bland soups.

TOO thick or too thin

- Thicken gravies or soups that are too thin. Make a paste with 1 teaspoon (5 ml) cornstarch or potato flour mixed with water into a smooth paste, then add it to the gravy or soup. Don't pour it all in at once; add small amounts and stir until you have the right consistency. Bring to a boil and season as needed.
- Gravies that are too thick can be thinned easily with water, wine, stock, milk or cream. Add seasoning if necessary.
- Pour lumpy gravy through a fine strainer to make it smooth again, or whisk it well.

BURNED foods

- If potatoes boil dry and stick to the bottom of the pan, carefully remove all but the last unburned layer, put them in a pot of fresh water to finish cooking, and add a dash of salt.
- If you burn the top of the roast, cut off the burnt bits and roast the meat in a clean pan with more fresh fat.
- If a casserole burns, remove the top layer, sprinkle it with cheese or breadcrumbs and dabs of butter, then finish cooking it.

If a soup or gravy contains too much fat, let it cool and skim off the fat.

Sauces, gravies and dressings

A good sauce or dressing can add color, flavor and even texture to an uninspiring dish. Rediscover this kitchen skill, once considered an essential culinary accomplishment, and create inspiring accompaniments for salads, pasta, rice and roasts.

Wine, all-purpose flour, cornstarch or puréed vegetables all contribute to good gravies. Oil and vinegar are the starting point for a tasty dressing.

DEGLAZING

Deglazing is the simplest way to get a good base for a meat gravy.

- After browning, remove the meat from the pan and add water, stock or wine.
- Bring to the boil, stirring constantly, to incorporate the dried meat juices and fat.

THE trick to thickening gravy

Thickening gives gravy the right consistency and improves flavor. Here are some tried and tested tricks.

- Purée vegetables cooked in the meat stock to thicken gravy and add taste.
- Add 2 teaspoons (10 ml) cranberry sauce or red currant jelly to give gravy a fruity kick.

When you deglaze meat juice with wine or stock, it develops a more intense taste.

- When braising meat, add a few small pieces of bread to the pot: They will disintegrate and make the meat stock creamy.
- All-purpose flour and cornstarch are good thickeners. Just stir them into a little water and add to the gravy before bringing it to a boil.
- A roux is a mixture of equal amounts of fat and flour, which is then cooked and combined with liquid to make a base for sauces. For a béchamel sauce, add milk to the basic roux; for brown sauce, add some meat or dark vegetable stock.
- A mixture of flour and butter (*beurre manié*) is good for thickening sauces shortly before serving. Work them together in equal proportions, then pull off small pieces and whisk them into the boiling sauce or gravy. Mixed flour and butter keeps for 2 weeks when refrigerated.
- Shortly before serving, sour cream, crème fraîche or thick cream can be beaten into a meat stock to thicken it.
- Mix a few spoonfuls of gravy with an egg yolk and add to the rest of the hot gravy while stirring constantly. Don't let the liquid boil or the egg yolk will "scramble" and make the gravy lumpy.

SUCCESS with gravies

- Season roux-based gravies only after thickening. Don't forget to taste them before and after seasoning.
- Boil a gravy thickened with roux for about 5 minutes to eliminate the floury taste. Add herbs such as thyme or sage to give gravy extra flavor.
- Prevent a skin from forming on light gravies by drawing a piece of butter over them with a fork.
- To enrich a gravy with butter, remove the pan from the heat and add the butter one piece at a time, letting it melt while swirling the pan a little.

Making a roux

1 Melt or sauté 4 teaspoons (20 g) butter in a pan and add 4 teaspoons (20 g) flour, while stirring vigorously with a spoon.

2 Keep stirring until the flour blends with the butter. To make a dark roux, lightly brown the butter-flour mixture.

3 Add your liquid (stock, water, milk, etc.) and bring to a boil, stirring constantly until the sauce thickens.

- Whisk gravies vigorously to be sure they are creamy and free of lumps.
- To test the consistency of gravy, dip a wooden spoon into it. It should coat the spoon.
- You can make gravy go further and add another flavor by adding stock, cream, sour cream, crème fraîche, wine, sherry or even the water from cooking vegetables or pasta.
- For perfect smoothness, strain gravy before serving.

THE perfect dressing

Vinaigrette is still the classic salad dressing—but it requires high-quality ingredients in the right proportions to work its magic.

- Use this one simple rule, for all vinaigrettes: Use vinegar and oil in a 1:3 proportion. If you are adding mustard, use about 1 teaspoon (5 ml) per 3 tablespoons (45 ml) salad dressing.
- Stir some salt and pepper into the vinegar, and whisk in the mustard. Gradually pour in the oil while stirring constantly, until the vinegar and oil combine to form an emulsion.
- If the ingredients start to separate, beat the vinaigrette vigorously again.
- If you are in a hurry, put the vinaigrette ingredients in a lidded jar and shake to combine.
- If the vinaigrette is too oily, add more vinegar, mustard and spices. If the vinaigrette tastes sour, add oil and salt. A little sugar won't hurt, either.
- You can make a vinaigrette in advance. It will keep in the refrigerator for about 3 weeks. Shake it thoroughly before use.
- You can vary the basic vinaigrette recipe by adding crushed garlic, mayonnaise, nuts, dried fruit, sesame seeds or herbs, depending on the dish to be served.

Use the correct proportions of oil and vinegar to make the perfect vinaigrette.

SEASONAL PRODUCE

Growing fruit and vegetables in your garden is satisfying, healthy and economical. However, you need to know each crop's best season—although geographical location or access to a greenhouse can make a difference.

FOLLOW THESE GUIDES FOR THE BEST SEASONAL PRODUCE.

Fruit • Peak season

Apples • August to February

Apricots • February to November

Bananas • All year

Blueberries • June to September

Cherries • June to August

Currants (black and red) • June and July

Figs • June to August

Grapes • June to August

Kiwi fruit • December to June

Lemons • All year

Mandarin oranges • March to May

Mangoes • March to May

Melons • June to August

Passionfruit • September to November

Peaches/Nectarines • June to August

Pears • September to November

Pineapples • September to November

Plums • June to August

Raspberries • June to August

Rhubarb • April to May

Strawberries • All year

SEASONS MAY VARY DEPENDING on the year and your LOCATION.

Vegetables • Peak season

Artichokes • March–June; September–December

Arugula • All year

Avocados • All year

Asparagus • March to July

Beans • June to November

Beets • March to August

Broccoli • October to March

Brussels sprouts • September to December

Butternut squash • October to March

Cabbage • All year

Carrots • December to April

Cauliflower • September to November

Celery • All year

Chile peppers • All year

Cilantro • All year

Cucumbers • June to August

Eggplant • June to August

Fava beans • March to May

Fennel • September to February

Garlic • All year

Leeks • September to April

Lettuce • All year

Onions • August to October

Parsley • All year

Parsnips • September to April

Peas • May to July

Peppers • June to August

Potatoes • All year

Radishes • March to May

Rutabaga • All year

Spinach • April to June

Sweet basil • June to August

Sweet corn • June to August

Tomatoes • July to September

Turnips • December to March

Zucchini • June to September

Shopping

People who shop and store their food logically save a lot, both in terms of time and money. Make a detailed shopping list and stick to it to reduce the risk of buying too much—and succumbing to impulse purchases.

Fresh, high-quality and often well-priced goods are available direct from fruit and vegetable stores or a local farmer's market. Wherever you shop, if you stick to seasonal and local products, you'll get fresher goods and save your budget as well as the environment.

PLANNING purchases

- Organizing a supermarket list by product category will allow you to shop more quickly.
- Keep the shopping list in a visible place in the kitchen so items can be jotted down as soon as you discover you need them. But don't forget to take the list with you when you shop.

Choosing seasonal and local produce saves you money and protects the environment.

- Making a meal plan for the coming week can help you to purchase wisely, buying only the necessary ingredients. But be flexible: Try to incorporate any specials available in the stores or supermarket.
- Never shop while hungry, as the danger of impulse buys rises exponentially and you are likely to spend more than you had planned.
- Opt for generic brands whenever possible. These tasty copycats are made by reputable companies and are much less expensive.
- You will often find good deals at weekly markets. Bear in mind that shortly before closing time the prices on fresh goods often drop significantly.

CAREFREE shopping

- To protect groceries from damage, put durable items (such as cans and bottles) into the cart first, then fresh foods on top.
- Always buy refrigerated and frozen food last, use insulated bags and put the food away as soon as you get home.
- It is usually cheaper to buy in bulk, especially if you can share groceries with neighbors or friends.
- To reduce trash, choose multi-use packaging or buy products in bulk.
- Beware of buy-one-get-one-free offers unless you are sure you will use the extra food, can freeze it or can share the purchase.
- You will generally find the most economical items on the lower shelves in supermarkets.
- Look for supermarket freezer cabinets that are neatly organized and not coated with thick ice. If the goods show any signs of freezer burn, walk away.
- Dented cans are best left on the shelves.
- The freshest beef will be deep red; pork should always be pink.

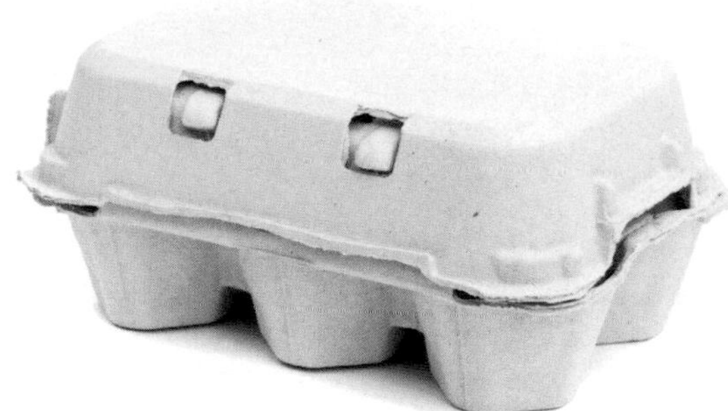

To retain moisture, leave eggs in their carton in the refrigerator.

STORAGE

Store foods properly. Temperature, light and moisture can affect their appearance, taste and vitamin content. Foods that are stored improperly can easily go bad and become a health risk.

- Prepackaged goods with a long shelf life, such as dried foods, are best kept in a dark cupboard or a dry pantry.
- Products kept in jars, bottles or clear plastic bags should be stored in the dark.
- Bread remains fresher for a long time inside a cloth bag, which takes up little room.
- Put new supplies behind those you already have on hand. Check use-by dates but don't be a slave to them. Use your eyes and nose to test for freshness. Yogurt and dairy products with bulging tops are almost certainly inedible.

KEEPING cool

- Avoid crowding your refrigerator—be sure there is good air circulation around each item.
- Foods that spoil quickly, such as fish, meat, sausages and prepared foods, belong on the middle shelves, but be careful that meat juices don't drip on the dairy products.
- Foods that need only minor cooling, such as butter and margarine, are best stored on the top shelf or in the door compartments provided for them. Opened jars and bottles—jam, chutney, fruit juices, sauces and milk—can also be stored in the door.
- To stop mold from forming, store blue cheeses separately from other types of cheese. Wrap each piece of cheese separately. Old-fashioned wax paper is excellent for cheese or use plastic wrap.
- Eggs are porous, so store them in their original carton to reduce moisture loss and avoid absorption of odors.
- Fruit and vegetables should go in the lower drawer, without packaging.
- To defrost meat, take it out of its packaging and place it in a bowl or on a plate in the refrigerator, covered with foil.
- Fresh fish will keep for up to a day in the refrigerator; if cooked, it will last for 2–3 days.
- In cool climates, less delicate fruits and vegetables can be stored in a cool part of the house if there isn't enough room in the fridge.

Spices

Pepper, ginger, saffron, nutmeg are just a few of the spices that can add taste and color to many dishes. Whichever ones you use, store them properly to preserve their flavor.

Use a ceramic mortar, as wood absorbs the flavor of spices.

Using spices correctly will enhance a meal, quite literally "spicing it up." Here is how you can keep them fresh and put them to good use.

STORING spices

- Store spices in airtight, opaque containers in a cool, dark place. They last longer when they are not exposed to sunlight.
- Since spices tend to give off and absorb flavors, always keep the same spice in a given container.
- Stored properly, spices keep for up to 2 years and many last even longer. But they are best bought in small quantities and used more quickly—ideally within 6 months.

Fresh curry powder

2 tablespoons (30 ml) coriander seeds
2 teaspoons (10 ml) cumin seeds
1/2 teaspoon (2 ml) mustard seeds
1 teaspoon (5 ml) black peppercorns
1 teaspoon (5 ml) fenugreek seeds
10 fresh curry leaves
1/2 teaspoon (2 ml) ground ginger
1 tablespoon (15 ml) ground turmeric
1 teaspoon (5 ml) chili powder or cayenne pepper

1 Dry roast the coriander seeds, cumin seeds, mustard seeds, peppercorns and fenugreek seeds over medium heat until the seeds darken and become fragrant, stirring constantly to prevent burning. Let cool, then grind to a powder.
2 Dry roast the fresh curry leaves, grind and add to the mixture along with the ground ginger, ground turmeric and the chili powder or cayenne pepper.

PROPER use of spices

Clever use of herbs adds subtle flavors that can help you to reduce the amount of salt you add to food.

- Spice meats and vegetables before cooking, when they are most absorbent. However, salt removes moisture from raw meat making it tough, so salt meat only after browning.
- Spices should heighten the taste of the food, not overpower it, so use moderately.
- Many spices, such as paprika, chile, garlic and curry, lose their flavor or become bitter when you add them to bubbling hot oil or butter. They release their aroma and taste better when lightly sautéed.

COMMON kitchen spices

- Use caraway to season bread, cabbage dishes, casseroles and curry.
- Cayenne pepper is dried, ground chilies. It adds pungency to sauces and stews, such as chili con carne. Use it in moderation and taste between each addition to be sure a dish is not too fiery.
- It's a good idea to wear rubber gloves when chopping fresh chilies. The oils in the inner membranes and the seeds can burn your hands, eyes and lips. For milder dishes,

discard the potent membranes and seeds. Dried chilies can be ground as required in a mortar or spice mill.

• Highly aromatic cloves are used as a spice in cuisines all over the world. Their spicy-sweet flavor works well in marinades, apple dishes, pear compote and with red cabbage.
• Cilantro (coriander) is used in Spanish, Middle Eastern, Asian and South American cuisines. The leaves should be used fresh and can be used like parsley on salads, soups and other cooked dishes. Coriander is the base of most curries and can be used for meat, poultry, fish and vegetables.
• Cumin gives a bite to plain rice and is used in many stews, curries, dry rubs and lamb and chicken dishes.
• Curry, a mixture of various spices, is used to add a savory punch to curry or rice dishes, sauces, poultry and meat.
• Paprika ranges from sweet to spicy or smoky. It releases its color and flavor when heated, but burns easily, so add paprika only when liquid ingredients are present and don't overcook it.
• Ginger adds a fresh, slightly pungent taste to baked goods, stir-fries, rice dishes and fruit.
• Raw horseradish is particularly pungent. It gives a kick to roasts and winter soups.
• No cook can get by without pepper. Unripe green peppercorns have a citrusy aroma. Black pepper is harvested shortly before ripening and then fermented. Red peppercorns, in contrast to white, are unshelled and have a delicate flavor.
• Star anise, which has a mild licorice taste, is a key flavor in Chinese cuisine.

GOOD TO KNOW

Take care with nutmeg

Nutmeg, along with mace (its outer covering), is an important element in many of the world's cuisines. Best freshly grated, it imparts a delicate taste and color to a variety of dishes, from puréed spinach to beef stroganoff, cookies, crumbles and béchamel sauce. But beware: Nutmeg is poisonous when eaten in very large quantities, so it should be stored well out of the reach of children.

• Allspice is a key ingredient of Caribbean jerk seasoning and an ideal ingredient for meat rubs of all kinds.

WORKING with spices

• Choose whole spices when possible. They retain their flavor better.
• Grind spices with a mortar and pestle just before use for maximum flavor. Add a little salt for friction.
• Spice mills are useful for nutmeg, pepper and other hard spices. Make sure they are easy to clean. Or buy a coffee grinder specifically for the purpose.
• Reserve special graters for ginger or nutmeg, as their flavors can be transferred easily.

Sweets and treats

Refined sugar should be consumed in moderation, but we all need the occasional treat. Many homemade goodies are easy to make and, if you use fresh, quality ingredients, are better than store-bought.

Homemade ice cream or sorbet on a hot day is delicious and refreshing, while truffles or candied fruit are a fitting finale to a meal with friends.

CHOCOLATE temptation

Ganache, a mixture of chopped chocolate and cream or butter, is the basis for many types of truffles and is simple to make. Use more chocolate in proportion to cream for a firmer ganache.

- While ganache is still warm in the pan, add liqueur, rum, sparkling wine or champagne, honey, coffee, peanut brittle, nougat, dried fruit, syrup or many other delicious ingredients.
- By blending ganache made from different types of chocolate, you can make marbled chocolates. For example, the contrast between a layer of white chocolate with vanilla and a layer of darker ganache with orange liqueur is both attractive and tasty.
- You can decorate truffles with many things, as long as they taste good and look pretty. Try icing, whole nuts, candied fruit or colored decorations made from marzipan. You can roll the balls in cocoa powder, confectioner's sugar or coconut, or use finely chopped nuts and chocolate crumbs.

ICE CREAM: ideal for hot days

Water is the basis for sorbets, while ice cream gets its creamy texture from milk and cream. You can flavor both with sugar, fruit and any number of other tasty ingredients.

- For sorbet, heat up about 1 cup (250 ml) water and 1 cup (200 g) sugar and boil for 2 minutes until sugar dissolves. Stir in about 1 pound (500 g) puréed fruit or 2 cups (500 ml) fruit juice and lemon juice. Let cool. Flavor with sugar or lemon and freeze.
- Ice cream is equally easy to make: Beat 3 egg yolks with ⅓ cup (80 g) superfine sugar until foamy, then stir in 1 cup (250 ml) cream and ¾ cup (170 ml) milk. You could also add puréed fruits, nuts, chocolate or yogurt.
- If you don't have an ice cream maker, put the ice cream or sorbet mixture in a shallow metal bowl in the freezer. When nearly frozen, stir thoroughly and freeze again. Repeat this process several times.

Making ganache

one In a small pan, quickly heat ⅔ cup (150 ml) thick cream. Bring to a boil, then take the pan off the heat to cool completely.

two In the meantime, chop up 10 ounces (300 g) good-quality chocolate, at least 70 percent chocolate; melt in a double boiler.

three Stir the cream and chocolate together to produce a smooth liquid. If necessary, stir in a little more cold cream.

TIPS for making ice cream

- Ice cream loses flavor when frozen, so the liquid should taste quite sweet and strong.
- If ice cream turns out too grainy, it may be because you have used too much water or too little sugar. Alternatively, the ice cream may have frozen too quickly or wasn't stirred frequently enough.

CRYSTALLIZED fruit

Fruits are crystallized by dipping them in a strong sugar concentrate to preserve and to give them a sweeter flavor. Alternatively, you can coat pineapple, apples, bananas, pears or strawberries with chocolate.

1 For the syrup, boil 1 quart (1 L) water and 2 pounds (1 kg) sugar until strings form.

2 Suspend 1 pound (500 g) fruit or pieces of fruit in a strainer in a glass bowl and pour the sugar solution over the fruit until it is completely covered.

3 Let steep for a day before removing and drying the fruit. Then boil the sugar solution and pour it over the fruit again.

4 Repeat this process five times. The last time, boil the sugar solution down further and let the prepared fruit dry on a cooling rack.

While melting chocolate, stir it continually to make sure it doesn't separate and get grainy.

- Strawberries can be crystallized but other berries aren't good candidates because they are too soft.
- For fruits such as grapes, which can be crystallized whole, it is best to poke a hole in them to allow the sugar solution to penetrate them. Crystallize orange and lemon slices with the seeds removed and peel intact, using only organic fruit.
- To coat fruit with chocolate, cut them into bite-sized pieces and spear them with a wooden toothpick before dipping them in liquid chocolate.

INVENTIVE snacks for children

Children can often be persuaded to eat fruit and other nutritious foods when appealing.

- Fashion an edible caterpillar by skewering melon balls, grapes and cheese cubes on an uncooked spaghetti strand.
- Pour melted chocolate over a mixture of dried fruit, cereal and nuts to create a delicious fruit-and-nut cluster.
- Cut pineapple pieces into triangles and arrange on a plate in a circle to create the rays of the sun. Spoon vanilla yogurt into the center for dipping.
- For the classic "ants on a log" treat, fill the center of a stalk of celery with peanut butter and sprinkle raisins (or "ants") along the log.
- Create a flower children will want to devour by using segments of a clementine or tangerine for the petals, a strawberry for the center and kiwi fruit sliced into the shapes of leaves.

THRIFT IN THE KITCHEN

With a little planning, skill and creativity, you can save plenty of cash in the kitchen—without giving up good food. Look for savings by altering household appliance usage, changing your shopping habits and making savvy use of leftovers.

Try these alternatives

- Instead of making a roux, thicken gravies or soups with mashed potato or another mashed vegetable, such as rutabaga or parsnip.
- If you don't want to buy a whole carton of buttermilk for a recipe, add 1 tablespoon (15 ml) vinegar or lemon juice to just under 1 cup (250 ml) milk and let it stand for 10 minutes.
- If you run out of cream for making sauces, use condensed milk or coffee creamer instead. However, these replacements won't froth up, so they can't be used as a substitute for whipped cream.
- Preserved fruit makes a delicious topping on a cake.
- Most nuts can be used for pesto, including walnuts and almonds.
- You can turn granulated sugar into confectioner's sugar easily in a coffee grinder or spice mill.
- Make stale bread into breadcrumbs and freeze, ready for use in everything from stuffing to toppings for dishes such as pot pie or a casserole.
- Make a funnel from a plastic bag by cutting off one corner.

Save energy

- Household appliances typically use up about 30 percent of your home's energy. It is worthwhile in the long run to replace energy-wasting appliances such as old refrigerators, freezers and electric stoves.
- Look for good-quality, heat-conducting pots and pans.
- Always place each pan on the burner closest in size to its bottom, and use a tight-fitting lid while cooking.
- Use residual heat by turning off an electric burner about 5 minutes before whatever you are cooking is done.
- A pressure cooker can save up to 30 percent of the energy used for top-of-the-stove cooking if the cooking time is more than 20 minutes.

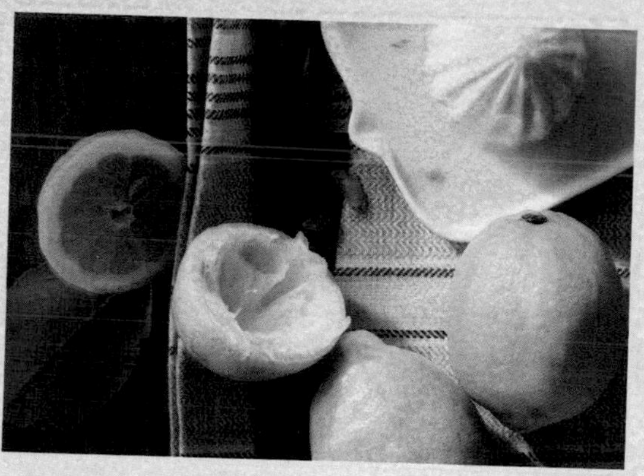

Enhance flavor

- Brush dried-out sponge cake with milk and bake it briefly in the oven so it tastes fresh again, or use it up in a trifle.
- Purée uncooked mushrooms with a little stock, freeze them and use later to add flavor to sauces or soups.
- Turn a hollandaise sauce into béarnaise with a pinch of tarragon.
- Add chopped gherkins, chives and capers, plus lemon juice to some mayonnaise for a flavor-packed tartar sauce.

Budget

- Plan your menu around supermarket specials.
- Seasonal items are not only cheaper but also tastier and fresher because they have taken less time to travel from producer to consumer.
- By tracking household expenditures for a month, you can get a good idea of where your money is going and modify your spending. An easy way to do it is to keep an envelope in your handbag or car and use it to store receipts, then tally them at the end of the month. Alternatively, you can find apps for your smartphone that help you track your food shopping expenses.
- Stocking up sensibly saves money. When berries become expensive, just take out the ones you froze in the middle of summer.
- Buy unsliced bread, as it stays fresh longer. If a loaf is too long, cut it in half and freeze one portion.
- Packaged foods always cost more. Prewashed salad, for example, will set you back an extra 50 percent.

With a little planning, skill and creativity, it's easy to save cash in the kitchen.

Cut down on food costs

- Try not to let foods spoil. You can make purées, jam, smoothies or compotes from fruit. Freeze leftover gravy and sauces (in an ice cube tray, for example).
- Shop thoughtfully: Brisket, bottom round, pork hocks and other less expensive cuts of meat are 10–30 percent cheaper but need longer marinating and/or braising to make them tender. Plan your meals in advance and take advantage of slow cooking to make the most of your money.
- After you have eaten a roast chicken or turkey, boil the bones to make stock.
- Even leftover alcohol can be repurposed: Use wine that has gone sour instead of vinegar in a dressing or marinade.
- Cooking twice the amount of potatoes or pasta you need saves time and energy. A day or two later, you can warm them up and serve them, or use them in a soup or casserole.

Style and comfort

Our surroundings should be havens, where we can relax, unwind and enjoy time with family and friends at the end of a busy day. Here are some useful tips to help you to enhance individual rooms and create the comfortable refuge you want your home to be.

Balconies, decks and patios

While the size and position of a balcony, deck or patio are often beyond our control, with a little effort and the right accessories any outdoor space can be turned into a relaxing oasis.

When thinking about how best to utilize these outdoor spaces, try to imagine an outdoor room. Choose appropriately sized furniture and consider how to protect yourself from the sun.

OUTDOOR furniture

- For small balconies, decks or patios it's a good idea to look at space-saving furniture, such as a wall-mounted folding table with a swivel-out table leg to stabilize it.
- Stackable stools and folding chairs fit into a limited space, which makes them convenient to store. This is especially important for homes with small patios, decks or balconies, or limited storage space.
- On a small balcony, chairs with adjustable backrests are more practical than lounge chairs.
- Multifunctional furniture makes maximum use of the space: Watertight chests make convenient seats as well as providing storage for chair cushions and pillows.
- Weather-resistant outdoor furniture is a sensible option. Garden furniture made of woven resin looks like wicker furniture but resists inclement weather and UV rays. Furniture made from aluminium, wrought iron, or steel comes in a variety of designs and can stay outside, but the latter two may require annual repainting to keep rust at bay. Add removable cushions for comfort.
- A canopied swinging seat can accommodate two to three people and has the advantage of built-in protection from the sun.
- Hammocks or hanging chairs are more appropriate for larger outdoor areas—you need room to swing and a stand or solid beam to hang them from.
- Big balconies, decks and patios are ideal for reclining sun lounges, deck chairs and clusters of sofas around an outdoor table.
- Large outdoor spaces can be structured into "rooms" with vine-covered trellis panels, plants in containers, raised flower beds and outdoor furniture.

GOOD TO KNOW

Vacation time

There is no need for patio plants to suffer while you are away. Put small pots into larger ones filled with wet sand or potting soil. Or use strips of capillary matting as wicks. Insert one end into a large bowl or bucket of water, the other into the soil in each pot. For large pots, collect plastic bottles and cut off the bottoms. Remove the cap, stuff the neck with cotton, then push the bottle, neck downwards, into the soil and attach it to a stake. Fill it with water just before you leave; it will slowly drain, and water the plant for a several days.

SUN protection

Most balconies and patios require some protection against sun and glare in the form of an umbrella, shade sail, awning or pergola covered in greenery. Here are a few of the more common choices.

- Umbrellas come in many sizes, shapes, patterns and materials. Buy them in the fall if you want a bargain. An umbrella usually stands on a pedestal but you can also get space-saving brackets that screw onto the railings or fixtures for the wall or ceiling.
- Retractable awnings are fabric or vinyl shades on a permanently mounted frame. With the help of a crank or a motor they can be fully or partly extended, depending on your preference and the location of the sun. Installing an awning can be difficult because the frames tend to be heavy and they must be firmly mounted. If in doubt, have a professional install it.
- Shade sails are made of a tough, sturdy cloth and secured to fastening points with cords or snap hooks. They come in standard shapes, but can be custom-made.
- Plants can also be used to provide some shade. Tall container plants, such as quick-growing bamboo, are a good choice. You can also plant grapevines and other greenery to climb a lattice frame or trellis, or train climbing plants over a pergola.

CREATE an outdoor room

Just like the interior of a house, an outdoor space needs to be well decorated if you want it to feel cozy and look complete. Small accessories can play a big role here, for example, by helping to create a maritime theme with colors or lanterns.

- Terra-cotta pots, ancient-looking sculptures or wrought iron furniture create a Mediterranean mood.

Lushly planted pots and planters beautify any outdoor space.

- A small pond with waterlilies or a large basin with floating candles helps to create a tranquil, relaxed ambience. The gentle splash of a fountain or small waterfall can have the same effect.
- Bright, colorful seat cushions and incense sticks add an Asian touch to your outdoor room, as do red and gold accents—and, of course, a bamboo plant or two.

Beautiful bedrooms

METAL BEDS ARE durable AND LOOK PRISTINE longer.

To create the right environment for a good night's sleep, make your bedroom a relaxing haven, adding all the trimmings of comfort and serenity.

Getting the correct amount of sleep is key to our health and well-being. Consider investing in a new bed, mattress and bedding if slumberland eludes you.

CHOOSING a headboard

Not every bed has a headboard, but they can add the finishing touch to a bedroom's decor.

• MDF (medium density fiberboard) may be inexpensive but it is less sturdy. Also, some MDF is made using toxic glues and binders that may affect the air quality in the bedroom. Check if there is particleboard beneath upholstered headboards.

SLATTED frames

These offer some real advantages in terms of bed height and weight.

• Rigid slatted frames vary considerably, depending on whether or not the frame has been reinforced in vulnerable spots. Some models allow you to adjust the supports to suit your sleeping position.

• Adjustable slatted frames let you alter the height of the bed—an advantage if you want to read before going to sleep. But a well-made adjustable bed can be expensive.

• Futons sometimes come with simple, adjustable wooden frames.

• Check the number of slats to determine the quality of the frame—the more the better.

• Electric bed frames let you adjust the frame effortlessly with a remote control.

• If you and your partner have different needs, consider two twin beds joined in the center—each tailored to your individual requirements.

CHOOSING a mattress

Selecting the right mattress means not only finding one that's the right size but also looking at the materials used and whether it suits your budget and needs. Here are the most popular mattress styles.

• Continuous-coil mattresses are the cheapest, but the coils often wear out more quickly and because the springs move as one unit, you are more likely to be disturbed if your partner moves during the night.
• Open-coil mattresses are one step up, and are constructed of single springs fixed together by wire.
• Pocket spring mattresses are the most comfortable. As each spring is sewn into its own pocket, it moves independently and provides better support.
• Memory-foam, or memory mattresses, are topped with a layer of temperature-sensitive viscoelastic material that molds and remolds to the body's contours. Although more expensive, they provide support and help to relieve pressure on painful joints. However, the foam is affected by room temperature so can be cold in winter and make you feel very hot in summer. You will find that the foam "loses its memory" after about 10 years.
• Latex or high-density foam mattresses offer a high degree of sleeping comfort, as they conform perfectly to your body and sleep position while minimizing pressure on your head, shoulders and hips. They are breathable, so you won't overheat, and are also a good option if you are allergic to dust mites.
• Protect a mattress and maximize comfort with a mattress pad.

THE right pillow

Always choose a pillow that conforms to your sleep position. If you sleep on your side, your pillow has to prop up your head so it should be thicker than a pillow for a back sleeper.
• If you have problems with your neck, opt for a smaller pillow—about 30 inches (80 cm) wide but only 15 inches (40 cm) long. A larger pillow could shift during the night, resulting in neck and back pain in the morning.
• If you have selected a pillow carefully but your neck pain remains, consult a doctor.
• Goose and duck down are the softest, lightest natural fillings, but they are not good if you are prone to allergies as they harbor dust mites. They need regular shaking to avoid lumpiness. Good alternatives are synthetic down or foam.
• Test pillows for their springiness—they should quickly return to shape after being pressed—and replace them as necessary.

QUILTS and sheets

You will probably want quilts and sheets made from different fabrics to cater for changing seasons.
• A quilt is the most popular form of bedding and, like pillows, may be filled with feathers and down, wool or synthetic material. While many quilts are medium warmth, suitable for year-round use and most sleepers, some brands offer various warmth levels to suit personal sleeping requirements and different seasons.
• Sheets and quilt covers, also know as duvets, are made from all kinds of materials, such as cotton, cotton and polyester blends, satin and silk. Flannel sheets will keep you warm in the winter, but cotton, cotton blends and linen are the best choices in summer.

Candlelight

Candles, together with oil and tallow lamps, were once the home's only light source. Today, we use their warm, soft light more as a decorative element or for creating an intimate atmosphere.

The use of candles dates back to ancient civilizations and over the centuries they've been made with a variety of substances, including tallow, beeswax and palm, coconut and olive oils. Today, most candles are made from paraffin.

GROUPS of arranged CANDLES are SIMPLE and ELEGANT.

MATERIAL

- Candles made from beeswax are of high quality but relatively expensive. Real beeswax candles give off a sweet fragrance when they burn.
- Petroleum-based paraffin is the material most frequently used in the manufacture of candles today. Paraffin candles are popular, as they are an affordable option.
- Soy wax is made from hydrogenated soybean oil. Because it is a natural substance, soy wax is a much more environmentally friendly choice than paraffin. Soy candles are also less sooty when they burn.
- Stearin, or stearic acid, is made from vegetable and animal fats. Adding stearin to paraffin candles makes them easier to control during production. The candles also burn more slowly.

CREATIVE candlesticks

A special meal is enhanced by elegant silver or crystal candlesticks. But what about a cozy evening at home or a romantic setting for a special dinner? Here are some time-honored solutions for adding candlelight to the occasion.

- You can also paint bottles, cover them with découpage or fill them with colored sand or ornamental stones.
- For an attractive dining room table centerpiece, create an arrangement in a pot with an oasis of floral foam and seasonal blooms. Tape toothpicks to the ends of candles and insert them in the center of the arrangement.

LANTERNS

Sometimes a lantern works better than a candle—outdoors, for instance, as candles can be too unstable or are blown out easily.

- Candles in jars can look like twinkling fairy lights on the patio. Use large jars with sand, stones or seashells filling the bottoms.
- Use glass frosting spray on jars containing candles to create a calm, soft light.
- Drop tea lights into well-cleaned baby food jars and arrange them in small clusters on the table and sideboard. They'll look fabulous.
- Make tin cans into lanterns by punching holes in a pattern with a hammer and nail. To avoid denting the can, fill it with water and freeze it for several hours.

PLAYING with fire

Candles are useful, warm and romantic. But they can be dangerous. Stay safe with these three simple rules.

1 Never leave candles unattended, not even for a short time—this includes tea lights and lanterns.

2 Use a container in which the candle can stand up straight.

3 Trim the wick down to about ½ inch (1 cm).

Choosing carpets

Both style and practical issues will govern your choice of floor coverings. In areas of heavy traffic, it's sensible to opt for hard-wearing fabrics. Elsewhere, color and effect will play a greater role.

There's an enormous selection of carpets, rugs and runners available. Before deciding what to buy, decide how the carpet is going to be used, whether it will fit in with the room's furnishings, what the floor currently looks like and how much you want to pay.

GOOD TO KNOW

Carpet quality

The main indicators of carpet quality are its density (how closely individual strands are packed), its twist (how many times the carpet's fibers have been spun) and the height of its pile. When you bend it backwards, the less backing you can see, the better the carpet. Look for individual carpet fibers that are tight and neat; loose or flared strands indicate substandard quality. As a general rule, the higher the pile, the better the carpet will wear.

THE right choice

- On wood, laminate or stone floors, a rug's primary function is to create an accent, so the design is extremely important.
- A rug in a child's room should be easy to clean. Make sure it is washable or its pattern hides stains.
- Today, indoor air quality (IAQ) is an top environmental consideration. The Carpet and Rug Institute gives their Green Label Plus to carpet products with very low emissions of Volatile Organic Compounds (VOCs).

TYPES of carpets

Different carpets are suitable for different situations. You wouldn't want a luxurious, deep-pile carpet in the hall any more than you'd put fake grass turf in the family room. Here are some of the things to bear in mind when you are choosing a carpet.

- Sturdy carpets have short, tough fibers. They are often made entirely or at least mostly from synthetic fibers.
- Carpets of higher quality are usually made from natural fibers such as wool with deep pile. They are softer but also get dirty more easily and require more maintenance.
- With loop-pile carpets, the threads of the pile, whether they are made of wool, synthetic or mixed fibers, are sewn into the basic weave. Since loop-pile carpets are relatively impervious to stains, they are a good choice for rooms with more traffic.
- Velour, plush or velvet carpets are cut-pile carpets in which the loop pile has been sheared off to produce a softer texture. Because of its velvety surface, this type of carpet works well for bedrooms or family rooms. A plush carpet in which the threads have been double-twisted under heat is particularly sturdy.
- Needle-felt carpets are high tech and durable. They're produced by electrostatic attraction of individual fibers, which results in a highly resistant carpet. Ultra-sturdy, they are most commonly installed in hotels and businesses rather than in private homes.

Choose hardy, woven carpets or runners for busy areas of the house.

TIPS for carpets and runners

Here are some things to bear in mind when it comes to the safety, maintenance and finishing of any carpet, runner or rug you decide to lay in your home.

- Look seriously at carpet tiles. They are a sensible option for busy areas of the home. You can replace worn or dirty squares rather than an entire carpet.
- Use cornstarch paste to stick down hazardous corners. When the paste dries, iron the corners flat (put a piece of wrapping paper between the iron and the rug just in case). Remove any remnants of the cornstarch with a small nailbrush.
- When choosing carpets, remember that solid colors tend to show dirt and marks more readily than patterns.
- Turn a runner 180 degrees occasionally to prevent excessive wear on one end, especially if that end is near the front door or another busy part of the house.
- Choose dry carpet-cleaning products rather than carpet foam for cleaning deep pile carpets. It can take several days for a damp deep pile carpet to dry completely.
- Hire a carpet steamer or cleaning machine once a year to clean all carpets thoroughly.
- Help to deter moths and eliminate unpleasant smells by sprinkling carpets and runners occasionally with a little cedar or lavender oil.

Make a play carpet for a child's room

one Get a low-pile, square carpet remnant from the carpet store and bind the edges with wide adhesive carpet tape.

two With tailor's chalk, draw the playing area for a board game—checkers, for example—or a roadway scene for toy cars.

three With fabric paints, go over the outline of the chalk drawing and fill in the shapes.

four Make play figures or tokens from old plastic bottles or fabrics.

- Renew faded colors by wiping the carpet with a solution of water and vinegar, mixed in a 10:1 proportion. Test an inconspicuous area for colorfastness first.
- Deal with indelible stains by covering them with a rug or, if you can afford to take the risk, by creating a carpet of many colors. Punch out the dirty spots with a metal hole punch. Then, acquire some discontinued carpet patterns (inexpensive) or samples (free). Punch out shapes to insert into the carpet's holes. If you get it right, you will end up with a creative design. If not, console yourself with the thought that you'd have had to replace it anyway.

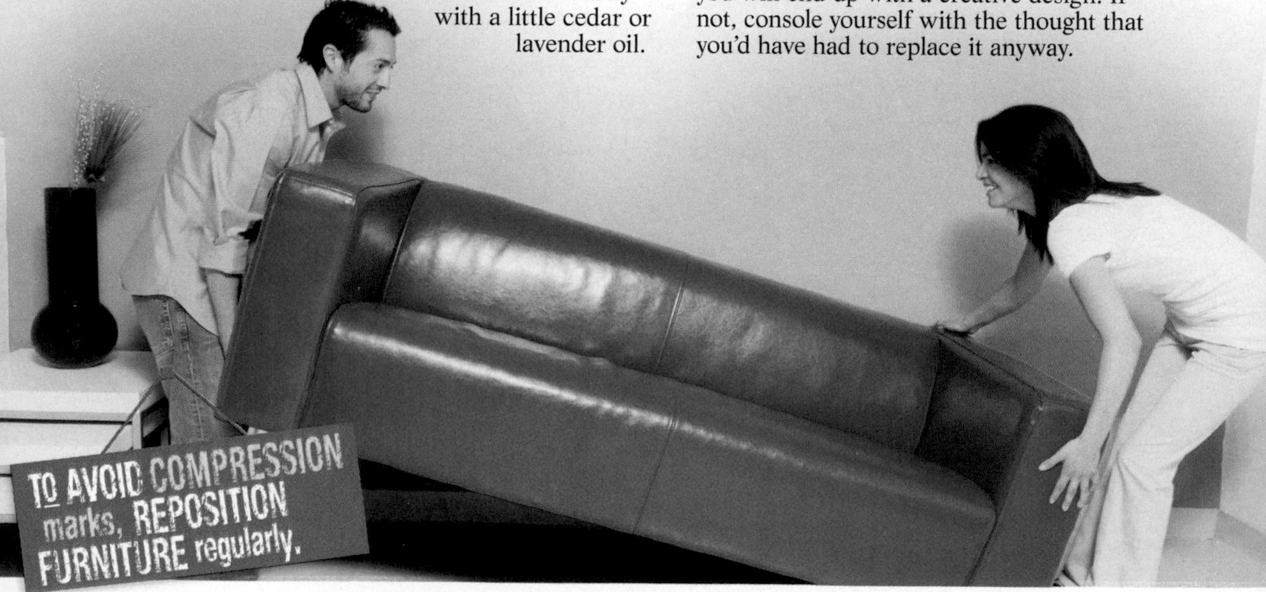

TO AVOID COMPRESSION marks, REPOSITION FURNITURE regularly.

Colors

The colors you surround yourself with at home can influence your mood and sense of well-being. In general, the function and style of a particular room determines whether you choose warm or cold, dark or light and strong or subdued colors.

Different colors have different characteristics. They can give a home a modern or traditional feel and by combining different colors, can add visual interest to a room.

Color charts display cold colors (green to purple) and warm colors (pink to yellow).

COLOR considerations

- Bright colors (vibrant shades of green, blue, red, yellow and orange) provide an expansive feeling. These are friendly, happy colors that encourage communication and are therefore especially welcome in the dining area and kitchen.
- Dark colors, such as deep red, purple, and dark shades of blue and green, can have a constricting and gloomy effect. But when applied in the right place or as accent elements, they can help to convey comfort and security.
- Warm colors (orange, yellow and pink hues, for example) raise the perceived temperature of a room. For that reason, they are best used in rooms that receive less sun. They inspire activity, so avoid them in rooms meant for relaxation, such as a bedroom. However, yellow in a bedroom is very good for combating SAD (seasonal affective disorder) and morning depression.
- Cold colors, such as icy blues and green, have a calming effect. They are especially suitable for bedrooms, helping you to relax in the evening and wake up refreshed the next morning. But they need to be used with care in sunless rooms.
- Navy blue can create a cold atmosphere that discourages conversation; don't use it in a family room or in dining areas.
- Red raises the energy level of a room, but it may also make people more irritable and hostile—so it is not a good choice for a child's room. Use it as an accent rather than a base room color.
- Gray should be avoided for the dining area and kitchen—unless you want to dampen your appetite.

HOW colors work in a room

The right choice of color can make a room appear bigger or smaller and the ceilings look higher or lower. This visual effect can compensate for some of a room's flaws.

- Use bright, light colors for small rooms; they will make the rooms appear more spacious.
- Choose warm, dark colors, such as deep shades of red, for large rooms to make them feel cosier.
- Use paler colors on low ceilings: The ceiling appears higher when it is painted in a lighter shade than the walls.
- Use darker colors for high ceilings. If you want to reduce the height of a room visually, opt for a dark-colored ceiling. The ceiling will also appear lower if you paint the bottom area of the wall in a lighter shade that gradually darkens as it rises towards the ceiling. If you want the ceiling to appear higher, the color should gradually become lighter as it rises from floor level.

• Opt for lively shades for narrower rooms; using bright colors on the walls makes a room appear wider to the eye.
• Darken wide rooms. If you paint two walls opposite each other in a darker shade, a wide room will look less cavernous.

THE right color strategy

To ensure a harmonious design for a room, you will need to choose attractive color combos for furniture, fabrics and accessories that complement the walls and ceiling.
• First, choose a basic color that you like and make sure it's appropriate for the room. Use this color for the walls, rugs and curtains, perhaps in varying intensities.
• Choose a consistent secondary color for furniture and accessories. For a unified look, choose a complementary color or design the room in color coordinates (for example, different shades of the same color). Or choose two secondary colors, but in that case the colors should appear next to each other in the color spectrum.
• Be careful when combining two colors of different intensities. For example, placing strong colors next to pastel shades forces the eye to jump back and forth between light and dark. This can create a visually disturbing effect and affect the room's atmosphere. All pastels mix well together.
• Pair neutral colors such as white or magnolia with some fresh accents in the form of cushions, artwork, accessories and throws in colors such as red, green, blue and even pink.
• If you are uncertain what color to choose, ask for advice from a paint store or interior designer. Buy sample jars and experiment before you commit.

Pair neutral colors with fresh accents in the form of cushions, artwork, accessories and throws.

GOOD TO KNOW

The color wheel

The primary colors (red, blue and yellow) form the basis of the color wheel. Secondary colors (green, orange and purple) are the colors formed by mixing the primary colors. Tertiary colors are the different shades formed by mixing a secondary color with a primary color (yellow-orange, red-orange and red-purple). Complementary colors appear opposite each other on the color wheel. Although they are the strongest contrasting colors, they go together well. The colors that appear next to each other on the wheel (analogous colors) are also considered harmonious. Finally, colors that appear together in nature generally go well together regardless of where they appear on the color wheel.

INJECT a little color

Want to make a few changes to liven up a room? Here are three easy do-it-yourself projects.
• Re-cover a lampshade. Trace and cut out the shape of the shade in wallpaper. Glue the ends with wallpaper paste for a slipcover. Summer calls for a fresh lime green against neutral furnishings. In winter, warm it up with a rich brown or red.
• Create a fabric wall hanging. Sew a hem across the top and bottom of a piece of attractive fabric and insert a wooden dowel at each end.
• Paint the wall behind book shelves an accent color that coordinates with the room.

Decorating

Each season has its individual charm, and this can be reflected in your home and garden. Bring the rhythms of nature into the house by choosing seasonal fabrics, table decorations, flower arrangements and embellishments.

SPRING

Tune in to spring by using colors such as bright and pastel yellows, pale and vivid greens and eggshell blue.

- Decorate a shelf or windowsill with early flowering plants, such as hyacinths, tulips and daffodils, in small terra-cotta pots.
- Opt for sheer curtains and tablecloths and choose bed linen that will lighten the look of a room. Look for plain, embroidered or printed designs that complement interiors.
- Rework your accessories. Bring out floral china or clear glass, and switch dark-colored sofa cushions for more cheerful tones.
- Rearrange furniture that focuses on the fireplace in winter and in spring, place it to take advantage of a garden view.

Opt for sheer curtains to lighten the look of a room and complement interiors.

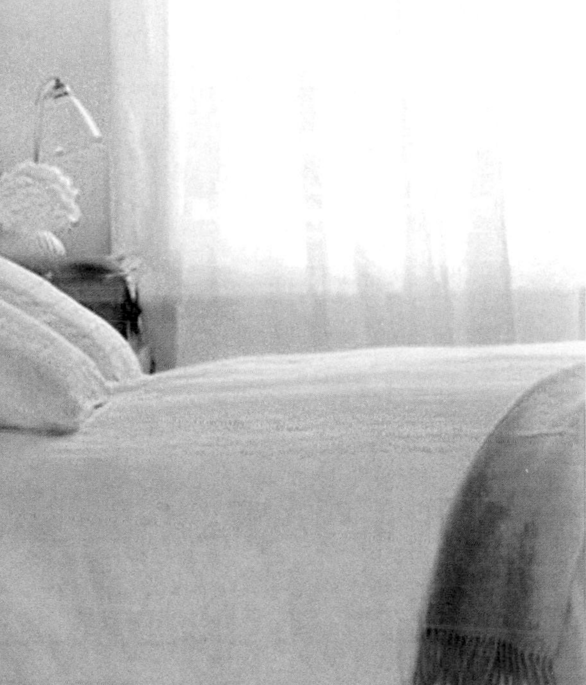

SUMMER

A varied mix of bright colors can express the fullness of the season. Here are a few ways to add summertime touches.

- Laying a white linen slipcover over the sofa helps to create a summery mood, especially if you use colorful cushions as accents.
- Counteract summer's heat with cool hues: Outdoor tables draped with blue and white are like a cool breeze in the garden.
- Create a maritime flair by filling glass tubes with sand of different colors and grain sizes, and setting them out on the balcony or patio.
- Swap a heavy, oriental carpet for a light and natural sisal rug.
- Replace fireplace logs with white candles of different heights and sizes.
- Arrange sunflowers in glass vases and light them up with lanterns at dusk to add a warm, decorative element to backyard barbecues.

AUTUMN

This season is characterized by nature's rich harvests. With just a little effort, you can decorate a house or apartment with foliage and fruit from field and forest—think pumpkins, gourds, red and golden leaves, rosehips and pine cones.

- Echo the changing colors of the leaves with accents in warm shades of orange and red. Dark green and harvest gold are also the perfect match for warm autumn hues.

• Let autumn usher in soft, textured fabrics such as suede, velvet and felt. Satin in autumnal tones adds glamor to table decorations.
• Place decorative elements such as fresh or dried leaves, unshelled nuts or seedpods in plain bowls to add interest to tables, shelves or windowsills.
• Create autumn room and table decorations from small pumpkins, dried wheat stalks, corn cobs and gourds: Simply spread them out on the table.
• Bright red apples and juicy pears in a large glass bowl make an attractive—and edible—centerpiece.

WINTER

Even though it may be cold outside, you can easily create a cozy atmosphere indoors by making a few changes. Turn up the heat and spruce up your home for winter with these tips.
• Bring cooler temperatures to mind with touches of white, turquoise and bluish-green.
• Alternatively, chase the winter chill out of your home by introducing rich shades of purple, gold and red.
• Choose winter decor fabrics such as soft wool, luxurious satin, chenille and lambswool for cushion covers, throws and drapes.
• Add warmth to a room (literally and figuratively) by swapping sheer or lace curtains for heavier drapes.
• Use brightly colored woolen rugs to warm up the floor in the family room or bedroom—it's quick and inexpensive.
• Make a colorful, cozy winter bolster by sewing two scarves together lengthwise, stuffing them with padding and securing the ends with ribbons.
• Use decorative glassware such as vases or lanterns to contrast pleasantly with rustic-looking decorations made of wood.
• Opt for a vase of evergreen foliage with berries, such as holly, or a bowl of green apples, lemons or other citrus fruits for an attractive winter touch.

Rich shades of red keep the winter chill at bay.

Door wreaths

These are an individual and friendly way to welcome guests to your home. Choose the basic components of a wreath according to the season and occasion. During the Christmas season, decorate wreaths with pinecones and ribbons to spread Yuletide cheer.

The proper wreath can set the right mood for any get-together—simply fasten decorations to suit the occasion. Every season brings with it a new collection of flora that would go well in a wreath.

AS the seasons change

- A simple wreath made with fresh new stems of any plant can be a lovely harbinger of spring.
- Decorative grasses, as well as flowers, make pretty components of a summertime wreath.
- In autumn, use tendrils of ivy or grapevines.
- In winter, entwined branches of evergreens or holly are welcoming.

SPECIAL occasions

- Use fresh fir branches with Santa Clauses, chubby-faced angels, bells, bows, pinecones and wooden toys to herald Christmas, and add colorful eggs to spring foliage for Easter.
- Explore the shape possibilities. Door wreaths don't have to be round. Other basic shapes include hearts and ovals, but there's no need to stop there.
- Spray evergreen foliage with gold or silver paint for an extra festive touch.

An autumn door wreath

one Decorate a wreath base with twigs, ivy tendrils or other greenery. Secure it in place with florist's wire.

two Add decorations such as flowers, fruit and other embellishments. Attach items that lack stems with florist's wire.

three As a final touch, decorate the wreath with colorful ribbons.

INCORPORATE DRIED FRUIT INTO A festive Christmas wreath.

- Ribbons, strings of pearls and dried flowers can add a wonderful romantic touch. To create a cheerful mood for an anniversary party, choose a variety of bright and colorful ribbons.
- Create unique designs with figurines, hearts and twinkling lights. For a wedding, weave a little bridal couple into a wreath of roses.
- Dried flowers give wreaths a lovely floral touch but they tend to be fragile, so don't use them on doors that are frequently opened and closed.
- To celebrate a child's birthday, display the boy's or girl's age in the center of the wreath using small, brightly colored flowers or beads.
- For a teenager who has just passed his or her driving test, make a clever wreath that includes little cars or traffic signs.
- Fragrant decorations such as herbs and spices look lovely and smell even better when incorporated into a wreath.

Fireplaces and woodstoves

The sound, smell and warmth of a crackling fire add ambience and a traditional welcoming feel to a home. Fireplaces and wood-burning stoves can also help reduce heating costs by lessening your dependence on more expensive fuels.

Attractive as they are, wood-burning fireplaces actually suck heat out of the home through the chimney, as well as releasing emissions into the environment. If you have an old wood-burning fireplace, consider putting in a insert or replacing the current one with a newer, high-efficiency model. No matter what type of fireplace you have, it is a potential hazard, so make sure you observe the appropriate safety regulations. Also you need to be sure you are not breaking clean air regulations. A woodstove may have to comply with emission standards. If you are unsure, check with your local authority.

OPEN fireplace

A built-in fireplace can be a source of cozy warmth, but you will need to take into account certain factors to keep it safe.

- Use a fireplace screen to keep sparks from flying.
- Clean the fireplace out after each use and regularly check and clean the chimney.
- Make sure you have the right fireplace tools but keep them out of reach of children: Bellows, pokers and tongs aid in stoking the fire. A small shovel is useful for removing ash.

WOODSTOVES and fireplace inserts

The contemporary variants of the open fireplace are woodstoves and fireplace inserts. In both cases, the fire burns in a closed chamber and is visible through a glass panel. You get all the appeal of a wood fire with none of the hassle, smell or soot. Here are a few things to consider.

- Install a wood-burning fireplace insert. It can help you to maintain a traditional look

by turning an inefficient masonry fireplace into a woodstove with an efficiency rating of about 70 percent. However, one disadvantage of woodstoves and inserts is that dust particles land on the stove and burn up there, making the air dry although the fire is closed off.

- Wipe the glass panel regularly with window cleaner to remove soot. Just remember to spray the window cleaner on a cloth rather than directly on the panel—and only when it is cold.
- If you are looking for something traditional, opt for a cast-iron stove.
- Find out the efficiency factor of a stove. It informs you how much energy is actually transferred to the surrounding air in a room.

GAS fireplaces and fireplace inserts

Gas fireplaces and fireplace inserts give you the look and warmth of a wood fire but with the added efficiency and ease of use of a modern convenience: You can turn them on or off with the touch of a remote control button or wall switch.

- Choose a gas fireplace to fit the decor of your home. A two-sided gas fireplace makes a lovely room divider, for example. But if you are fond of the antique mantelpiece, buy an insert to fit the fireplace rather than replacing the whole thing.
- Follow the manufacturer's instructions for using your gas fireplace and be sure to have it checked periodically to maintain maximum efficiency. And remember to turn off the pilot light at the end of winter to save energy costs.
- Check the chimney flue for blockages, such as bird nests and leaves, before using the heater for the first time in the winter. Have the chimney swept every year, when it can also be checked for safety.
- Gas fireplaces don't produce smoke and other by-products that affect people with asthma or allergies. They are easy to maintain and don't require you to sweep up ashes or deal with stray sparks.

GOOD TO KNOW

The right fuel

Modern woodstoves burn logs; fully cured hardwood is best. About 1,400 pounds (700 kg) dry, seasoned firewood can replace the energy from about 7,000 ft^3 (200 m^3) of natural gas. Light gray to gray ashes are a sign of efficient combustion, containing no carbon remnants—you can even use them in the garden as a high-potash fertilizer. Add dried orange peel as you start a fire. It burns well and gives off a pleasant aroma.

A cast-iron stove adds a traditional touch as well as contributing heat to a room.

Fresh, bright bathrooms

The bathroom is the perfect place to relax at both the beginning and end of the day, so it is worth spending a little time creating a serene, spa-like feel. A few small changes are often all it takes to add a comforting ambience even to an older bathroom.

New mirrors and lighting can help freshen up a tired-looking bathroom, and changing the fabrics, towels and tiles sets a new tone. But ventilation and hygiene should remain a top priority as mildew will damage the room's appearance and can be harmful to health.

THE right setup

- Use a softer bulb as dim lights can help create the right ambience for a relaxing bath. Also, artfully placed candles can add to the spa feel and provide flattering lighting for almost any skin type.
- Use light colors such as white, pale blue and beige or light-colored wood to make smaller bathrooms appear larger. If you can't replace tiles or repaint the room, choose accessories in lighter shades.
- Install a new shower partition. This can be done without much trouble and it works wonders, especially in older bathrooms.
- Clear out the clutter: The only things on display should be those in daily use.
- Store towels in a bathroom cupboard if space is limited. Or, for a chic yet practical solution, roll them up, secure each with a ribbon and place them standing up in a basket by the bath.
- A larger bathroom is ideal for humidity-loving, exotic bonsai trees and tropical plants.
- Add suitably upholstered furniture to create a stylish, inviting place to relax. Stools with terry cloth seats are practical and provide comfortable seating while you paint toenails or moisturize your skin.
- Bring in soothing scents such as lavender, orange and vanilla in the form of aromatherapy candles, lotions or scent diffusers.
- Keep a waterproof clock in the bathroom —one that can be attached to the tiles with suction cups is perfect—so you can keep an eye on the time while getting ready.
- Get a waterproof radio if you like to start the day with music.

Replacing damaged tiles

Damaged tiles can cause bigger problems in a damp environment. If you discover a cracked or chipped tile, follow these simple steps as soon as possible to limit the damage. If you can't match tiles exactly, use contrasting replacements.

one Remove the grout around the damaged tile and use a dry-cut saw drill attachment to slice diagonally through the tile, or make several holes with a drill.

two Chip off fragments of the tile with a hammer and flat chisel until the whole thing comes loose. Remove as much of the old adhesive as possible.

three Cover the back of the replacement tile with bonding material and press it onto the wall, using tile spacers to position and fit it correctly.

four Let the glue dry overnight (or as directed by the manufacturer). Then apply grout and clean.

• Repair small cracks in the tiles with matching paint from an art supply store. Mix a small amount of the paint with grout and apply to the tiles to fill hairline cracks. Rub smooth.
• Refresh older tiles by repainting the grout (special grout-coloring kits are available). But remember that grout paint can't be used on nonenamel tiles or on top of water-resistant joint sealer.
• Visually enlarge the bathroom with adhesive mirror tiles. They are a good choice when replacements for old tiles are no longer available. Or paint over unwanted tiles with tile primer and lacquer to cover them.
• One simple but effective solution is to apply a new layer of tiles over unsalvageable existing ones. This is cheaper and easier than removing the old layer and resurfacing the wall.
• Even easier is to paint over tiles with tile paint—but only if tiles aren't going to get wet regularly.

BEST fabrics

Well-chosen fabrics can turn the bathroom into a comfortable, attractive space. They should also be kind to skin.
• Choose a shower curtain that complements the rest of the bathroom furnishings. Waterproof fabric curtains are more chic and attractive than plastic ones but need regular cleaning, so make sure they are machine washable.
• Opt for matching towels in different sizes to give the bathroom a coordinated look. Thick, high-quality towels will make drying off after a bath an absolute joy and will last for years.

PROBLEM tiles

If old, cracked tiles, graying grout or 1970s decor are cramping your style, don't begin demolition right away. Take a cue from earlier generations and fix rather than discard.
• Try thoroughly cleaning the existing tiles, which injects new life at once. For stubborn stains, use water mixed with ammonia or alcohol, and remove scale with vinegar. Rub old tiles with a little linseed oil to make them shine again.

THE mildew menace

The best remedy for mildew is good air circulation, which gets rid of moisture so mildew can't take hold. Turning on the bathroom fan is the first step, but try some of these tips, too.
• Wipe condensation from the shower wall and tiles with a squeegee after each shower.
• Use vinegar to clean the corners between the shower or bath and the tiled wall regularly.
• Paint untiled wall surfaces and the ceiling with a mildew-resistant paint.
• Remove the grout where mildew has taken hold, clean thoroughly and seal the cleaned edges with new grout.

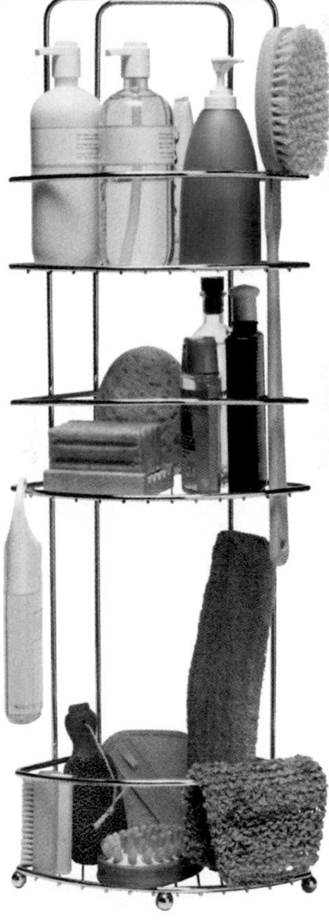

A compact unit of shower shelves keeps the bathroom tidy.

Furnishing for comfort

Plush, upholstered furniture can add style or period appeal to a living room. Remember, however, that its most important qualities are hidden beneath the fabric covering.

Sofas or armchairs are likely to be used on a daily basis, so as well as looking attractive and harmonizing with the existing furnishings, they need to be practical, sturdy and hard-wearing, both in terms of construction and fabric covering.

SELECTION criteria

- For a seat in a lighter or plain dark color, check whether it has removable covers that can be washed or dry-cleaned.
- See if the upholstery fabric has a stain-resistant coating. This will help to keep your furniture looking like new.
- Consider buying an easy-to-clean leather sofa, particularly if you have children who are more likely to spill things or a pet that likes to be curled up beside you on the sofa.
- Keep a new armchair or sofa away from direct sunlight to prevent fabrics from fading.
- You can buy high-quality upholstered furniture with different degrees of firmness. The heavier you are, the firmer the cushions should be for comfort.

GOOD TO KNOW

Modern upholstered furniture

Today's armchairs and sofas consist of a basic frame, several layers of inner springs or foam and soft padding. Look for frames made of sustainable hardwoods rather than pine. Opt for seats made with spring coils, webbing between the frame and the springs that is tightly woven and taut, and cushions with even stitching and seams. Loose threads can signal low-quality work. Microfiber, leather and textured fabrics tend to last longer.

- If you have weak legs, consider an armchair with a mechanical or electric power lift. They help you to stand by raising and tilting the seat in an ergonomically appropriate way.
- Measure it out. You won't really know whether a sofa is a good fit until you get it home, but you can get a sense of whether the size is right by taking the measurements of a potential purchase and then laying out squares of newspaper in that exact size in the living room.
- Give yourself plenty of time before deciding what to buy. However stylish, a sofa and chairs need to stay comfortable even after a long evening spent in front of the television.
- Stand about 3 feet (1 m) back from the sofa you are considering and look at it with a critical eye. Does the pattern line up? Does the sofa look symmetrical? Do the cushions fit together in a straight line? Does everything look right?
- Don't buy a sofa or armchair without first sitting in it just as you would do at home—even if this includes lying down or slouching. Noticing the flaws in a piece of furniture only when you have it home can be an expensive mistake.

Heating and cooling

By managing a home's heating, cooling and ventilation properly it's possible to save on energy costs, create a healthy interior climate, reduce greenhouse gas emissions and banish mildew before it sets in.

A CEILING FAN KEEPS AIR MOVING during hot and cold SPELLS.

Heating and cooling account for the largest amount of energy used in the home, but with a few simple strategies, you can keep your home cozy in winter and cool in summer without running up huge bills.

HEATING sensibly

- A portable space heater may be sufficient for a small house or apartment, especially if you only need heating on the coldest days of winter.
- Where a number of rooms need to be heated regularly, choose fixed space heaters for living areas and portable heaters for bedrooms.
- Investing in central heating may only be worthwhile if you need to heat most of the house for 3 or more months of the year.
- Check regularly that your heaters are working efficiently. If unsure, have them serviced once a year.
- Turn heating off when you leave the house and before you go to bed.
- Let the sun's warmth in on winter days by opening up the house to the south and west.
- Keep cold drafts out by sealing gaps around doors and windows and using heavy curtains.
- Move heaters away from windows to avoid unnecessary heat loss.

STAYING cool in summer

- Cool south- and west-facing rooms by installing temporary shutters or awnings that can be removed in winter. Or train a deciduous climber over a pergola on a south- or west-facing wall—when it loses its leaves in winter, it will let the sun in.
- On hot days keep the heat out by closing windows, blinds and curtains.
- Portable or ceiling fans are cheap to run and effective. They move air over your body and evaporates moisture and keeping you cool.
- When the temperature drops at night, open doors and windows to let the cool air inside.
- To cool a hot interior quickly, open two windows opposite each other to create cross ventilation.

THE right ventilation

Too much moisture creates a breeding ground for mildew. Improper ventilation is usually the cause.

- Short, periodic bursts of ventilation are best to maintain air quality. Open windows three times a day for up to 10 minutes in winter and a little longer in warmer months, unless you suffer from hay fever.
- If the kitchen or bathroom steams up, air the room at once by opening a window or turning on a fan.
- Leave about 1–2 inch (2–5 cm) clearance between wardrobes or bookcases and outer walls. Mildew can easily develop behind tall furniture.

Adequate ventilation helps to reduce humidity in the home.

Home safety

By taking care and using common sense when planning a renovation or arranging furniture, you can make life more comfortable and reduce the risk of accidents in the home.

Safety issues can affect every room and area of the house, including the bathroom, balcony and backyard.

GOOD TO KNOW

Avoid accidents

Most falls occur indoors, so look for problem areas in the home. Are there obstructions such as raised thresholds? Or electrical cords you could trip over? Are there rugs or runners that could slip or cause someone to fall? Is the lighting in each room adequate?

USEFUL aids

- Be sure there is a light switch right next to the front door so that you won't have to stumble around in a dark house when you come home at night.
- Choose stylish light switches that contrast with the wallpaper or paint to make them more visible.
- Plug in a small nightlight in the hall for safe passage to the bathroom in the dark.
- Opt for shatterproof glass patio doors to prevent accidents. Use decorative aids, such as adhesive designs or stickers, to make the glass visible.
- Use sound-absorbent curtains or floors to reduce echoes and other noise.
- Choose dining room chairs with armrests for comfort. They also make it easier to stand up after a meal.
- Sitting down and getting up are much easier if you choose sofas and chairs that have raised seats. Similarly, make sure that a new bed is a comfortable height before you buy it.
- Make sure you don't forget your keys or mobile phone by designating a storage area next to the front door that is invisible from the outside.
- Attach timers to table lamps so that they turn on automatically once or twice a day to deter burglars and let you come home to a lighted house at night.

BATHROOM and kitchen

The bathroom and kitchen probably offer the most potential for disaster in a home. Here are some preventive strategies.

- Install sturdy bath rails to help you get in and out of the tub.
- Stick water-resistant, adhesive antislip stickers on the bottom of the bathtub. They offer better protection against slips and falls than a bath mat.
- A shower or bath seat is not only helpful for older people—it can simplify bathing children, too.
- Install a single-handle faucet. It's a safe and easy-to-operate fixture that allows even little ones to regulate water temperature, protecting against scalding.
- Consider purchasing a space-saving, folding stepladder. It will let you to reach top cupboards in the kitchen and high bookshelves without risk, and can be stored away neatly.

BALCONY, deck and patio

An outdoor area is a relaxing place to unwind after a hard week. Just make sure that it provides a safe environment as well.

- Flat surfaces as you enter or exit a deck, balcony or patio reduce the risk of tripping. For a balcony you step down to, it may be worth adding a wooden step to raise the level.
- A screen that protects against the wind can let you to enjoy an outdoor space even on the coolest days.

A tasteful outdoor wall light adds a touch of class as well as security.

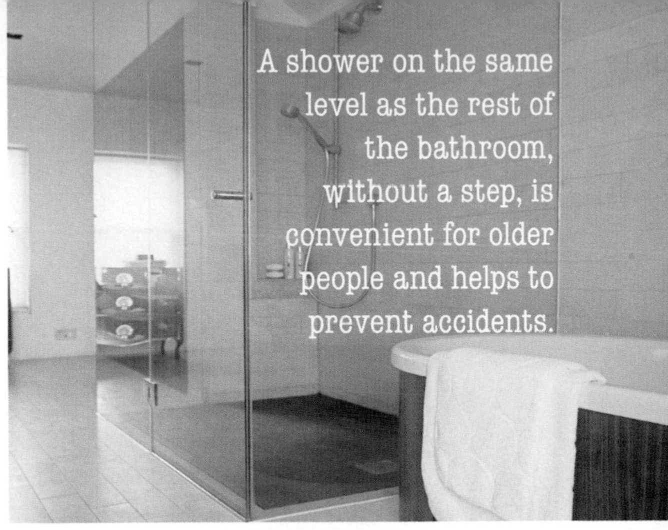

A shower on the same level as the rest of the bathroom, without a step, is convenient for older people and helps to prevent accidents.

- Make sure the height of the railings on the balcony complies with building regulations. Take special care to make sure children are constantly supervised if they are able to access balconies.

BACKYARD and entrances

Steps from the patio to the backyard can be an attractive feature but they need to be safe. Install a handrail and make sure there is no loose mortar that could make a step unstable and cause a fall. Here are a few other things to consider.

- Repair uneven pathways and keep them clear of leaves, broken branches and overgrown plants.
- Illuminate the entrance to the yard and steps with solar lights to avoid tripping in the dark.
- Install motion detectors on lights outside the house and in the garden so that when someone approaches the surroundings light up. This is also a useful security feature.
- Lay nonslip doormats that are flush with the floor to make entrance areas safer.
- Install an easily accessible doorbell and a legible house name or number to help visitors find the right home. The postman and delivery man will also appreciate a house number that is clearly identifiable from the street as will police, fire, ambulance and other emergency personnel.
- If you have an outdoor water feature, install a pump in it to deter mosquitoes. Mosquitoes can only breed in standing water.

Indoor plants

Plants add atmosphere to a home. Tall specimens such as ficus or palm trees act as accents, while smaller ones can decorate a windowsill. When choosing a plant, consider carefully where you are going to put it in order to enhance the decor and ensure its survival.

When properly cultivated, orchids will flower over and over again for years.

Armed with a few tips and patience, anyone can care for a variety of plants that will help enhance a living space. And remember, a room with plants is known to help lift the spirits.

GOOD TO KNOW

The right location

Besides water, plants need light to thrive. A window facing south that gets plenty of sun is ideal for cacti and succulents. Ferns, orchids, peace lilies and palms prefer a north-facing window or relatively dark areas of a room.

A HEALTHY room climate

Plants are not only beautiful, they also increase the humidity level and oxygen content of a room during the daytime. This is good for the climate and, ultimately, for your health. It's especially important in winter, when heating can dry the atmosphere.

- Plants are particularly effective at counteracting the release of volatile and potentially harmful chemicals from various substances (such as insulation, plywood or varnish) at normal atmospheric pressure—and contributing to balanced internal humidity. Good varieties to choose include braided money tree (*Pachira aquatica*), dragon tree (*Dracaena*), ficus, rubber plant, weeping fig, umbrella tree, Boston ferns, palm trees and peace lilies.
- Don't keep plants in a bedroom because they use up oxygen and produce carbon dioxide at night.
- Bear in mind that big plants such as dragon trees and palm trees produce more humidity than smaller ones.

WATERING plants correctly

Many plants do well when watered from above, but there are myriad factors to consider, depending on the size and species of plant. One general guideline to follow is that you should always use water at room temperature. Another is always to water plants with furry leaves, such as African violets, from below to avoid damage.

- Put bulbs and other plants with sensitive roots, such as poinsettias, in a large bowl and water them from below to keep the bulbs or roots from rotting. Also, check planters about an hour after watering and drain off excess water.
- Keep rainwater and stale mineral water handy, as both are good for watering plants, as is cooled, salt-free water that has been used for boiling eggs.
- Let tap water sit overnight before you water plants with it. Fluoride and other minerals dissipate or settle when the water is left to sit.
- Immersion can be beneficial to many plants, including cacti and citrus species. Immerse the root ball in its pot in a large container of water. It is saturated when no more air bubbles rise.
- Spray plants occasionally. Use lime-free water to keep limescale from building up. Pamper plants (especially cacti and those

with large leaves) with a cleansing shower twice yearly: Put them out in the rain or spray them with a showerhead. Tip cacti pots to prevent water from running directly into them.

REGULAR care

With a little tender care, plants will reward you with healthy foliage and gorgeous flowers.

- Check new plants thoroughly for pests before buying. Indoor plants can be susceptible to mites, aphids and other troublesome creatures that spread easily.
- Dust plants carefully now and then to let leaves breathe, giving particular attention to the undersides.
- Wipe plants with larger leaves with diluted beer to make them shine.
- Remove wilted flowers and leaves immediately to keep plants looking good and to help to prevent them from attracting bugs.
- Prevent a harmful accumulation of water by occasionally loosening the soil. When repotting, be sure the new pot's drain holes are clear and always use new potting mix. Choose a good-quality mix that has controlled-release fertilizer and water-absorbent crystals.

A garden in a bottle

A terrarium is the perfect way to bring a little greenery to a cramped space. This is how to assemble one.

one Line the bottom of a large, big-bottom bottle with gravel. Then, use an ice cream stick to extend the handle of a spoon and a fork (use some tape to attach them).

two Put a layer of soil on top of the gravel and smooth it out. Use a cardboard funnel to keep the sides of the bottle clean.

three Insert suitable plants, such as ferns, small trailing figs and ivy, using the spoon and the fork as tools. Don't plant them too close together, as they need room to grow.

four Water the plants carefully with cooled boiled water, and keep the bottle tightly sealed. If the bottle fogs up, you have overwatered it.

five Don't place the bottle garden in direct sunlight or on or near a heating unit.

- A mixture of sieved compost, garden soil and sand makes good potting soil. Also, eggshells (for calcium), coffee grounds and black tea make excellent natural fertilizers.
- Leaving plants exposed to heat or drafts is the equivalent of leaving outdoor plants unprotected from the elements.
- Water plants more sparingly during the colder months, as winter is a time of rest. Also, keep them in rooms with cooler temperatures if possible.

CUTTING back

Trim fast-growing plants regularly during the summer. Careful pruning controls plants and encourages growth. It will help them grow stronger and is a good way to shape certain species.

- Prune woody plants once a year, but timing depends on the type of plant. Plants that flower before midsummer are best pruned immediately after flowering.
- Increase the number of shoots and flowers by cutting back the main shoot. This will cause the plant to sprout new shoots.
- Make the cut clean, no matter why or where you prune. Use a sharp knife or pruning shears.

Light conditions

Make the most of natural light in your home to safeguard the environment and reduce electricity use during the day. Open the curtains wide to let the morning sun into your home and it will provide a positive energy boost at the start of the day.

It makes sense to situate the kitchen and living area where they get the maximum amount of daylight. But unless you have designed the house yourself, that's not always possible. Even so, there are plenty of tricks to help you make a dark home (or an overly bright one) more appealing.

PROVIDING the proper lighting

- A dark and windowless hallway can create a gloomy first impression. Illuminate it evenly, perhaps with recessed lighting along its length.
- If natural sunlight only penetrates the part of the room that is close to a window, capture that elusive light with a mirror and reflect it wherever you wish.
- Very pale-colored or well-illuminated walls give a room an expansive feeling because they appear to reflect the sunlight. They can also make a room appear larger and more friendly.
- By designing windowsills and patios to look like a continuation of the interior furnishings, you can cleverly enlarge a room. The natural light will evoke the same colors inside as well as outside.
- Dark walls absorb light and therefore seem visually closer to the observer—an optical trick that you can use for large or long, narrow rooms.
- To reduce glare, place the TV out of the path of direct sunlight and reflected light.

PROTECTION from sunlight and glare

Although bright, sunlit rooms are generally pleasant, too much sunlight can be stifling in the heat of summer. Here are some ways to cool things down.

- Shutters deflect sunlight when placed on the outside of windows.
- Equally important is protection from glare. Antiglare devices such as louvered blinds and interior shutters go on the inside of windows and usually have adjustable wood or plastic slats that direct the light up or down, or otherwise control it.
- Panel curtains mute the direct light from the outside yet still allow light to enter, keeping all areas of the room free from glare.
- Antiglare screens reduce eyestrain when using a computer monitor on a sunny day.

To prevent eyestrain, reduce the contrast between a computer monitor and a room's ambient light.

Lighting

Lighting has an obvious function, but it is important to light a room properly. Harsh, glaring lights in the study can cause headaches or eyestrain, while insufficient lighting in the kitchen or workshop could be dangerous.

A CLASSIC floor lamp ADDS ELEGANCE AND DIFFUSES soft light.

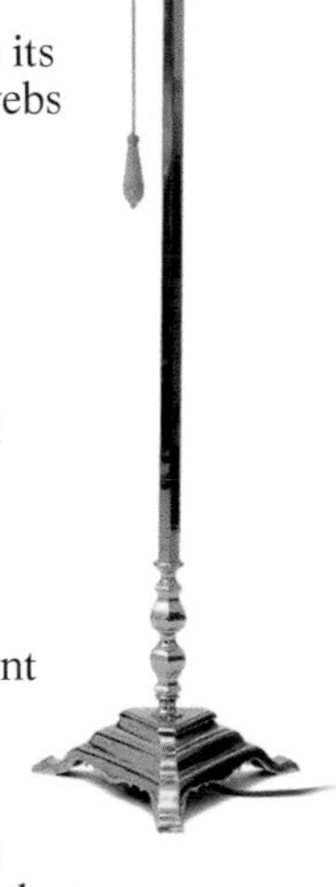

To keep you and your family safe, observe the manufacturer's guidelines when hanging lamps, chandeliers and wall lamps and follow lighting tips for each room. Seek professional advice on all electrical matters.

BASIC lighting

- The light source should illuminate the room fully and evenly.
- Light projected from the ceiling should not reduce the effect of nearby floor or table lamps.

GOOD TO KNOW

The end of incandescence

In 1880, Thomas Alva Edison patented the incandescent light bulb. Today, the bulb's fate is sealed: Many countries have either banned incandescent bulbs or will begin phasing them out. Energy-saving bulbs (such as CFLs or LEDs) use a fraction of the energy of traditional bulbs and come in many different forms, colors and temperatures. By making the switch you can reduce lighting energy consumption by up to 80 percent.

HANGING lamps

A hanging light fixture is a common sight in a modern home, but not all are properly hung. Follow these suggestions when installing one.

- Pendant lights are perfect for casting light on dining room tables. Hang them about 30–34 inches (76–86 cm) above the table for an 8 feet (2.5 m) high ceiling so they provide enough light without disrupting sight lines or blinding guests.
- If the ceiling is higher and you plan to use large, table centerpieces, hang a pendant light higher so guests can see one another.

CHANDELIERS

Glittering crystal chandeliers are the most elegant forms of hanging lamps. They have become much more affordable through the use of glass-like synthetic materials. However, a chandelier won't show a dining room to its best advantage if it is draped with cobwebs and a layer of dust, so it needs to be cleaned regularly.

WALL lamps

Wall lamps supplement the main light source in a room and play an important role in mood lighting. Here are some suggestions for using them to their best advantage.

- A beam of light shining up or down on the wall can visually separate different areas of activity in a room from each other.
- If you want wall lamps to help spread the light evenly in a room, make sure that more light is shining upwards than downwards.

FLOOR lamps

Portable floor lamps come in many different attractive styles and will always brighten up dark areas of a family room or den.

- Floor lamps create a cozy atmosphere, lighten dead corners and provide reading light.
- Torchières (lamps on tall stands) can add a striking accent and may also be used as reading lamps.

TABLE lamps

Table and desk lamps can be both decorative and useful.

• They can look pretty on an occasional table or they may be essential for bedtime reading or for close work in a study.

• You can make an imaginative lamp base from a clay pot, clear vase or ceramic urn, using a lamp kit from a hardware store. Be sure to use only materials that aren't combustible, as the bulb will emit heat.

KITCHEN

Basic lighting is provided by a ceiling light, but halogen spotlights or fluorescent tubes installed under hanging cabinets can illuminate key working areas much better.

• Recessed downlights over the sink or stove can create good task lighting for cooking, baking or scouring pots and pans.

• Kitchen islands and breakfast bars can be effectively lit and highlighted with a series of pendant lights.

• A pendant over the kitchen table provides lighting for doing homework, tackling paperwork, undertaking hobbies and more.

LIVING room

The living room is more about ambience, so torchière lamps can provide basic lighting but they will reveal any bumps on the ceiling and walls, so place them carefully. Here are several other things to consider.

• Islands of light created by several small table lamps accentuate certain spaces.

• Colored lights can create a fun effect, depending on the color and position.

• To relieve eyestrain, illuminate the wall behind the TV with a soft light source.

• Indirect lighting, mounted, for example, along baseboards, in glass cabinets or behind a curtain rod can provide a pleasing lighting effect.

DINING area

• Choose a hanging lamp with a pleasant and glare-free light to install over the dining table. A dimmer switch that allows you to adjust light conditions is ideal: Turn the light up for a family dinner, down for an intimate meal for two.

BEDROOM

• A ceiling light that can be turned on and off at the door or from the bed generally provides the basic light source in a bedroom. However, it is also important to invest in a good bedside reading lamp if you enjoy reading in bed.

BATHROOM

• Halogen lamps or fluorescent lights provide basic lighting in many bathrooms these days. For a more focused illumination of the vanity area, you can install additional lights that don't cause glare or shadows above or on both sides of the mirror.

THE DINING AREA should be STYLISHLY LIT and FREE from glare.

Maintaining your home

Use a few tried-and-tested tricks and you can keep your new furniture or freshly varnished floor looking pristine and your sofa and armchairs in showroom condition.

Slipcovers, armrest covers, throws and furniture cups or felt pads all work well to keep furniture and floors free from damage.

SEATING

Living room chairs and sofas experience heavy wear, but a few well-chosen covers will reduce the need for repairs and increase their life expectancy.

- Slipcovers prolong the life of upholstered furniture. They come as either custom-made or loosely draped coverings that protect the sofa from small, sticky fingers and four-legged friends. When slipcovers get dirty, just remove and wash them. They can also be changed with the seasons.
- Slipcovers also serve a decorative purpose: They enhance seating arrangements and ensure that sofas and different types of chairs are well coordinated.
- The armrests of chairs and sofas wear out the quickest. Use armrest covers to protect against abrasion and sweat.
- Throws that cover an entire sofa can have a modernizing effect on older or outdated furniture, giving the living room a new look.
- A decorative blanket draped over the seat of a chair or sofa can save seating from wear.

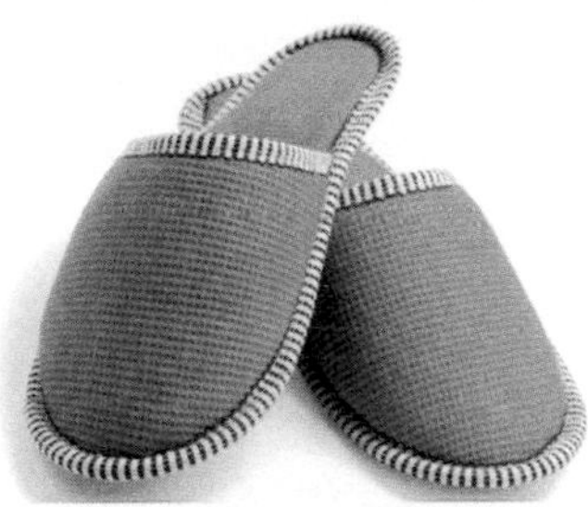

Wearing slippers indoors will help to protect floors.

If you can't get the stains out of upholstered fabrics, opt for an elegant, custom-made slipcover.

- It may be possible to have removable covers dyed if you want a change of color.
- Discourage your cat from damaging furniture by investing in a scratching post and placing it near where the cat sleeps or eats. Or try a cat repellent (available at pet stores) to keep it off furniture.

FLOOR

A new floor enhances any house. Although wear and tear may be unavoidable, you can reduce damage by taking a few simple precautions.

- Always put floor protector pads under tables and chairs. Self-adhesive pads often come loose, leaving ugly remnants of glue. Opt for more durable, screw-on pads instead.
- Put a protective mat under the desk chair. Even casters specifically made for hardwood floors can mark them.
- Prevent dirt and stones from being tracked through the house by asking people to remove their shoes at the door. You could even provide some warm slippers or wooly socks for visitors to wear.
- Use rugs to protect any section of the floor that might be susceptible to spills or extra wear.

NATURAL MATERIALS

Go green when painting, decorating and choosing home decor, avoiding chemicals and pollutants that damage the planet. Natural, eco-friendly materials tend to be good for your health and the environment.

Tile or stone floors are long-lasting, stylish and free of toxic materials.

Floors

Today, beautiful, eco-friendly and stylish flooring is well within the reach of anyone who is renovating their home or having a new house built.

- Cork flooring is warm and springy underfoot. You can even sand down a cork floor and apply a new polyurethane finish. But check first with the manufacturer that it is safe to do so.
- Linoleum is also a natural product. Because of its noise-reducing, antibacterial and antistatic qualities, it is currently undergoing something of a renaissance.
- Naturally oiled wood floors are an alternative to engineered hardwood, laminates or glued parquet floors. You can sand off scratches as they occur and repair them with oil.
- Tile or stone floors are extremely long-lasting and free of toxic materials, unlike many types of synthetic flooring. Cared for properly, they look good and enhance most types of property.

Walls

From plaster to paint, walls play a huge role in the quality of a home's interior environment. It's not difficult to find materials that don't emit harmful fumes. These are some of the choices available.

- Lime plaster (not to be confused with lime-based render) is made of finely sifted sand and lime. It is good for controlling humidity and offers tremendous durability. Application requires considerable expertise.
- Clay plaster also has a positive effect on the climate of a room. It can be used as a base or a top coat. It's application also requires skill.
- Clay paint consists of clay, chalk, water and pigments. It is nontoxic and affordable.
- Whitewash is ideal because it resists mildew. It is best applied to lime and clay plaster, but will also stick to oil paint or wallpaper.
- Milk paints are good for allergy sufferers. Based on a centuries-old, nontoxic formula made from casein (a milk protein), water, limestone, clay and natural pigments, they come as a fine powder that can be mixed at home. They stick only to unfinished, porous surfaces such as wood and plaster.

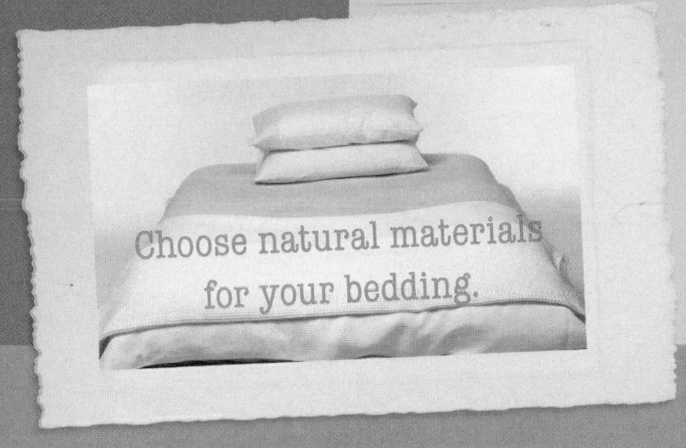

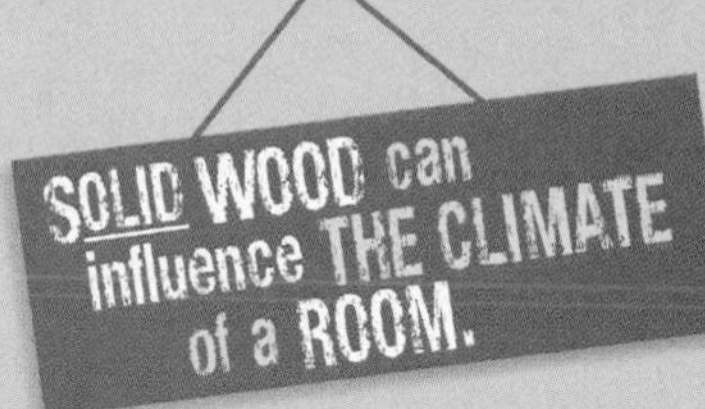

Beds

For maximum comfort and sound health, it's a good idea to stick to natural materials when it comes to your bed. A solid wood, wrought iron or stainless steel bedframe is a good choice.

- Opt for eco-friendly materials when buying a mattress. In terms of energy consumption, all-natural latex (free of synthetic latex) rates much better than synthetic latex made from petroleum, even when you factor in harvesting and transport.
- Before buying a futon, check the stuffing to see if it has been enriched with breathable, warming, natural fibers such as horsehair, virgin wool, coconut fibers or natural latex.
- Choose down, feathers, cotton and linen for blankets and bedding. If you are an allergy sufferer, opt for blankets that can be washed in water up to 140°F (60°C) or hotter, and pillows and quilts that are made of synthetic fibers.

Household fabrics

When choosing the fabrics and linens for your home, going green means looking a little more closely at the labels before you buy.

- Look for blankets made of wool or organic cotton.
- Choose organic cotton, bamboo and linen for bedding and sheets. The absorbency of the natural fibers contributes to a dry, warm sleeping environment. They are also cool in summer.
- Consider felt-backed bedroom curtains for allergy sufferers. Not only does this have an insulating effect, but these curtains tend to absorb the vapors and scents in the air.

Furniture

Furniture made from natural substances and finished with chemical-free stains or varnishes not only looks beautiful, it is also nontoxic.

- Furniture made of solid wood is preferable to pieces made from MDF or veneer, which can emit formaldehyde. A bonus: By absorbing and releasing humidity, solid wood polished with beeswax improves a room's atmosphere.
- Wicker furniture made of cane, bamboo, rattan or willow provides a natural ambience. Just moisten the furniture with a damp cloth to freshen it up.
- Wrought iron or stainless steel furniture is a good alternative, especially for allergy sufferers.
- When buying upholstered furniture, look for pieces made with natural materials—soy or vegetable-blend cushions, for example, as well as cover fabrics such as hemp and organic cotton.

Pictures

Design a tasteful arrangement and use the right lighting and suitable frames to draw attention to oil paintings, family portraits or photos from your last vacation.

A little preparation will ensure that pictures are hung properly, arranged stylishly and shown in the best lighting conditions.

ARRANGING pictures

The basic principle when arranging pictures is that the horizontal center of each picture or group of pictures should line up at eye level on the wall. You can drop the centerline 12–24 inches (30–60 cm) in areas where the admirers will mostly be seated, such as a living room. Beyond that, you are free to arrange them as you like, but observing the following rules does help.

- Hang pictures that are the same size and shape next to or underneath one another in strict geometrical order.
- Create a harmonious arrangement by organizing pictures of different sizes according to imaginary lines that go through the middle and the lower or upper border of the specific picture.
- Be creative: Arrange a larger group of pictures in a square, oval or circle. Alternatively, orient them according to an imaginary cross in the middle of the arrangement.

A neat, geometric arrangement looks cohesive and clear.

PLACING pictures in the best light

- Even in a well-illuminated room, a picture light can accentuate a piece of art or group of photos.
- Well-placed lamps either below or above can cast a mellow light on pictures.
- To bring out the glow in a photo, illuminate it from behind. Press a photo to a piece of plastic wrap, glue it on matte glass, and install a light behind it so that it shines through the picture.

HANGING pictures properly

Besides the good old picture hook in the wall, there are many other options for hanging pictures almost invisibly.

- Hang pictures from a rail or molding using nylon line that matches the color of the ceiling and is almost invisible. You can move them back and forth and adjust them for height, too.
- If a picture always hangs askew, use a little adhesive or masking tape behind the corners of the frame to hold it in place.

Pillows and cushions

Bedroom pillows and toss pillows provide a fresh, creative and inexpensive way to decorate, as they come in a wide variety of shapes, sizes, fabrics, textures, colors and patterns. They can liven up any room, create a dramatic effect or provide the perfect finishing touch.

One of the main jobs of pillows and cushions is to provide comfort and support. Just follow a few simple guidelines to take full advantage of their potential benefits.

FOR everyday use

- If you prefer a soft, warm pillow or cushion choose one filled with down and/or feathers.
- Take a look at specialty pillows filled with buckwheat, latex or memory foam, which offer better support for your neck.
- If you suffer from neck pain, consider a neckroll pillow that can relieve neck strain. Inflatable neck pillows are ideal for travel and don't take up much room in luggage.
- For back pain, try adding a relatively firm wedge cushion to the chair. The tapered angle of the wedge encourages correct posture, providing relief for your spinal column.
- Why not get some general purpose seat cushions for hard chairs, benches or stools? The cushions will increase comfort considerably.
- Choose fabrics that will harmonize with the rest of the decor.
- Floor pillows are both portable and comfy to stretch out on. They make wonderful spots for sleeping pets or napping children to curl up, while beanbag chairs provide remarkably comfortable, portable seats.

DECORATING with pillows

Providing comfort isn't a pillow's only function. When covered in attractive and appropriate fabrics, cushions and pillows can also play a central role in a home's decor.

- By decking out a sofa, armchair, futon or bench with accent or matching pillows, you can create a connection between the different kinds of seating or complement the overall design and color scheme of the room.

Clusters of pillows add a splash of color to a plain sofa and can tie in with a room's decor.

- Arrange pillows of different shapes and fabrics on a plain sofa. Vary patterns but stick to the same color for a pleasing effect.
- Opt for floral patterns, paisley or brocade for a country look. By contrast, simple upholstered furniture and a contemporary ambience tend to call for cushions with geometric patterns or brightly colored silk and velvet fabrics.

Decorating cushions

Cardboard stencil
Plain-colored cushion cover
Fabric paint
Fabric adhesive

First, cut your stencil to the desired shape or buy one ready made from a craft store and glue it on the cushion cover with fabric adhesive. Apply the fabric paint over the stencil then carefully remove it to reveal your new pattern.

Space saving

When the cupboards are bursting, bookshelves are overflowing and the computer is sitting on the dining room table, it's time to start finding ways to save space. Every home has a few empty nooks and crannies that can be pressed into service.

Most parts of the house have the potential to provide extra storage space, including the kitchen and family room, dining room, bedrooms, hallways and corridors. Evaluate all the potential space-saving areas that are available for extra storage before you decide how to proceed.

ADDITIONAL cupboards and shelves

- Create additional storage space under a pitched roof or a sloping staircase by adding a moveable closet on casters or a custom-built cabinet door.
- Turn a nook into a cabinet by installing a rod for clothing. The space between the clothes rod and the back wall should be the width of half your widest hanger. If there's no room for a door, install a roller blind or a curtain.

CREATE space in the bedroom

Bedrooms, especially children's bedrooms, can be a perennial problem but are not difficult to organize effectively. Here are a few ideas for making the best possible use of the space available.

- Use the space under the bed. Tuck away extra blankets or pillows for guests in drawers, low chests or sturdy boxes that are low enough to fit under the bed. A chest of drawers with casters and handles or loops is particularly easy to move in and out. This works best with a bed on a taller frame.
- If there is no space under the bed, hang shelves above it instead. If you want to store important but not particularly attractive objects on open shelves, use a set of matching decorative boxes to hide them away while keeping them in view.
- If you have a high-ceiling bedroom, consider installing a platform for the bed to turn it into a loft-style bed. In this way you will have created more space and can put the area beneath it to good use. What works best in this case will be a chest of drawers, a trunk or a set of shelves covered with cabinet doors.

USING hallways and corridors

Hallways and corridors can make up a large percentage of a home, yet they are rarely used as storage spaces. Why not put every nook and corner to work with custom-fitted shelves? Storage and hardware stores offer modular, multi-use shelving systems that can stretch the available storage space without stretching your budget. But there are all sorts of other solutions as well.

- Install a shelf or shelves over the front door or along one wall in the hall, as well as some hooks. This will make it easy to organize coats, boots and shoes, scarves and

There is plenty of extra room beneath a loft-style bed for cabinets and shelves.

GOOD TO KNOW

Proper storage

Pack articles of clothing in white tissue paper to protect them. A layer of blue tissue prevents white clothes from yellowing, and cedar chips between clothing help to guard against moths. Vacuum-sealed bags with vents make practical space-saving storage devices for bulky clothes and blankets—just put the items in the bag and suck out the air with a vacuum cleaner. Finally, store hats in hat boxes and stuff leather handbags with tissue paper so they keep their shape.

sporting equipment. You can use matching pull-out baskets to make everything look tidy and attractive. Or you might want to conceal it all behind a curtain or blind.

- Alternatively, instead of hiding the shelf away, why not try showcasing it instead? If you equip the shelf with halogen spotlights, it will become a welcoming island of light in the hallway.
- Another great idea is to build a small custom-made office or chest of drawers to go beneath a staircase in the hallway. A desk made exactly to fit and one or two shelves is perfect for using this potentially dead space.

STORAGE in the kitchen and dining room

A cozy kitchen will quickly become the hub of a home, so it is essential that there is enough storage space to keep it neat and uncluttered.

- Store larger items such as pots, pans and small appliances in the kitchen's floor level cabinets. For higher up, choose overhanging cabinets that are the right height. The topmost shelves, which you may only be able to reach with a stepladder, should contain any appliances or other items that you don't use frequently.
- Or, hang pans and utensils from a custom pot rack attached to the kitchen ceiling.
- Use unused nooks or corners to stow the kitchen garbage and recycling bins or a rack for kitchen towels.
- Install tall cabinets with vertical slide-out drawers that are accessible from two sides. They are versatile space savers, while a corner cabinet with a carousel makes good use of a space that often goes to waste.
- Remove large, rarely used items, such as catering-size pans or dishes, and keep them in the attic or a storeroom. Keep a list of what you have put away.

MORE space in children's rooms

Over time, most children's bedrooms accumulate a mind-boggling assortment of toys, clothes, books and crafts that all have to be stored somewhere.

- Here, again, a loft bed can provide valuable extra space. Put a desk underneath it.
- If there is no shelf space, hang a bag made from sturdy material or a mesh net from a ceiling hook for storing stuffed animals, balls and other toys.
- Use colorful baskets, boxes and chests to store toys. Make it easy for children to sort and put away their own toys at the end of the day by gluing a magazine picture of the contents (for example, cars, blocks, doll clothes) on each container.

Storage solutions

Cupboards, closets, dressers and shelves can easily become dusty and untidy. Organize your belongings in neat and decorative ways with functional furniture and a system that can help you create order from chaos.

In times past, people managed with much less space. Granted, they probably had fewer belongings, but even today it's possible to organize storage to make better use of the room available.

A TIDY closet

- Never overload clothes hangers, shelves and drawers. Clothing should be easy to remove and to put back.
- Select multi-armed hangers for use in a smaller closet.
- Make the best possible use of space by installing two clothing poles in the closet: One for longer clothes such as dresses and another for shorter ones such as shirts.
- Keep accessories such as scarves, ties, belts, stockings and gloves in a drawer. Alternatively, hang handbags, belts and ties from hooks on the inside of the closet door.
- Use drawer inserts for keeping items neat, organized and accessible.
- When you pack away seasonal clothes, dust your shelves. Dust mites are bad for fabric and people with allergies, and can make clothing appear dirty.
- Donate garments to charity if they no longer fit. Even if you do manage to get back into them, the chances are they will be out of fashion.

CHEST of drawers

Drawers of different depths can be useful. Store undergarments in shallow drawers and sweaters in deeper ones, for example. But consider the following when looking for a new chest of drawers.

- Check that the drawers slide smoothly.
- When stowing clothing in a drawer, leave about 1 inch (2.5 cm) clearance between the top edge and the contents so it can be opened and closed smoothly.
- Arrange the chest so you have enough room to put items in and take them out easily.
- Avoid storing heavy items in drawers or you'll risk breaking the bottoms.

SHELVES and glass cabinets

These are an obvious solution for storing and organizing, which is why they are everywhere. But there are a few things to consider.

- Open, decorative shelves make excellent room dividers—tastefully separating the dining area from the living room, for example—and they also provide storage. But, they do need to be dusted regularly.
- Opt for a cabinet with a glass door if you are not fond of dusting.

• When buying shelves, make sure they can accommodate the weight of whatever it is you are planning to store. Lightweight shelves may buckle or even break under a load of heavy books or tools.

CHESTS, dressers and sideboards

Nice as they are, a shelving unit or glass cabinet won't fit in every room. Sometimes a sideboard or dresser is the best solution.
• You can use a lovely old chest with no partitions to accommodate either large items of clothing or children's toys.
• Put a dresser or sideboard in the dining room or a large kitchen as a decorative storage place for dishes, glasses and silverware. It will also provide extra space for laying out food and drinks during a dinner party. If you don't have room for an attractive but heavy old antique piece of furniture, there are many streamlined models available today.

PRACTICAL aids

With a little creative flair it's possible to find a storage solution for practically every problem.
• Use decorative boxes to store off-season clothing or footwear, as well as seasonal decorations. Store them inconspicuously on the top shelf of the closet, under the bed or in the attic. By adding peepholes covered with plastic wrap or a photo of the contents, you can find what you need at a glance.
• Store clean cashmere and sweaters in ziplock plastic bags to prevent attack by moths.
• Wheeled trolleys allow you to store diverse items in an organized manner. A tool trolley is a classic example—it can be rolled out of its niche as needed.
• Magazine racks are practical, too—just don't forget to empty them regularly.
• Put up a peg-board with hooks to keep workshop tools neatly organized. Traced and painted outlines of the tools make organizing easy.
• Hooks are great for kitchen utensils and magnetic strips work well for knives.
• Sturdy plastic boxes are good for storing general household items.
• Paper clutter on countertops is a constant problem, from bills to school notices. Keep an expandable file folder in the kitchen with sections for significant categories. Tuck it away out of sight when not in use.
• Store all your instruction manuals in a box or binder in the kitchen.
• Store toys in see-through stackable containers that are clearly labelled. That way, kids can put them away themselves easily and favorite toys won't get buried at the bottom of a large box.
• Store bath toys in a mesh bag and hang it from the faucet or showerhead until it is fully drained.

A partitioned box with a transparent cover lets you see at a glance what's inside. Just store it under the bed when you don't need it.

Do-it-yourself decorative boxes

If you need some boxes for storing small household items, you don't need to spend a fortune. Shoe boxes can be spruced up with inexpensive art supplies.

one Select a suitably sized shoe box for the items to be stowed.

two Select wrapping paper or wallpaper that matches the decor and cut it to size.

three Spread wallpaper paste on the box and glue on the decorative paper.

four Glue the paper to the box. When it is dry, stow items away.

Wallpaper

Wallpaper is making a comeback. Not only can it look richer than paint, it gives rooms more dimension and can mask a wall that is uneven. Whether you opt for a muted color or bright patterns, wallpaper should create a unified look with the fabrics and the style of furnishings in a room without overwhelming the space.

Wallpapering is easier than you think. A few tips, some basic instructions and a little imagination are all you need to change the atmosphere of a room.

The color of this wallpaper works well with the sofa and accessories.

THE effect on a room

Wallpaper can have a significant impact on a room. It can subdivide and structure a room, as well as making it appear larger. The trend these days is to wallpaper only one or two walls rather than the entire space.

- Large patterns tend to dominate a room, making them ideal in a big room. In a small room or one full of nooks and crannies they can be overwhelming.
- Cover small rooms with a bright, monochromatic color or small patterns.
- To best show off a striking wallpaper pattern the furnishings should be low-key.
- Vertical lines on the wall make low ceilings appear higher, particularly if the ceiling is painted white.
- Before you start, get an idea of how a chosen wallpaper will look by holding a large piece of it against the wall.
- Textured wallpaper covers up small holes or lumps.
- Make a note of the serial or model number of the wallpaper you are buying so that you can find it again if you need more.
- To be sure you have enough, buy an extra roll or two—especially if you can return it if unused.

THE right choice

Your choice of wallpaper will depend on personal preference and where you will be using it, as well as on the skill of the installer.

Making fabric wall panels

By creating fabric panels for walls, you get all the drama of wallpaper but can easily change the patterns and colors.

one Pick up wooden frames for stretching canvas from a craft store (they can be different or uniform sizes) and cut the fabric so it is slightly bigger than the frames.

two Iron the fabric, position it on the frame and tack it down on one long edge with a staple gun.

three Stretch the fabric taut over the frame and staple the opposite long edge, followed by the short sides.

four Finish the corners by folding down the fabric as if wrapping a present, then staple it down. You now have a dramatic wall feature for little money or effort.

- Vinyl wallpaper is easy to handle and stands up to scrubbing and moisture fairly well, so it can be used in bathrooms, kitchens and children's bedrooms.
- Flocked wallpaper has raised "velvet" patterns and works well for creating decorative highlights and for formal areas such as dining rooms. It is washable, but can be damaged by rubbing and scrubbing.
- Grasscloth, made from a weave of grasses, is suited to areas that sustain little wear and tear.
- Fabric wallpaper is made of silk, cotton or linen, which is sometimes laminated to regular paper. It's not the easiest to keep clean and is fairly difficult to work with but is stunning in a formal setting, such as a dining room.
- Foil wallpaper is made of patterned metal foil. It can add an interesting touch and reflects light well but is unforgiving if it gets wrinkled or folded.

WALLPAPERING made easy

Once you have selected the wallpaper, roll up those sleeves and get to work.

- To remove old wallpaper, pierce it with a scoring tool and moisten it with water. A little white vinegar added to the water acts as a glue solvent.
- Turn off the electricity at the fuse box before moistening wallpaper, as power outlets and light switches can pose a danger.
- Repair holes and cracks in the walls with filler and sand them until smooth.
- Check the undercoat by sticking a piece of tape to the wall and pulling it off with a jerk. If the paint remains on the wall, the wallpaper will stick.
- Sand down painted walls to help the glue stick and eliminate unsightly bumps.
- Apply a coat of primer on dry plaster before beginning so that the wallpaper will stick.
- For a perfect finish, apply lining paper before adding the final paper.
- Repaint the room's trim and ceilings before you begin wallpapering, and protect furniture and rugs from drips with drop cloths.
- Always begin wallpapering at the edge of a window.
- Using a carpenter's level or plumb line, draw a vertical line from floor to ceiling as a guide to keep the paper straight. Repeat for each strip.
- Cut lengths of wallpaper about 4 inches (10 cm) longer than the height from ceiling to baseboard.
- Fill a tray with lukewarm water and dip each length of prepasted wallpaper for 30 seconds or more. Change the water every six to eight lengths.
- Match the edge of the first length to the plumb line you have drawn on the wall, leaving 2 inches (5 cm) of extra paper at the top of the ceiling.
- Match patterns exactly, and allow for them when calculating wallpaper amounts.
- Be especially thorough when gluing down the edges and corners of wallpaper seams.
- Trim excess paper at the top and bottom of the wall with a utility knife and ruler.
- Wipe wallpaper and baseboards with a damp sponge to remove excess glue. Rinse the sponge well or streaks will appear as the paper dries.

Draw a vertical line before positioning.

Window dressing

Coordinate curtains, drapes, blinds and accessories with the overall decor and proportions of a room. Choose window fabrics and decorative elements only after you have decided on the look you want to achieve.

Window coverings have to be functional as well as attractive. They protect a home from drafts, extremes of temperature and bright light, as well as from prying eyes.

CURTAINS for every style

There are several different kinds of window dressings, each with certain advantages.

- Voile or sheer curtains should limit the view outside as little as possible but, at the same time, they offer occupants their privacy.
- Heavier curtains can keep out blinding light and act as a privacy screen.
- Blinds are often a better alternative to sheer curtains in contemporary homes.
- For a classic contemporary look, use distinct shapes, geometrical patterns and bright colors.
- To create a luxurious effect, combine light sheer curtains with drapes of silk, cotton ubiquitous or damask.
- Heavy valences of tufted cord, brocade ubiquitous or velvet look sumptuous. They can be combined with curtains of tulle and gauze. But this striking combination requires a room with a high ceiling or it can look stifling.
- Pleated pull-up sheers or curtains made from light fabrics with flowery patterns set a romantic and playful theme.
- Use decorative tie-backs to add interest and maximize light levels in a room.

BLINDS are ADJUSTABLE AND infinitely variable.

SHORT or floor-length?

- Short curtains look rustic and suit ubiquitous short and square or wide, low windows. They stop just above the windowsill or a little below it.
- Arched sheer curtains are a good choice for windows with window boxes, because the floral contents remain in full view.
- Floor-length curtains enhance the high, narrow windows often found in older apartments and houses. They should reach to about 2 inches (5 cm) above the floor so that you can vacuum underneath easily.

THE effect on a room

- Choose floor-length curtains to make a room's windows look longer and the ceiling look higher.
- Install the curtain rod a little higher than the frame to make the window look taller.
- Use wide curtains to make a narrow, high window look broader.

• Create uniformity between windows of differing heights by hanging all curtains at the same height.

CURTAIN rods

These days, many windows are covered by venetian or other kinds of roll-up blinds, but the good old curtain and rod still have their place in many homes. Of course, hanging curtains isn't quite as simple as hanging the blinds that cover so many windows but, if done correctly, they can bring a comfortable, old-world allure to any room. Here are a few things to consider.

• Display window treatments to their best advantage by installing curtain rods not less than 6 inches (15 cm) above the window frame, extending at least the same distance beyond the sides of the window.

• If a windowsill sticks out a lot further than the wall, it is a good idea to install wood molding on the wall around the window first. Then, mount the brackets for the curtain rod on the molding.

• Install the rod so that it is almost touching the ceiling, or is attached to it, if you want the ceilings to appear higher.

DECORATION

Blinds and curtains aren't the only way to dress up a window. With a little creativity, you can use all sorts of items to add visual interest.

• Install stained glass windows to give a room an individual appearance and shield you from prying eyes outside, too.

WINDOW TREATMENTS GIVE free rein to YOUR CREATIVITY.

• Use the windowsill as a ready-made shelf for flowering or green plants. Or, add accessories such as elegant vases, pretty stones, ornaments or artistic flower arrangements.

• Install a glass shelf across the center of the window, then place small plants on the shelf. This is especially good for bringing a touch of green to the kitchen or any area that doesn't require the same level of privacy as, say, the bedroom. Just make ubiquitous sure that the plants are not too heavy.

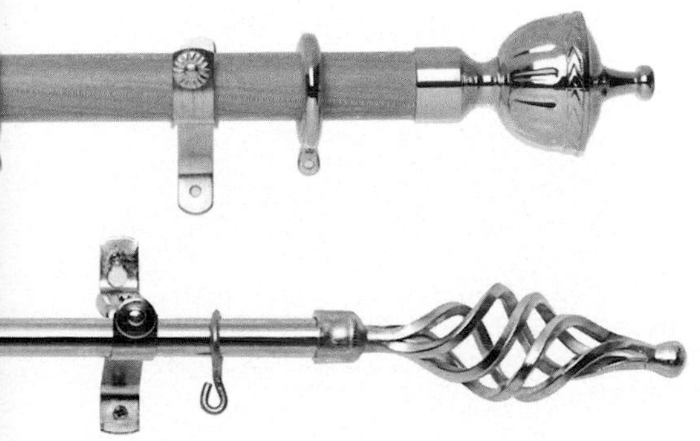

Curtain rod finials come in many shapes and materials.

Gardening with nature

Long before high-tech gadgets and chemical compounds were available, generations of gardeners combined art, nature and horticultural know-how to create flourishing gardens that were both productive and beautiful.

Bulbs

Crocuses, snowdrops and daffodils are among the first messengers of spring, whereas dahlias, gladioli and autumn crocuses flower into late autumn. These traditional garden plants don't require a lot of care and can easily be used to add color to a balcony or patio area if grown in pots.

The saying "the bigger, the better" really does apply to flowering bulbs, because the biggest bulbs are generally healthier and flower better.

MAKING the right selection

- Buy bulbs with undamaged outer skins and firm cores. If they are sprouting or exhibit decay, throw them out.
- Store bulbs that you can't plant right after purchasing in a cool, dark and airy place. Store rare and valuable varieties in the vegetable drawer of the refrigerator until they are ready to be planted.
- Plant lilies, lilies of the valley or glories of the snow (*Chionodoxa*) in shady areas; wood anemones (*Anemone blanda*) flourish in full shade. Daffodils will tolerate partial shade.

PROPER planting

- Flowering bulbs grow best in loose, porous soil. If the soil is heavy, fill planting holes with a layer of sand about ½–1 inch (1–2.5 cm) deep to keep bulbs from rotting when weather is wet and cold.

Plant spring-flowering plants such as irises, crocuses, grape hyacinths or tulips in the fall.

- Remember that the depth for planting should always be at least twice the height of the bulb.
- Follow the instructions on the packaging of lily bulbs carefully, as there are various considerations that will determine at what depth they are planted.
- Plant bulbs at different depths to get a nice, thick flowering. This produces better results, especially in restricted spaces such as a terra-cotta pot.
- Lightly water daffodils and fritillaries after planting. Their roots will grow more quickly in moist soil.
- Plant bulbs in plastic baskets, nets or wire mesh if you plan to take them out later. They will be easier to remove and will also be protected from rodents.
- Plant the tubers-flowering dahlias, gladioli or crocosmia in well-loosened, aerated soil with good drainage.

CULTIVATING bulbs

Most bulbs flourish beautifully without special care. They need little watering, which makes them ideal for areas with less rainfall or for gardeners who have little time.

- Put a stake in the ground at the same time as you plant tall-growing plants, such as gladioli or dahlias, that will need support later on. If you wait until the root system is already developed before driving a stake in, you risk damaging the plant.
- In damp regions, remove tulip bulbs after their leaves have wilted and store them until the autumn in a bed of sand or sawdust in a dry, dark place.
- Snip off the flowers of bulbs after they wilt in order to save them the energy needed to form seeds. Don't touch the leaves, however—the plant needs them to store nutrients for the winter. Keep them well watered, too, until leaves have died down.

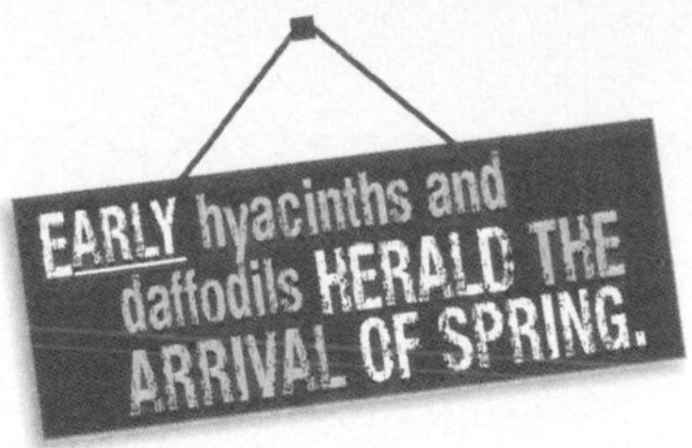

• If possible, plant bulbs, corms and tubers in different places each year to avoid the buildup of diseases caused by fungi or bacteria.

PROPAGATING bulbs

The propagation of bulbs is easy. Many form small bulbs or sprout tubers by themselves. These simply have to be detached from the parent plant and stored in a cool and sheltered place over the winter.

• Dig up bearded iris rhizomes every 2–3 years after plants have finished flowering. Divide them into several pieces and trim the leaves. Dispose of the oldest parts of the plants.

• Divide and move snowdrops immediately after flowering when they are still "in the green."

• Divide dahlia tubers with a knife before planting in spring. Each division should have a budding sprout.

PROPAGATING lilies through bulb scales

• Dig up the bulbs in the autumn and gently pull off four to six of the fleshy outer scales. Dust the wound on the parent plant with charcoal powder and replant.

• Place the scales to half their depth in a mixture of potting soil and sand. Keep them moist at room temperature by covering with plastic wrap. Don't expose to direct sunlight.

• When small bulbs with delicate roots form (in about 8 weeks), plant individually in small pots so that only the tips are visible and store in a dry, dark place at about 40°F (5°C). Or put the bulbs in a ziplock bag with propagating mix or fairly dry sphagnum moss and keep in the vegetable crisper in the fridge.

• Carefully plant bulbs as soon as the first delicate leaves sprout in the spring, choosing a day when it is not too cold.

A multilayered effect is created by planting low-flowering bulbs in front of high-stemmed lilies, narcissi or tulips.

Companion planting

A traditional means of repelling pests, companion planting has been used for many years to protect prized vegetables. Aromatic plants such as garlic, marigolds and peppermint are all reputed to send a signal to unwanted insects to go elsewhere.

Companion planting is a kind of botanical buddy system. It works on the principle that plants that grow together may interact and influence one another. Apart from removing certain nutrients from the soil, individual plants give off substances and fragrances that can be good or bad for their botanical neighbors.

To introduce companion planting, start by adding the new plants in the center of the bed. Partners that are harmonious generally have similar seeding or planting times.

Root excretions from French marigolds help to keep ravenous pests away from broccoli.

GOOD TO KNOW

Harmonious partners

Make sure that plant varieties tolerate one another when introducing companion planting. Tomatoes go well with lettuce, cabbage, carrots, radishes, beets, celery, spinach and parsley, but not with potatoes, cucumbers, fennel and peas. Potatoes go well with horseradish but not with sunflower, tomato or cucumber. Improve spinach crops by combining them with peas and beans.

ADVANTAGES of companion planting

- Companion planting uses far less water. Since the companion plants grow close together and shade the ground more effectively, less moisture is able to evaporate.
- Because the plants are closer together, you get a higher yield per surface area.
- Companion planting tends to require less fertilizer because the plants absorb different nutrients from different soil depths, as well as excreting beneficial elements into the soil.
- Many plants enhance their neighbor's flavor. Caraway and cilantro improve the taste of early potatoes, and dill intensifies the taste of carrots.
- Pests are less drawn to gardens where companion planting is employed because some plants form a protective shield for others by means of their scent.
- Garlic can prevent mildew and kills many fungi when planted near fruit trees.
- Nematodes can't stand the root excretions from lilies or marigolds, while tomatoes and basil drive away asparagus beetles.
- With carrots and onions you can kill two flies with one blow: They help protect each other from both carrot fly and onion fly infestations.
- Grow fennel to attract aphid-eating ladybugs.
- Nasturtiums deter aphids, protecting a whole range of garden plants.
- Choose the right companion plants to reduce, if not eliminate, the need for pesticides. Eliminating pests will result in higher yields.

Compost

There is no need to spend large sums on modern plant feeds—the simplest and least expensive fertilizer is compost from your own garden. When well mixed over the course of a year, kitchen and garden waste turns into nutrient-rich humus, one of the best fertilizers you can find.

GOOD TO KNOW

Do not compost

Weedy trees or shrubs; root-spreading perennial weeds; newspaper printed in color; thick paper and cardboard; fresh leaves, which are best put in large plastic bags and allowed to rot for six months to a year, but can then be composted; food remains such as meat and meat products that attract pests (although eggshells are fine—they just need to be crushed first).

With a compost pile you are basically recycling nature, and the greater the variety of materials used, the richer the subsequent compost will be. After as little as 3–4 months it may be possible to have raw or fresh compost, which is best for mulching or autumn fertilizing of the vegetable patch. However, compost needs about a year to ripen fully. You will know when it is ready because it becomes fine, crumbly and dark, like fresh soil.

MATERIALS for the compost pile

All healthy, organic materials that rot within a year can be added to the compost pile. The following things can all be added.

- Kitchen waste, including vegetable and fruit peelings, cores, pods and stems (as long as they haven't been sprayed with pesticides); spoiled or dried-out foods; coffee grounds, tea bags and tea leaves; crushed eggshells; and paper filters.
- Paper from napkins, paper towels, uncoated paper and paper bags for disposal of biodegradable waste: best shredded before adding.
- Garden waste such as shredded tree, hedge and shrub cuttings; residue from flowers and perennials; roots (but not those of perennial weeds); and weeds without seeds.
- Grass cuttings can be added in thin layers, preferably mixed with coarser material so that enough air still gets into the compost pile. It also prevents grass from turning slimy in the bin.
- Potting soil, cut flowers, potted plants with soil and small pieces of untreated scrap wood.

Keep animals out of the compost by securing the opening with chicken wire.

MAKING a compost pile

- A compost pile should be formed right on the top of the soil, never on stones or concrete. It needs contact with the earth, so creatures that contribute to rotting can easily get in and the resulting seepage can run off easily.
- A partially shaded location is ideal for a compost pile. In bright sunlight the compost will dry out and in the shade it may rot. However, give an enclosed plastic bin full sun, as it helps contents to rot quickly.
- Use the three-pile method for large gardens. Use the first pile for garden waste, which can be moved into a second heap in the winter. This can be left to ripen. By the following winter, the ripe compost can be sifted and moved to the third pile for use in the garden.
- Lay coarse wood cuttings to make up the first layer of the compost. Place a little soil on top and then pile on the compost material to a depth of about 3 feet (1 m).
- Add a judicious sprinkling of lime sand or rock dust on each layer to provide the compost with important minerals and trace elements.
- A composter with sliding panels at the bottom enables you to remove compost from the base. Removable sides are also helpful.
- A wire-bin composter with a hinged front provides easy access.

COMPOST must be ACCESSIBLE SO IT CAN be turned regularly.

Cress test for readiness

one Plant a little cress in a bowlful of material from the compost pile.

two If it sprouts in two to three days and develops green leaves, the compost is ripe and okay to use even for sensitive plants.

three If nothing sprouts or the cress develops yellow leaves, the compost is still too fresh for using in the garden—you'll have to wait.

ENCOURAGING the composting process

- A few shovels of garden soil or a herbal slurry (*see page 212*) can be used to speed up the rotting process. Or use a biologically formulated compost accelerator.
- Occasionally spray the compost with an undiluted slurry made from dandelion or nettle, or a thinned-down borage extract.
- Plant comfrey beside your composter and add a few leaves each week to the mix. The chemical allantoin contained in comfrey encourages the rotting of plant remains that contain cellulose.

SPECIAL considerations

- Compost needs a certain amount of moisture and should feel like a sponge that has been squeezed out. A grayish-white coating or lots of ants mean that the compost material is too dry and must be watered.
- Good ventilation is also crucial. Use a pole to poke ventilation holes down to ground level.
- Turn the compost every six months or so.
- Surround a fairly small compost pile with a trellis on which nasturtium, vetches or other climbers can grow. Sunflowers are also good for concealing a compost pile.
- Fragrant plants can be used to combat the smell of rot but they are often unnecessary. A well-balanced compost should smell like fresh forest soil.
- Collect leaves separately in a covered circle made of wire mesh. They'll decompose more quickly and their acidic qualities will promote the growth of azaleas and camellias. Or pack leaves into large plastic bags and let them rot for two years.

Feeding and revitalizing

For centuries, gardeners relied on natural nutrient sources such as cow manure. Then chemical fertilizers became popular because they were inexpensive and easy to handle. But as concern for the environment grows, it is time to go back to organic methods to improve the soil and grow lush, healthy plants.

Green fertilizing involves improving soil quality by planting specific crops with roots that will penetrate the earth to provide thorough aeration. Generally, they are dug into the soil before they flower to enrich it. The results may not be immediate but you will be rewarded with a healthier garden.

Mix compost and cow manure into new garden beds with a pitchfork.

GREEN manure

- Leave small quantities of grass clippings and leaves spread out across the garden and lawn to decompose and enrich the soil.
- Use green fertilization for empty areas and places with some permanent crops such as strawberries, rhubarb, roses and asparagus.
- Green-fertilizing plants that are sown in the spring should be mowed or cut down shortly before they flower, then chopped up and raked in to enrich the soil.
- Leave green-manure plants sown in the autumn to stand through the winter, then mow or dig them in during the spring.
- Prevent diseases by ensuring that green-fertilizing plants belong to a different plant family from that of the next vegetable crop.
- Sow seeds of phacelia (blue tansy) in any kind of soil in spring and summer. It grows quickly, is easy to care for and attracts bees and dragonflies.
- Dig green-manure plants in just before they flower, when they are most nutrient rich.
- Plant fava beans, fenugreek and vetches in the cooler months. They are frost-tolerant, can help to break up clay soil and add plenty of organic matter.
- Use mustard for medium–heavy soils, but don't plant vegetables from the cabbage family in that soil for the next two to three years.

NATURAL fertilizers

Organic fertilizers spread easily and continue working for a long time.

- Use compost from waste from the garden and kitchen, a good source of nitrogen for the soil when added to the garden in the spring. Work it in to a depth of 1–2 inches (2–5 cm).
- Before applying horse manure, make sure it is well rotted or composted or it will burn the plants. If you buy it fresh, first pile it in a heap, water it thoroughly and cover it with a sheet of plastic so that it stays moist and rots. Spread it in the autumn and work it into the soil well. You can plant cabbages, lettuces and pumpkins immediately, but wait a year before planting beans, peas, carrots and radishes.
- Spread commercially available dried manure on the beds as a top dressing or use it as an effective composting accelerator.
- Spread blood and bone—which contains phosphorus and calcium—in springtime. Mix it into the soil to encourage healthy growth in young shrubs and dose potted plants on occasion, too. Water it in well.
- Hoof and horn meal is an organic fertilizer that is easily absorbed by the soil and offers a quick supply of nitrogen, phosphorus and potassium. It can be spread throughout the year, especially before sowing. Use ¼–½ cup (60–90 g) per 10 square feet (1 m^2).

• Fertilize potatoes, carrots, tomatoes, celery and roses with wood ash from an indoor fireplace or wood stove. In spring, spread the fine powder thinly in furrows or holes and lightly work it into the soil.
• An occasional milk fertilization benefits ferns, roses and tomatoes. Mix milk or whey with water in a 1:5 ratio. The plant roots will drink up the amino acids from the milk. If sprayed on the leaves, the solution helps prevent mildew.
• Sandy soil needs fertilizer and added nitrogen, as rain leaches away many of its nutrients. It also needs compost to improve its texture and water retention.
• Crushed eggshells are a good source of calcium and they are especially useful in acidic soil as they raise the pH level. Another benefit: If you scatter them around tender young plants, their jagged edges discourage slugs and other pests.
• Put coffee grounds directly on the flower bed to fertilize plants and keep slugs and snails away. You are unlikely to generate enough coffee grounds to fertilize the entire garden, so you will have to use other fertilizers as well.

Nettle slurry

4 cups (1 kg) fresh or 2/3 cup (150 g) dried nettle leaves
10 quarts (10 L) water

Crush the nettles in a large bucket. Add water and thoroughly immerse the plants. Cover with plastic wrap or a lid and let ferment for 3 weeks, stirring daily; strain. Use diluted 1:4 with water as a plant tonic to strengthen resistance to disease, but only on overcast days.

FEED your garden naturally

Natural preparations made from herbs and leaves can be used as tonics to fortify plants against pests, diseases and fungus. Dilute them with rainwater if possible or otherwise with tap water that has been allowed to sit so that the chlorine and fluoride it contains can dissipate.
• Create an extract by soaking 4 cups (1 kg) leafy plants in 10 quarts (10 L) cold water for at least 24 hours. Strain the liquid and use diluted 1:4 as a plant spray. Nettle extract will help to keep pests away; garlic extract with a little added liquid soap combats aphids, and prevents and treats fungal diseases.
• Make a herbal broth by mixing equal parts of the herbal extract (made as above) and cold water. After letting the mixture sit for about a day, boil it gently for about 30 minutes. Allow to cool and apply around plants as a tonic.
• Basil infusion is an excellent spray weapon to use against aphids and two-spotted mites. Place 8 teaspoons (40 g) dried leaves in a bowl and pour 1 quart (1 L) boiling water over them. Allow the mixture to steep for about 10 minutes. Strain and use the liquid undiluted when cool.
• Make a slurry by soaking about 4 cups (1 kg) fresh herbs or leafy plants—or ⅔ cup (150 g) dried in 1 quart (1 L) water for 10–20 days, stirring daily. Use diluted 1:10 with water. Birch leaf slurry (made with fresh leaves) helps to prevent fungus on leaves and fruit; fresh dandelion leaf slurry promotes a better-quality yield from most berry bushes and fruit trees.

Flower beds and borders

When planning and planting a flower bed, bear in mind that the soil condition and position of the bed each play an important role. Ideally, you should choose plants that flower at different times so your garden always looks colorful and fresh.

If you select plants carefully, your garden will reward you with an almost constant display throughout the seasons, whether in sun or shade.

THE right plants

- Make a seasonal bed that positions early-flowering alliums next to colorful perennials. French marigolds, geraniums and pansies all flower for a long time.
- Shade-loving plants include cyclamen, begonias, anemones, epimediums, lady's mantle, lilies of the valley, bergenia and plectranthus.
- Damp, shade-tolerant flowers include hellebores, foxgloves, hostas and periwinkle, as well as primulas and snowdrops.
- In the summer, plant ornamental grasses to create an attractive visual island within a flower bed. These grasses are eye-catchers until late autumn and can also be used to add a romantic note to summer flower bouquets.
- Plant some poppies, lupines and delphiniums for an early summer flower bed. Peonies and multicolored hollyhocks are also a good choice.
- To add structure during winter, mix in some small evergreen shrubs. Good choices include gardenia and rhaphiolepis, as well as winter-flowering daphne and hellebores. Fill gaps with winter annuals such as pansies and primulas.
- Create flower bed variety by using plants with attractive leaf shapes or shrubs with colorful bark or fruit. Try crepe myrtle or hibiscus.
- Look for lots of buds, good branching and a well-developed, moist rootball when you are choosing plants to buy.

SALVIAS, RUDBECKIA and COSMOS add vibrant COLOR in SUMMER.

GOOD TO KNOW

Cutting flowers

Here are the ground rules: Cut flowers in the early morning and buds in the evening. Cut irises, daffodils, carnations, marigolds, roses, daylilies and tulips as buds. But gladioli, anemones, snapdragons, lupines, peonies, liatris and delphiniums should be partly open when picked. Asters, azaleas, chrysanthemums, dahlias, rudbeckia and sunflowers are at their best in the vase only when you pick them fully opened.

PLANNING the layout of the flower bed

Use a detailed plan to make the work much easier. It will reduce costs as well, because you will end up with the right plants in the right quantities. If you are a novice gardener, start with a few fairly easy-to-care-for varieties.

- First prepare a sketch, complete with a planting diagram. Take into account the size of the plants when grown and note sunny or shady areas.
- Bear in mind that flower beds should never be too narrow. Many plants like to spread out, so leave enough space between them.
- Use a vertical planting scheme for a tiered effect: Set out taller plants in the center of the garden or at the back edge; place the medium-sized plants in front of them; and put the lowest plants right in front.

EDGING and maintaining the bed

A flower bed doesn't have to be angular. You can create precise outlines in other shapes, too.

A set of hand tools comes in handy for smaller jobs.

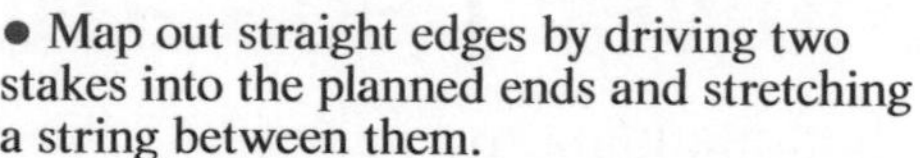

- Map out straight edges by driving two stakes into the planned ends and stretching a string between them.
- Lay out round, oval and elliptical beds by using a garden hose as a guide.
- Create irregularly shaped flower borders by outlining them in sand or stones.
- Use stepping-stones to make it easier to access hard-to-reach spots in the garden without treading on the plants. They also help to keep the soil looser as you won't compact it by walking on it.

Draw everything in the garden to scale, including intended plantings.

- Add a layer of mulch between plants to keep soil damp and weeds at bay.
- For a more formal or Asian-style flower bed, use white gravel or pebbles for the same purpose.

PROBLEM locations

Use a little forethought and effort to establish flower beds in some of the problem areas of the garden.

- Protect new plants from sliding down a slope in the rain by covering the soil with mulch. Or terrace a slope to create flat areas for planting.
- Put plants that tolerate more moisture at the foot of a slope where runoff accumulates.
- Situate plants that tolerate dry soil in front of a wall. The soil there warms up more, especially if it receives plenty of direct sun.
- Lay drought-tolerant plants at the corners of a garden, because these areas often dry out quickly.
- Create shade for sensitive plants in sunny gardens by using shrubs and small trees.

Gardening tools

You don't have to spend a fortune filling the toolshed with every gadget on the market, but you will need some basic gardening equipment to keep your garden looking its best.

"You get what you pay for" is a traditional adage, and you will pay a premium for high-quality gardening tools. But well-made, sturdy tools—a spade, rake, watering can, garden hose, shears and trowel—will last a long time, so it is worth the extra expense in the long run.

LOOKING for quality

- Opt for spades and pitchforks made from stainless or chrome-plated steel. They are expensive but the most durable and don't rust.
- Choose small garden tools in bright neon colors—they'll be easier to find in the grass or among weeds. The handles themselves can also be painted.
- Avoid buying gardening tools from a catalog or online. It is a good idea to try them out and see how they feel in your hands—and to check that they are not too heavy or too large.
- Where possible or appropriate, select tools that have extendable handles to make garden work much easier on the back.

Avoid damage to gardening tools by cleaning them thoroughly, then drying the metal and wood parts.

GOOD TO KNOW

Protection for working in the garden

Gloves and sensible footwear are key for working effectively and safely in the garden. For jobs that require kneeling, such as weeding or planting, knee protection is a good idea. Even a bag stuffed with rags or an old cushion will do the trick. In order to keep your fingernails clean, scratch them over a bar of soap before heading out to the garden. By filling the space between your nails and your fingers with soap, you can help keep dirt at bay.

CARE extends the service life

- Remove soil, grass cuttings or dirt immediately after using a gardening tool.
- Clean stubborn dirt from the cutting edges of clippers with warm, soapy water.
- Prevent rust on metal surfaces by wiping them with an oil-moistened rag after use.
- Wrap uncomfortable handles with a little foam material for extra cushioning.
- Use a medium wire brush to remove encrusted grass clippings from under the lawn mower.

PREPARATION for storage

- Sharpen the large blades of scythes or sickles with a whetstone and smaller blades with a file. Store in a toolshed or indoors, safe from the elements—but away from small fingers.
- Oil wooden handles and shafts with linseed oil to keep them smooth.
- Clean metal parts of tools with fine steel wool. Remove a light coat of rust by sanding it with medium-coarse sandpaper.
- Don't keep metal tools on the floor. To prevent them from becoming damp and rusting, place them on a shelf or hang them from hooks screwed to the wall. Store the lawn mower on a wooden plank.
- Do not leave any wood or metal tools in the garden. Keep everything in a toolshed or indoors for protection against the weather.

Herb gardens

Herbs were once a standard feature in a kitchen garden, grown for both flavoring and medicinal properties. A ready supply of fresh herbs is just as useful today—home-grown plants look good in the garden and are often tastier and cheaper than store-bought ones.

Most herbs like a sunny area with loose soil, although some, such as parsley and chervil, do best in partial shade. Raised spiral herb gardens built up with rocks and soil have been used for many generations to get maximum productivity out of small spaces. They also tend to suffer from fewer pests and the garden is accessible from all sides. The basic design calls for a spiral or layer of rocks, enclosing soil in which many species of herbs can be planted. The rocks warm the soil and the design allows for a wide variety of soil conditions.

GOOD TO KNOW

Fertilizing in moderation yields better taste

Only natural fertilizers should be used in an herb bed, if any are used at all. The plants lose flavor if they get too much of a good thing. A little compost worked into the soil is ideal, plus weekly liquid fertilizing.

CREATING an herb spiral

- Plant an herb spiral in spring or autumn on at least 32 square feet (3 m^2). Sketch the shape in advance.
- Add a small pool about 30 inches (80 cm) deep at the beginning of the spiral. Line it with pond liner and reinforce with stones.
- Dig out the remainder of the herb bed to the depth of a shovel and fill it with an 80:20 mixture of soil and well-rotted compost or manure. Create a small mound about 3 feet (1 m) high in the center of the bed and reinforce it in a spiral shape with stones.
- Fill the upward-spiraling bed with different types of soils to create the following areas.

1 In and around the pond at the base of the spiral, the loamy soil should stay moist. Watercress and water mint will thrive here.
2 The next level provides a sunny, compost-rich moist zone. Plant basil, chervil, dill, garlic mustard, parsley, peppermint, sorrel, chives, garlic chives and wild arugula.
3 The middle sector may be partly shaded, with rather dry humus soil creating the best conditions for fennel, cilantro, lovage, tarragon, oregano, marigold and hyssop.
4 Plant warm-climate herbs in the dry zone at the top of the spiral. This is where savory, lavender, marjoram, sage and thyme grow best. The soil is permeable and water will drain down naturally to the lower levels where you have planted herbs that need more moisture.

Plants find ideal conditions in the limited space of an herb spiral, and more plants can fit in a small area.

Pick leaves and flowers by hand, but cut off tougher stems with gardening scissors.

MAINTAINING the herb garden

- Give tough-leaved herbs such as bay and rosemary only a little water—they don't usually require much.
- Make sure water is able to run off effectively through a drainage layer of gravel or topsoil.
- Hoe the ground between herbs regularly to keep it loose and let the water soak in.
- If the pH of the soil is less than 5, add garden lime to give herbs an additional source of calcium and magnesium. Varieties that thrive with its help include savory, tarragon, caraway, marjoram, mint, parsley, rosemary, chives and thyme.
- Plant a hedge of boxwood, lavender or hyssop to protect herbs from wind and frost.
- Cut back bushy herbs like lavender and thyme in the autumn to prevent frost damage.
- Keep herbs from spreading out too much by cutting them regularly. Thin out perennials like oregano each autumn.
- Plant mint and lemon balm in pots to restrict their growth. They can form strong runners that quickly take over the entire bed.
- Seed annual herbs in a different location every year. This form of herbal crop rotation will help to keep the soil from becoming too depleted.
- Many herbs need room: Lovage and fennel have large roots that can damage adjacent plants.

HARVESTING herbs and seeds

- Gather herbs and seeds in late morning for the best flavor.
- Collect the seeds of dill, fennel, cilantro and lovage when they turn from green to brown.
- Dig up garlic before plants flower and before the leaves dry up—that way the bulbs keep better.
- Harvest most herbs before they flower, otherwise their flavor fades or (in the case of sage) disappears. Lavender, thyme and oregano can, however, be harvested at flowering time.
- Pick lemon balm in the afternoon when the leaves develop their greatest intensity before, or just after, the flowers open.

Kitchen gardens

A kitchen garden is a long-standing part of horticultural tradition and garden design. Part of its charm is that it combines the beauty of flowers with useful plants like herbs and vegetables, which you can pick fresh and enjoy while they're still bursting with flavor.

We can thank medieval monks for developing gardening culture. As they became aware of the benefits of mixed plantings for protecting gardens from pests, these monks increasingly grew medicinal plants and flowers along with their vegetables and fruit. As early as the 16th century, the rural population of Europe used these cloister gardens as a model for their own gardens.

THE structure of a kitchen garden

- A kitchen garden can offer so much more variety than a simple vegetable patch. A kitchen garden should be laid out on flat ground so that it's sheltered from the wind but receives plenty of sun. If possible, the minimum size of the kitchen garden should be about 270 square feet (25 m^2).
- To avoid bending over, consider making raised beds. Constructed from stone, brick or wood, they become an attractive feature, add height and structure to your garden and improve drainage.
- Plant carefully. It's important to consider the height and width of growth to be sure that one crop doesn't shade another from the sun. And take into account which vegetables should or shouldn't be grown together (*see "Companion planting," page 208*). Select varieties that will mature or ripen at different times during the summer and autumn, so that you are guaranteed a continuous supply of fresh produce.
- Before you cultivate the patch, make a sketch. It should show the location of beds, pathways, possible sitting areas and desired plantings. This will make seeding and harvesting much easier.
- For a traditional kitchen garden, use a four-square design based on the intersection of two major paths within a symmetrical, enclosed area. When laying out the pathways, take into account the width of the plants that will grow along their edges.
- Use intersecting pathways in the plan so you can reach garden beds to plant, care for and harvest fruit, vegetables and flowers easily.
- Delineate pathways with ease by lining them with hedges that grow no taller than 20 inches (50 cm).
- Save space in a smaller kitchen garden by edging individual beds with marigolds,

Plant marigolds—they add color and help to deter aphids.

other perennials and even chives and herbs.

- Start laying out a kitchen garden in the autumn by planting the trees and shrubs, keeping in mind their eventual height and the shade they will create.

CENTER and edging

- If you have enough room, consider planting a circular flower bed in the center, perhaps with a fountain or standard rosebush as a focal point.
- Alternatively, you could place a wooden or cement basin in the center for collecting rainwater. Disguise a less attractive rain barrel with climbing plants.
- Or install a small gazebo or bench under an arch covered with climbing plants in the center of the kitchen garden.
- For larger areas and a more formal look, enclose the kitchen garden with a fence, hedge or shrubs. The solid green foliage of hedges and shrubs provides an attractive backdrop for multicolored plantings and keeps the kitchen garden from looking too busy.
- Incorporate trellis plants if the garden abuts a wall of the house. Beans are a good option.

PLANTS for a kitchen garden

In a kitchen garden, plants are generally laid out close to one another in mixed plantings. The benefits are that soil doesn't get depleted, vermin and diseases don't spread, you don't have to fertilize too much and you get a large yield with little effort.

DELINEATE PATHWAYS by lining them WITH low hedges.

- Include heirloom varieties of vegetables such as parsnips, beans and tomatoes, with fun-to-grow orange beets and purple potatoes and carrots.
- Plant medicinal and culinary herbs such as valerian, savory, dill, oregano, chamomile, garlic and peppermint between the vegetables.
- Introduce aromatic plants, such as sweet pea, phlox, sage and centifolia roses. They attract butterflies and bees, important for pollination.
- To ensure variety, include self-propagating perennials like columbine and fennel, and biennials such as foxglove and evening primrose.
- Plant marigolds, as they flower abundantly in summer and autumn. The flowers can be eaten or used as a medicinal herb to prevent infections. In addition, they help to ward off aphids and nematodes.
- Place tall flowers such as delphiniums and sunflowers against a fence or hedge, where their long stems can get support.
- Crop rotation reduces the need for fertilizer and helps to prevent pests and diseases.

Lawns

A well-kept lawn is a huge asset to a property, and can even add value. But whether it consists of decorative grass, a play area or simply ground cover, it needs to be laid out and maintained properly.

There are a few important considerations before seeding a lawn, including soil quality and what type of seed would grow best. For routine care you'll need a lawn mower, rake, pitchfork, hose and sprinkler.

PLANNING a new lawn

- Check the soil quality (*see "Soil," page 236*). Is it heavy, light, rocky, acidic or alkaline? You will need to know in order to prepare the ground properly.
- Choose sod or grass seed according to how you plan to use the lawn. If children or animals are going to romp around on it, opt for a heavy-duty variety.

PREPARING the soil and buying seed

The first step is to remove all roots, rocks and any construction waste, and thoroughly dig up the ground at least 2 weeks before sowing a lawn.

1 If the soil is very heavy, mix in some sand for better aeration and permeability. Enhance soil that's lacking organic matter with compost until it's dark in color.

2 At the same time, level out uneven areas with a rake and, on fairly large surfaces, pack it down with a light lawn roller. Then let the soil settle. Be careful not to overcompact it.

3 For best results, sow seed in spring while the ground is damp.

4 Spread the seeds evenly by first practicing with sand, or make a spreader by drilling small holes in the bottom of an old can.

5 Choose a day with as little wind as possible. Spread half the seeds in one direction and half in the opposite direction.

6 Sow by sections and, on larger surfaces, mark off individual sections with string. Sow more heavily at the edge, so the lawn comes in thicker there.

7 Rake the seeds into the soil just a little so they don't blow away and can sprout properly. Pack down the seeds with the

Lay the sod rolls close together on well-prepared level soil.

Water can soak in more effectively through aeration holes made in the lawn with a pitchfork.

lawn roller or opt for a low-tech solution: footboards tied to the bottom of your shoes.
8 Finally, sprinkle water on the seeds, but avoid washing them away. Don't apply mineral fertilizer during the first two weeks—it will retard rather than enhance germination.

MOWING and watering the lawn

How often the lawn requires mowing depends on the thickness of the turf. The cut grass should be no shorter than about 1 inch (2.5 cm). Shorter lawns burn easily in the summer.

- Mow a new lawn for the first time when the blades of grass are around 2–2½ inches (5–6 cm) long.
- Shorten the lawn by no more than about 1¼ inch (3 cm) per mowing. If it's still longer than you want, wait for a few days before mowing it again
- Leave the cuttings where they fall to provide nutrients to the soil and shade the lawn's roots. Excess cuttings can be composted.
- Water thoroughly once a week during summer dry spells. The soil should be moist down to about 6 inches (15 cm), so the grass can form deep roots.
- During hot weather, minimize evaporation by watering in early morning or after 6 p.m.

LAWN care

Dethatching or aerating will help to get old or untidy lawns back in shape.

- Dethatching involves using a rake to pull out the thick mat of dead grass and roots that accumulate under the living green blades of the lawn. Normally, you should dethatch or scarify the lawn in spring or early fall, every 1–2 years.
- Aeration helps combat waterlogging. Make holes about 3–4 inches (7–10 cm) deep with a pitchfork.
- Spread fine sand over the surface of the lawn to deal with minor waterlogging. Worms will bury it when it rains.
- Use nitrogen fertilizers in the spring; in the autumn, opt for a fertilizer that contains more phosphate to stimulate root formation. Apply fertilizers high in nitrogen only in wet weather.
- Keep off the grass in freezing weather or the blades could break and leave unappealing tracks.
- If a section at the edge of the lawn is damaged, cut it out vertically and put it into the resulting hole upside down. Then even out the spot with a little soil, sprinkle some seeds on it and carefully water the area.

Patching bald spots on the lawn

one Dig up the area with a spade and loosen the soil with a rake.

two Remove all weed roots and smooth out the surface.

three Add a mixture of sand and compost to the area and sow grass seed. Compress and water.

Organic pest control

A spray gun loaded with noxious chemicals may combat attacks by aphids, but at what price? Plants survived for years before pesticides appeared on the scene, and there are still natural ways to deal with pests.

You can fight aphids, flea beetles, wire-worms, cabbage white caterpillars, slugs, snails, two-spotted mites and ants with plant-based sprays, or use other plants that will repel the unwanted invaders with their scent or excretions from their roots.

Nasturtiums protect ornamental and vegetable plants from aphids.

ANTS

- Sprinkle ant trails that lead towards the house or patio with the leaves of fragrant herbs such as chervil, lavender, mint, thyme or juniper, with spices such as chile pepper or with salt. The pungency of the herbs or spices not only repels the ants, it disrupts the scent trail that the scouts leave behind for other ants to follow.
- If you plant ferns, lamb's lettuce or tansy, ants will avoid rather than enter your garden.

Fighting aphids with tansy

1 cup (200 g) fresh or 2 tablespoons (30 g) dried tansy leaves
1 quart (1 L) water

Boil the leaves in water and steep for 1 hour. Dilute the tea with water in 1:1 ratio and spray on affected plants. Or pour or spray a tansy slurry made of 1¼ cups (300 g) of fresh leaves and 10 quarts (10 L) of water twice a week. Tansy is poisonous, so take special care around children and animals.

APHIDS

- Plant fennel or cilantro between plants to protect shrubs. For roses, you can plant garlic, lavender or French marigolds.
- If plants are already infested, spray them in the morning with a strong jet of water or a mild detergent solution. A spray made from tansy or nettle tea will also help.
- Encourage ladybugs in the garden—their larvae devour aphids.

FLEA beetles

- Flea beetles attack brassicas of all kinds, including arugula and bok choy. They like to take up residence in planters, but if you stick a few matches (the wooden variety is best) head first into the soil, they disappear. The sulfur dissolved by watering drives them away without harming the plant.
- Tuck one or two cloves of garlic in potting soil to get the same effect.
- Sprinkle wood ashes or sawdust in the pot or flower box in dry weather.
- If you plant peppermint, lettuce or onions, flea beetles should avoid your garden.
- Coat a piece of cardboard with Vaseline and run it through a row of plants. Flea beetles will stick to it.

WIREWORMS

Wireworms can eat their way into crops of carrots, turnips, beets and celery—but potatoes are the most susceptible of all.

- Make carrot traps by cutting pieces of carrot and pushing them 2–4 inches

Garlic and chile spray

¼ cup (50 g) crushed garlic
4 hot chilies
⅔ cup (150 ml) liquid paraffin
10 cups (2.5 L) water
⅔ cup (150 g) pure soap

Pour the paraffin over the garlic and leave for 48 hours. Add the remaining ingredients and mix thoroughly, then strain the mixture well. Store the solution in a glass bottle, away from sunlight. To spray, dilute at the rate of one part garlic and chile solution to three parts water. Wear gloves and take care when using, as chile is an irritant to skin and eyes.

(5–10 cm) below the soil surface. Pull them up and dispose of them—and the wireworms they have attracted—every 2–3 weeks.
- Harvest potatoes as soon as they mature rather than leaving them in the ground.
- Sow a crop of green manure (*see page 211*), such as mustard, next to potatoes in late summer. It will attract wireworms away from the crop.

CARROT flies

These pests lay their eggs on young plants, and then the developing larvae riddle the crop with tunnels. They locate plants by scent. As plants are vulnerable after thinning or weeding, do these jobs on dry days.
- Separate each row of carrots with two rows of onions or garlic. Mulch each row with grass cuttings.
- Mix carrot seed with a packet of mixed annuals, such as French marigolds, and sow. Or plant sage and rosemary close to carrots to help deter them.

CABBAGE white butterflies

The larvae of these butterflies are harmful to all types of cabbage and other plants in the mustard family, including horseradish, kale and broccoli.
- Collect the caterpillars and kill them if the infestation is not too severe. The worst time for these pests is in spring and summer.
- Plant mixed crops including mugwort, peppermint, sage, celery, thyme and tomatoes as a preventive measure, or protect vegetables with fine netting.

SLUGS and snails

These pests are a threat to all young and soft-leaved plants. Address as soon as possible.
- Place scooped-out grapefruit halves cut side down in garden beds. Slugs will accumulate inside overnight.
- Sprinkle coffee grounds around garden beds—the caffeine they contain deters and poisons slugs and snails. Reapply the grounds after a rain.
- Bury a glass jar or smooth plastic container in the soil and half fill it with beer. The slug sniffs the brew, crawls in and drowns.
- Use gravel on garden beds. The sharp edges cut slugs on their soft underbellies, killing them.

TWO-SPOTTED mites

Fine webbing on the underside of leaves indicates an infestation of two-spotted mites. They munch on the leaves of cucumbers and bean plants, but are most troublesome in greenhouses and on houseplants.
- Spray with insecticidal soap, neem oil or a garlic and chile spray.
- Use predator mites, available in well-stocked gardening centers. They will search plants for pest mites, kill them and move on.

MICE

These rodents nibble on bulbs and corms, devour newly sown peas and beans, and attack stored fruit and vegetables if not well protected.
- Cover newly planted seeds with twigs of barberry, rose, or some other thorny shrub to keep them away.
- Toss seeds in wood ash before you plant them. Give bulbs and tubers the same treatment before storing.
- Plant mint near vulnerable plants—rodents do not like its aroma.
- Get a cat. Its mere presence may be more than enough to deter the pests.

Ornamental shrubs and trees

These undemanding plants add beauty and fragrance to a garden, providing a visual framework or drawing the eye to significant spots when grown singly on the lawn. Their foliage, flowers and berries can be used to provide colorful accents to any home.

Take your garden's light and soil into account when you are planning where to put trees and shrubs to avoid having to transplant or replace them later.

CHOICE and location

- Ornamental shrubs and trees that offer a visual treat all year round are perfect for smaller gardens that lack the space for a larger selection of plants. A compact ceanothus produces a glorious display of blue flowers in late spring, while a selection of hardy fuchsias will create a stunning display of pinks and purples from late spring to early winter. Butterfly-attracting asters are ideal for a smaller garden, as are dwarf Japanese maples with their glorious autumn leaf colors.
- Flowering shrubs such as winterberry and chokecherry will attract birds to your garden, too.

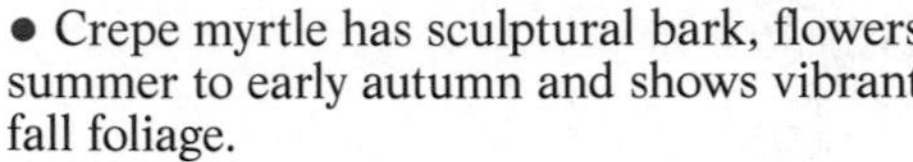

- Crepe myrtle has sculptural bark, flowers summer to early autumn and shows vibrant fall foliage.
- Plants that thrive in the shade are begonia, bromeliad, hydrangea, plectranthus, flowering quince, camellia, azalea and abutilon.
- For damp locations, select cannas, St. John's wort, hosta, calla lily, astilbe, various ferns, papyrus and water iris.
- Never plant Japanese maples or flowering cherries next to flower beds or vegetable plots. Their shallow roots make it difficult to cultivate the soil.
- Shrubs and trees take water and nutrients from the soil, so be sure other plants can tolerate their proximity.

COLOR in autumn and winter

- Provide glorious autumn color with the purple princess flower (tibouchina).
- Brighten up winter days with mahonia, daphnes, witch hazel, winter jasmine and Kaffir lily.
- Find pretty red berries, even during the colder season with ardisia, clivia and nandina.
- Rich blue fruit adorn the mahonia, purplish-pink fruit the beautyberry (*Callicarpa* spp.).

PLANTING

Spring and autumn are always the best times to plant shrubs and trees because they are either still in a state of rest or are preparing for winter after shedding their leaves.

- Loosen up matted rootballs with a pitchfork before pulling the roots apart.
- Clip the roots and shoots to promote the growth of new and healthy plant parts.
- Place the supporting stake in the planting hole before inserting the tree, which will avoid damaging roots after the tree has been planted. The stake will also be much easier to handle.

GOOD TO KNOW

Plants that like radical pruning

Many flowering ornamental shrubs compensate for audacious pruning with good growth and a bountiful flowering. Plants such as butterfly bush, Yuki cherry blossoms and spiraea respond well to a radical pruning.

- Use old tights to tie the tree to the stake. They are cheaper than store-bought tree ropes and cords and, because of their softness and elasticity, they provide greater protection, especially for younger trees.

PRUNING and cultivating

Ornamental trees and shrubs, including natives, need pruning to supply them with light and air.

- Prune in early spring, shortly before plants sprout. Don't prune during a severe frost. Prune the plants that flower in spring immediately after they have finished flowering, but wait until the following spring to prune those that flower after midsummer.
- Do not prune evergreen shrubs and conifers, laburnum, dogwood, magnolia or witch hazel regularly—it can do them harm.
- Thin out shrubs that have become scrubby and have stopped producing flowering branches.
- Clip azaleas and camellias to shape them after flowering has finished in early spring.
- Put layers of mulch around the base of shrubs and trees to keep the soil from drying out during the heat of summer and to provide protection against weeds.
- Protect the trunks of young trees from damage with a slit plastic bottle or chicken wire.
- Try adding wood ash to the soil if a shrub fails to flower. There may not be enough potash in the soil.

Use figure-eight knots to tie a rope around a tree and its supporting stake.

Plant diseases

Using chemicals to combat plant diseases has become the norm. However, many gardeners are now returning to tried-and-trusted traditional methods to counteract pests and keep plants healthy.

Certain chemicals used in fertilizers and pest controls have now been banned. Fortunately, nature can help combat many garden diseases.

CAUSES and prevention

Fungus in garden plants is often weather-related. Extremely damp or dry weather can encourage fungal growth. In addition, viruses, bacteria, and nutrient deficiency or over-abundance can cause health issues.

- Avoid overfertilizing. Fortify plants with slurries (*see "Feeding and revitalizing," page 212*).
- To prevent disease, consider location and observe the rules of mixed cultivation and crop rotation.

> **GOOD TO KNOW**
>
> **Disposal is the only cure**
> Phytophthora is a fungus that destroys a plant's root system, preventing it from taking in water and nutrients. Leaves may develop brown patches at the tips and edges, then yellow, dry out and die. Limit the spread of the disease by disposing of the plant, including roots, and don't replant in the same hole. Practice good garden hygiene by keeping tools, machinery and boots clean.

CHLOROSIS

In this metabolic disorder, the plant doesn't produce enough chlorophyll so the leaves or plant parts turn yellow and withers. This occurs as a result of too much lime in the soil, dense soil or waterlogging. Raspberries, hydrangeas, roses, geraniums and rhododendrons are most likely to be affected.

- Water plants with rainwater or douse them occasionally with a nettle slurry (*see page 212*).
- If chlorosis is already present, loosen up the soil and improve it by working in plenty of compost.

APPLY HERBAL SPRAYS in the evening OR ON OVERCAST days.

MILDEW

This fungal disease—subdivided into powdery mildew and downy mildew—is a common problem. It is characterized by a white or gray fungal growth.

- Powdery mildew is a threat to apples, apricots, peas, strawberries, cucumbers, peaches, delphiniums, roses, crepe myrtle and grapevines. It is prevalent in hot, dry conditions and appears as a whitish, floury layer.
- Downy mildew attacks strawberries, peas, lamb's lettuce, cabbage, lettuce, horseradish, radish, salsify, spinach and onions. It sets in during damp weather or in a moist greenhouse and spreads quickly. You will notice light spots on the top of the leaves and a grayish coating on the underside.

The grape leaf (left) shows chlorosis. The raspberry leaf (right) is afflicted with rust.

• Prevent both by purchasing mildew-resistant strains. Choose a sunny location to grow them and space the plants out well. Plant garlic between them or spray with a solution of 1 teaspoon (5 ml) baking soda in 1 quart (1 L) water.
• For a powdery mildew infestation, cut off sick leaves, shoots and branch tips; compost them.
• Spray every 2–3 weeks in spring and summer with garlic spray. Chop one or two garlic bulbs; cover with boiling water in a lidded jar. Soak overnight, strain and mix with 1 quart (1 L) diluted soap solution.
• To prevent or control downy mildew in seedlings, steep 1½ teaspoons (7 ml) dried chamomile flowers in 1 quart (1 L) boiling water. Cool the infusion and spray it on the seedlings.
• If plant parts are affected, remove the entire plant.

BOTRYTIS blight (gray mold)

A fungal disease, it attacks fruit and vegetables such as strawberries, peppers, lettuce, tomatoes and grapevines. Ornamental plants can also be affected.
• Afflicted produce develops a grayish-white fungus and may rot and die.
• Space plants out well and prune to ensure good air circulation as prevention.
• Place straw underneath strawberry plants to keep the fruit from lying on the ground.
• If botrytis has gained a foothold, remove diseased plants and burn or bury them away from healthy ones.

BROWN rot

This fungal disease takes hold on trees and wood, as well as on stone fruit, especially peaches and plums. Infections on wood and flowers tend to occur when there is prolonged wet weather during flowering. Fruit rot occurs when the skin of the fruit is damaged.
• Blossom and twig blight occurs frequently with apricots, cherries, peaches and plums. The blossoms wither and the shoots die from the tip back. Affected leaves don't fall off.
• Fruit rot is characterized by small, squishy brown spots that rapidly grow in size until the whole fruit is rotten. It especially affects the fruit of apple, cherry and plum trees. The fruit don't always fall off.
• Prune endangered trees and open up for good ventilation. Fortify with tea made from leaves and roots of horseradish; try garlic spray (*see "Mildew" page 226*).
• If brown rot is present, discard all diseased fruit on both the tree and the ground, and toss or burn. Cut back diseased branches to the healthy wood.
• Spray with an organic fungicide such as Bordeaux mixture or lime sulfur in autumn as the leaves fall, and again at bud-swell. Apply a copper-based fungicide as flowers open and as the petals fall, then again a month and 2 weeks before harvesting fruit.

RUST fungus

A fungal infection, it appears on leaves and stems. Rust species tend to be host specific (for example, beans, leeks or asparagus), although some do change host plants. They spread by tiny spores and grow best in humid, moist environments.
• Orange or red pustules appear on the underside of leaves, as well as yellowish-red spots on the tops.
• For prevention, plant in a sunny, well-ventilated area and loosen the soil frequently.
• Remove diseased leaves immediately and add them to the compost pile.
• Garlic spray is also a good treatment for rust.

Planting for privacy

A garden should be a refuge in which you can unwind. To achieve this sanctuary you will need visual cover, whether it's a wood fence, a hedge or some artfully placed planting.

Apart from sheltering you from prying eyes, cover can be used to hide unattractive trash bins or compost piles. Fences come in a variety of materials, styles and colors. Planting hedges is a more permanent cover option, and using potted plants as visual cover allows you to maintain maximum flexibility in your use of space. By replacing plants and moving pots around, you can continually come up with new combinations and surprising accents.

FENCES

- Natural materials such as brush or bamboo work well in most gardens. Attach bamboo matting or visual screens such as a trellis to a newly erected fence for added privacy.

Fast-growing bamboo, even when planted in tubs, helps to create visual cover on a patio.

- Green up an existing or a new wood fence with climbing plants and hanging baskets.

TALL potted plants

Many plants grow well in planters, though they may not get as tall as they would in the garden.

- Opt for hydrangeas and weigela. They produce abundant flowers and thick foliage.
- Plant conifers or palms in buckets for an evergreen visual cover.
- Elevate the plants by putting them on a flat stone, a block of wood or an old, low bench. Or choose very tall containers.

PLANTED trellises

When planning visual cover in the form of a trellis, take into account the prevailing wind direction and angle of the sun, as they will play a role in determining whether the climbing plants will thrive. Excessively tall trellises sometimes cast unwelcome shadows.

- Wooden trellises or pergolas should be made from weatherproof, pressure-treated lumber so you don't have to use toxic wood preservatives to maintain them.
- Annual runner beans grow especially quickly on trellises. In just a few weeks they will produce a green wall with attractive red flowers. From late summer, you can eat the beans.
- Trellises provide perfect visual cover even in the winter, with evergreen climbing plants such as star jasmine and mandevilla.
- Make a trellis out of bamboo poles for annual climbing plants that are not too heavy. Place the poles on top of one another in a grid pattern and tie them together at each intersection with garden wire, then attach the trellis to the wall.
- A trellis thick with climbing roses produces abundant flowers and, depending on the variety of rose, a wonderfully fragrant privacy screen.

• Cut back trellis plants regularly so they retain their shape and don't become too heavy—which could result in the trellis breaking.
• Fragrant plants, including honeysuckle and jasmine, can be doubly useful. When trained on a trellis around the compost pile or in front of a trash bin, they can cover up the view and simultaneously mask the smell.

HEDGES

A hedge is a living fence defining a boundary. It can also provide visual cover, depending on its plants.
• Grow a flowering hedge around a bench in the garden. Mix ornamental shrubs that flower at different times, such as hibiscus, plumbago, camellias, brunfelsia and mock orange.
• Choose nearly impenetrable shrubs like barberry, flowering quince, mahonia, hawthorn and wild roses for even more privacy and security against intruders. They all have spines or thorns.
• Provide evergreen visual cover with American holly, Italian cypress, arborvitae, juniper and Japanese yew (*Taxus*).
• Choose fast-growing plants such as burning bush and viburnum and conifers like western red cedar (*Thuja plicata*) and Leyland cypress (*Cupressocyparis leylandii*).

GOOD TO KNOW

Low-maintenance visual cover

Annual climbing plants such as sweet pea, nasturtium, purple bell vine and Spanish flag grow quickly, don't take up much room and don't need to be trimmed. Plant them in the spring, providing the shoots with something they can cling to. Remove the dead plants in late autumn.

• Use tall bushes or sunflowers for quick-growing visual cover. Ferns and tall ornamental grass varieties, such as giant feather grass (*Stipa gigantea*), also achieve vertical height quickly.
• Consider bamboo, which makes an ideal privacy hedge. The multicolored canes remain vivid even in the winter. They grow quickly and reach a good height, and some varieties have especially thick foliage for providing visual cover. Use a combination of different color leaves or stems to provide visual interest. Only plant clumping bamboo—running varieties will quickly take over.
• Low, dense-flowering shrubs, which are also often spiky, provide shelter and food for small native birds. Good choices include shrub rose, mountain laurel, winterberry and chokecherry. Grasses and similar plants such as switchgrass, big bluestem, miscanthus and Indian grass also attract birds.

Pot and container plants

Plants in pots can beautify a balcony, veranda or patio with refreshing greenery and colorful flowers. In frost-prone areas, both the plants and their containers may need protection.

Plants will grow in anything that will hold soil, such as baskets, boxes, wheelbarrows, buckets or a small wine barrel. You may need to modify your chosen container slightly to be sure plants remain healthy.

THE selection

- Choose containers made from terra-cotta, as they are permeable to water and air. Look for frost-resistant ones for plants that will be kept permanently outdoors in frost-prone areas. They are a bit more expensive, but well worth it.
- Prevent the similar but much flimsier plastic pots from falling over in a strong wind by dropping a few heavy rocks in the bottom before adding soil.
- Use plastic pots to line metal and wooden containers and prevent rust or rot. Alternatively, line the containers with plastic or foil.

PREPARING the containers

- Thoroughly clean all containers, including new ones and rinse off any residue.
- Scrub off the unattractive white lime deposits on the outside of clay pots with vinegar and water and only apply water that has aerated for 24 hours to prevent the deposits from returning.
- Use a hammer and a screwdriver to punch a drainage hole in the bottom of a clay pot that doesn't already have drainage holes, or use an electric drill to make several small holes in the bottom—but be very careful or the pot will break.
- Prevent soil and nutrients from washing away while watering by covering small drainage holes with a piece of mosquito netting. A coffee filter placed over larger holes allows the water to escape but retains soil.
- Potting mixes are formulated to provide excellent drainage, so there's no need for crocks or stones in the bottom of pots. Far from improving drainage, they impede the flow of water through soil.
- Be environmentally friendly: Choose coco peat and peat-free potting mixes to prevent the depletion of natural peat resources.
- Premium potting mixes have added controlled-release fertilizer, wetting agent and water crystals to give potted plants everything they need to grow healthy and strong.

Plants will grow in just about anything that will hold soil.

GOOD TO KNOW

The secondhand store: a place of discovery

You can find all kinds of things that can be used as flowerpots at secondhand stores: colorful ceramics from other countries, tubs or pans, metal buckets or an old basin. Flowers can even feel at home in discarded cooking pots.

INSERT A FINGER ½ INCH (1 cm) in THE SOIL. If it's dry, WATER THE PLANT.

- Be sure the area where planters are kept has good water runoff. If necessary, place the containers on large stones or pot feet.
- Lift pots up to protect the roots on cold nights, when the chill from the ground could do some serious damage. If frost threatens outdoor potted plants, wrap them in fleece or bubble wrap.

MOST plants thrive in a container

In addition to boxwood and small conifers, small, slow-growing ornamental shrubs such as gardenias, azaleas and dwarf camellias will thrive all year long in plant containers.

- Provide a splash of color among winter-hardy evergreens with frost-resistant hellebores, crocuses, or any plants that flower in early spring.
- Climbing plants such as passionflower, clematis or a potted rose can live comfortably on a balcony or patio, where they will disguise unattractive concrete walls.
- If your garden soil isn't hospitable for rhododendrons, azaleas or other acid-loving plants, put them in the appropriate soil in tubs and place them in the flower beds.
- If snails are a problem, grow dahlias, verbena, hydrangea or marigolds in tubs so that snails can't get to them. Or secure copper bands around pots. Snails and slugs will be deterred by the feel and taste of the metal.
- Choose impatiens, fuchsia, hydrangeas, lobelia, bromeliads, crotons or ferns for shady or partially shady areas.

CARE and winter protection

- Stick your finger ½ inch (1 cm) into the soil to see whether a plant needs water. If the soil feels dry, water the plant.
- Loosen crusty topsoil regularly to allow water to penetrate better.
- As the soil contains fewer nutrients during the growing season, use a little more plant fertilizer on potted plants.
- Pour cooled water used for cooking vegetables and eggs and any tea remnants on potted plants. The liquid contains plenty of minerals that are good for flowering plants.
- Depending on the region in which you live, plants that are not winter-hardy should be indoors in their winter quarters before the first frost.
- Make sure that plants' winter quarters are bright and cool. Optimal temperature is 40–45°F (5–8°C).
- Wrap the containers of even winter-hardy potted plants in fleece or bubblewrap if a frost is forecast. Protect everything above the top edge of the pot.
- If you do water potted plants in the winter, make sure that it is on frost-free days because any cold winter winds will quickly dry out their roots.

If your garden soil isn't hospitable, plant azaleas in tubs.

Roses

The rose is perhaps the quintessential garden flower. A symbol of love, beauty, passion—even war—its countless colors and shapes and delightful fragrance earn it a place in any garden—from borders to a trellis or pergola.

Planting and caring for roses is not as difficult as it may seem. Armed with a sturdy pair of gardening gloves to protect you from their thorns, some clippers and patience, your garden can soon include a wide variety of roses that will delight you and your visitors.

ROSE cultivation

The original rose species and natural rose hybrids grow wild in most Northern Hemisphere temperate climates. Gardeners have cultivated the rose for hundreds of years, developing the double flower and, eventually, modern hybrids with a high, pointed center in which ancestral floral characteristics are almost totally submerged.

PLANTING roses

Potted plants are available to plant throughout the year. Bare-rooted roses are available in winter and should be planted by the end of August.

- Soak bare-rooted plants in a bucket of water with added seaweed tonic for several hours before planting. This helps to alleviate transplant shock.
- If there are any damaged roots, cut them off cleanly before planting.
- Plant roses so that the graft area is just above the surface of the ground. Usually a change in color on the stem shows the depth at which the rose was planted at the nursery. Plant at this depth.
- Create a mound of soil in the bottom of the planting hole. Spread the roots over the mound and backfill, firming the soil around the roots.
- Use a seaweed tonic when planting or transplanting to give roses a great, natural boost.
- Pay attention to the distance between plants: It should usually be 16–18 inches (40–45 cm); for dwarf roses, 8 inches (20 cm) is adequate; climbing roses need at least 5 feet (1.5 m).
- Provide roses with at least one botanical companion, which will help to keep many

Maintenance involves regularly deadheading wilted flowers and removing dead plant parts.

pests away: Lavender, rosemary and thyme repel aphids; French marigolds kill nematodes; chives helps prevent powdery mildew; and the sulfur in garlic and onions wards off fungus growth.

ROSE care

- Remove any winter protection from roses on a cloudy, overcast day. Too much sun and warmth can give the plants a shock after their winter's rest.
- Fertilize roses in early to mid spring.
- Use water-soluble fertilizers only when the weather is damp.
- Nurture roses with manure and water: Add a large plant pot of dried manure to 8 quarts (8 L) of water and let it soak for a couple of days. Dilute the liquid so that it is the color of weak tea and pour on the root area.
- Rake finely chopped banana skins into the soil to provide the plants with lime, magnesium, sulfur, nitrogen, potassium, phosphate and silicic acid.
- Water roses thoroughly but not daily during dry periods. Depending on the plant's size, during a drought a rose will need 10–20 quarts (10–20 L) of water per week to produce luxurious flowers.
- Never water roses from above as this could result in fungal diseases.
- Prevent fungal diseases by spraying roses in the morning with a solution of 1 teaspoon (5 ml) baking soda in 4 quarts (4 L) of water. Adding 2–3 drops of liquid soap blends the solution more effectively.
- Stop fertilizing roses at least 1 month before the first frosts are likely to occur. Fertilizing for too long into autumn encourages roses to produce tender new growth that will get nipped by the cold.
- In frost-prone regions, keep bush roses from lifting in the winter by covering the root area with compost. Tie large bush roses or climbing roses with string to keep them from breaking in the wind or under a heavy load of snow.

PRUNING roses

Prune roses properly to encourage growth and the formation of buds.

- Wear gloves and use good clippers. It's particularly easy to injure yourself when cutting climbing or bush roses.
- Twist off suckers that sprout from the ground at the base. They look different from the main plant.
- Remove prunings immediately from the garden as they can be a haven for insects and disease pathogens. Add this garden waste to the household trash rather than the compost pile, since many disease pathogens can withstand even the high temperatures inside the compost.
- Cut back bush roses by about a third in summer to produce bushier growth and autumn flowers.

GOOD TO KNOW

Color into winter

Regional climate permitting, in the autumn a number of rose varieties, including *Rosa canina*, *Rosa rubiginosa* and *Rosa rugosa*, form large, shiny red rosehips—as long as the spring flowers aren't cut off. These fruits make excellent purées and fruit teas.

SEASON BY SEASON

There's a comforting rhythm to the cycle of the seasons and the timing of the corresponding chores that need to be undertaken in the garden. The reward for that year-round love and attention will be a horticultural haven.

LOCATION AND CLIMATE CAN alter the timing OF CHORES.

Spring

In ornamental gardens, plant or cut back roses, bushes and shrubs, divide and transplant existing perennials, and sow annual summer flowers such as pansies, snapdragons and sweet peas.

In the native garden, clip winter flowering shrubs such as ardisia and clivia into shape. As individual flowers die, cut back stems about 2 inches (5 cm) behind the spent bloom.

Plant cold-hardy vegetables such as peas, spinach, asparagus, broccoli, cabbage, kale, fava beans and onions.

When there is no further danger of frost, plant carrots, beets, Swiss chard, cauliflower, potatoes, celery and radishes.

Plant warm-climate fruiting plants such as mangoes, avocados and passion fruit as the weather starts to warm up.

Late spring

Plant shrubs in the ornamental garden, prune early-flowering bushes once the flowers have wilted, tie up climbing roses and move potted plants outdoors when the danger of frost is past. Plant biennials and those that flower early, as well as summer bulbs such as dahlias and gladiolus.

Add mulch or straw around strawberry plants. Thin out excess fruit on the trees and prop up branches overloaded with fruit using boards. Water fruit trees well if necessary.

Plant tomatoes, peppers, chilies and other frost-tender vegetables, as well as herbs like dill, oregano and basil.

Harvest early beets, radishes, rhubarb, lettuce, arugula and spinach, plus the first berries.

Late spring is the time to plant shrubs in the ornamental garden.

Colorful spikes of lupine embellish the early summer border, adding structure and cottage garden appeal.

Early summer

Trim deciduous hedges, remove wilted flowers, deadhead perennials, plant autumn-flowering bulbs and cut back to the ground the stalks of all early summer flowering plants. In addition, divide iris and lily of the valley bulbs once they have finished flowering. Wait to remove the foliage of spring bulbs until it has died down.

Support heavily laden branches on fruit trees and, after the harvest, begin the first pruning and trimming to remove dead or diseased wood. Trim berry bushes after the harvest.

Plant pumpkin, squash, zucchini, leeks, onions, beets, sweet corn and more in the vegetable garden so you will still have fresh vegetables in the autumn. Remove all the side-shoots from tomato plants (except for bush varieties) and stop growth once about five fruit clusters have formed.

Harvest the first potatoes and tomatoes, in addition to lettuce and many other vegetable varieties, berries, early apples and stone fruit.

Late summer

Trim evergreen hedges in the ornamental garden, tie up late-flowering perennials and plant biennial summer flowers.

Plant berries and strawberry runners in the garden—new passionfruit shoots must be tied up. Fruit trees shouldn't be cut any further.

Plant late crops of spinach, fennel, bok choy and radicchio. Keep checking veggies for pests like snails and caterpillars. Pick off and squash any you find.

Harvest nature's bounty: apples, pears, blackberries, plums, hazelnuts and walnuts. Enjoy tomatoes, leeks, late potatoes and late carrots.

Autumn and winter

Now you can plant the bulbs for next spring and remove annuals entirely once they have faded.

Plant rose bushes in the flower garden and in frost-prone areas, earth-up hybrid tea roses with soil or straw to prevent them from freezing.

In cool regions, remove dahlias, gladiolus, tuberous begonias and ranunculus from the ground after the first frost and store in a cool, dry place. Cut back herbaceous perennials.

Prune ornamental shrubs and cover perennial gardens and borders with compost, bark mulch or leaf litter. Prune repeat-flowering roses in July or August. Leave roses that flower only once in spring; they should be pruned after flowering is finished.

Plant bare-root roses, shrubs and fruit trees such as figs and olives in the garden when there is no frost. Prune trees and remove dead or damaged wood on frost-free winter days.

After harvesting the last crops, remove spent vegetables and compost. Ripen green tomatoes on a sunny windowsill. Sow green manure in empty beds to improve soil before spring.

Plant garlic and overwintering varieties of fava beans and onions.

Soil

A loose soil rich in humus and nutrients, with a slightly acidic to neutral pH value, is optimal for most garden plants. You will rarely encounter such ideal conditions but, fortunately, you have centuries of garden wisdom to call on to help improve the soil in your beds.

Most soils are a combination of sand, clay and silt, and the proportion of each determines the type of soil you have. You might have anything from light sandy soil, which contains mostly sand, right through to heavy clay—a soil that is predominantly clay—and any combination in between. The ideal is a loamy soil, which has roughly equal parts of sand, silt and clay, plus plenty of added organic matter and a crumbly texture.

SOIL types

- Sandy soil is loose and easy to work and plant roots can spread out easily in it, but water and nutrients are poorly absorbed. Use compost to increase the amount of humus and mulch to prevent rapid drying.
- Clay soil makes it difficult for roots to spread. The soil can be so tightly compacted that the roots of many plants can't penetrate it to reach water and nutrients, so the plants will wilt quickly. Loosen clay soil by adding large amounts of organic matter. Clay soil is nutrient-rich and holds water well.
- Loamy soil offers the best conditions for gardening. It stores water and nutrients effectively and the soil structure is loose enough for plants to root easily and reach the nutrients. By adding a little compost or organic fertilizer each year, you can be sure that the soil doesn't become depleted over time.

SOIL analysis

Determine the type of soils you have before you get started on gardening so you choose the right one for your plants.

- Take a spade sample at several places in the garden, digging to about 12 inches (30 cm).
- Sandy soil will feel gritty when you rub it. Dampen a handful of soil. If you try to form a "ribbon" of soil by pushing it between your fingers you'll be able to form only an inch (cm) or two.
- Clay soil will feel smooth and may stain your fingers. You may be able to form a ribbon of soil several inches (cm) long.
- Loamy soils are crumbly and there could be lots of plant material in it, due to the high organic matter.
- Alternatively, determine soil conditions by examining the roots of plants currently growing in the garden. A small rootball and crooked, intertwined root strands point to impenetrable soil.

HYDRANGEA FLOWERS ARE blue in acid soil, pink in alkaline.

Sandy soil is dry, grainy and crumbles easily; good loam soil first smears then crumbles after some time.

• Look for creepy-crawlies. The presence of many helpers such as woodlice, earthworms and millipedes in the soil is a sign of good soil quality.

ACID and lime content

The health of garden plants may well depend on the acid content of the soil. Some plants grow well in acidic or alkaline soils, while others don't. Look at neighbors' gardens to see what plants thrive there.

• Alkaline soils are indicated by the presence of yarrow, hellebores, bergenias and Solomon's seal.

• Acidic soils: camellias, azaleas, and blueberries.

• A high lime content is indicated by the presence of bellflowers, marigolds, alliums, delphiniums, cornflowers, and lavender spurge.

• Spray a little vinegar on a clump of soil. The vinegar will bubble when it comes into contact with soil containing lime.

SOIL improvement

The type of soil you have does not determine whether your plants will grow well. Although generally fertile, clay soil can be compacted, while sandy soil, even though well-drained, can be lacking in nutrients—both of which affect plant growth. Adding the right substances improves most soils.

• Add compost or manure to sandy soil regularly to improve the structure and increase the amount of water the soil can hold.

• Dig garden lime or dolomite into highly acidic soil in autumn, and add phosphate and potash in the form of wood ash.

• Heavy clay soils can be broken up by adding compost or manure regularly—in spring and autumn is ideal.

• Use organic mulches such as lucerne, sugar cane, coco peat or bark, as they break down over time and add extra organic matter to the soil.

Determining pH value with a kit

1 Place 1 teaspoon (5 ml) of soil on the test card and add drops of the indicator liquid a few at a time, stirring, until a thick paste forms.

2 Dust with the white powder provided and wait for 1 minute until it changes color.

3 Match the color to the nearest pH value on the color card. Purple is alkaline, yellow is acid, and green is neutral.

Tasks for winter

In frost-prone regions it pays to be ready for the colder weather. Prepare your garden well so that all the plants, including the more delicate ones, can survive the harshest winter.

With a bit of preparation, much can be done to help your garden to survive the winter. This includes trimming trees, applying a coat of paint or even bringing part of the garden inside.

GOOD TO KNOW

Potted plants

Potted plants will appreciate being in the ground during winter. If at all possible, find a sheltered spot in the garden to either plant your potted beauties temporarily for the winter or bury them pot and all. Mulch with 2–4 inches (5–10 cm) of bark or leaves once the soil has frozen.

NATURAL protection

Opt for leaves, spruce and fir trimmings, straw, burlap and jute when covering or wrapping plants.

- If you can get them, consider using spruce trimmings for optimal winter protection. They gradually lose their needles and let more light reach the plants. Arrange cuttings like a small roof over the plants, but make sure that air can get to them or they may rot or become diseased.
- Check leaves for pests, fungus and other diseases before deciding on winter protection.
- Burlap is light and smooth, so it won't harm plants. For better protection, put straw between the plants and a burlap wrap over them.

PROTECTION from the cold

Plants from warmer regions and newly transplanted or young plants will make it through a tough winter only if they are well wrapped in sturdy burlap or spruce trimmings.

- Wrap fruit tree trunks in cardboard to keep them from cracking during major temperature changes.
- Make teepees of bamboo canes around individual plants and pack them with straw.
- Protect delicate perennials and late autumn plantings with dried leaves or straw, and use spruce cuttings to protect evergreen varieties.
- Tie tall ornamental grasses together in bunches to protect them from frost and snow and to provide winter shelter for helpful creatures.
- Press soil back down around perennials that may have buckled due to frost. This will protect the roots.
- Wrap lower branches of tender climbers and shrubs with straw held in place with burlap and string.

OTHER winter options

- If you have room, bring potted plants indoors for winter. They will bring color and extra oxygen to the home. Just remember to give them adequate light and water, and be careful not to place them too close to the cold of the window or any heat sources.

In a hard frost, place pots on wood so they don't freeze to the ground.

Transplanting

Redesigning your garden may involve transplanting perennials, shrubs or even trees. It's not a daunting task, but remember that timing is key because no plant should be kept out of the soil for too long.

The best times for transplanting are late summer or early autumn, which gives plants the chance either to put down roots and start growing before the onset of winter or to start growing in spring before the onset of hot summer temperatures.

THE right timing

- Try to transplant during wet and cooler weather to reduce stress on the plants. Avoid hot spells.
- Transplant evergreen trees and shrubs in April or October, when the soil is moist and warm.
- Transplant shrubs that are sensitive to frost, such as magnolia, hibiscus or hydrangea, in spring.

TRANSPLANTING large trees and shrubs

Trees and older shrubs should be prepared before being relocated or they won't tolerate the change. It takes two to three seasons to root-prune a tree fully but, in the end, a compact, well-branched root system will greatly increase a tree's chance of survival once it is moved.

1 In spring, dig a furrow 15 inches (40 cm) deep by 10 inches (25 cm) wide a third of the way around a tree, slightly closer to the trunk than you will eventually be digging when the tree is moved. By doing so, you can break long, unbranched roots, prompting the regrowth of new roots nearer the main trunk of the tree. Cut off the roots around the main shoots, at a slight angle toward the shrub or tree.

2 Fill the trench with fresh soil and compost and keep watering the plant well to promote the growth of new fibrous roots.

3 In autumn, dig around the next third of the roots and in the following spring, dig a furrow through the remaining roots. Don't transplant until the following autumn.

4 Prune the shoots of the transplant by up to a third of their length to prevent harmful effects from damaged roots.

5 A handful of bone meal and some mature compost will give the tree or shrub a good start once it's positioned in its new hole.

6 Keep transplants, whether perennials, shrubs or trees, from dehydrating by spreading a thick layer of mulch on the ground around them.

TRANSPLANTING perennials

- Transplant perennials after they have finished flowering. If you transplant in the spring, don't expect them to flower that year.
- Transplant in late autumn so you can save yourself the work of extensive watering.
- Add compost or humus to the hole for perennial plants to help them to sprout new shoots.

MAKE SURE the plant is sitting at the SAME LEVEL in the new hole.

Vegetable and salad beds

Plant greens in the sunniest and flattest part of the garden to ensure a good supply of vegetables throughout the summer and fall. Plan vegetable and lettuce beds well so that they are easy to maintain, accessible for weeding and watering and protected against garden invaders.

How you plan your beds will help you greatly in the long run. It will save time and effort, make it easier to harvest crops and could prevent you from developing a sore back.

USE CARDBOARD egg cartons for STARTING SEEDLINGS.

MAKING a new bed

Keep vegetable beds no wider than 4 feet (1.2 m) and for accessibility, don't place them next to a wall or hedge. The paths between individual beds should be about 12 inches (30 cm) wide.

- Lay wood boards on the paths so you won't sink into the mud during rainy weather.
- Remove all roots of perennial weeds before you plant. Dig the soil well.
- Divide the vegetable bed into two: one with things you harvest daily, such as carrots, radishes and lettuce; the other with permanent crops, such as herbs and horseradish, cabbages and asparagus, and with crops such as potatoes.
- In cool climates, use berry and hazelnut bushes to provide attractive protection against cold wind.
- Plant potatoes and Jerusalem artichokes to loosen the soil and restrict weeds.
- Add basic fertilizer, preferably with compost, about 3 weeks before the first planting.
- Plant low-growing vegetables on the sunny side of taller ones so they get adequate light.
- Allow for varying ripening times when you are laying out the bed, so you can grow different plants close together.

This small vegetable bed is located next to the compost pile, making it easy to fertilize.

SEED propagation indoors and sowing

- Use plastic starter trays. They are easy to clean, which makes it difficult for diseases to take hold.
- Don't forget to label individual starter trays with the name of the vegetable and the date of planting.
- Don't plant too many seeds in one tray. The fewer seeds you plant in a container,

Sow seeds in straight rows by stretching a string between two stakes at either end of the row.

the less work you'll have when it's time to thin out the plants.

- Sow larger seeds farther apart, singly or in pairs, just in case one of them fails to sprout.
- Scatter smaller seeds, such as spinach and Swiss chard, directly into shallow furrows in the bed. Cover them lightly with soil.
- Mix very small seeds with a little sand so they don't fall too close together when you are sowing them and are easier to spread.
- Soak the seeds from legumes or vegetables such as pumpkins or tomatoes (which are really fruit) in a milk marinade for 24 hours so that they will sprout faster.
- Warm the ground by covering it with a black tarp or black plastic sheet for a week in advance and you can seed outdoors earlier.
- Plant zucchini and cucumber seeds on their sides to speed germination.
- Make optimal use of space by planting slow-growing vegetables such as carrots between fast-growing lettuce.

BED maintenance

- Dig irrigation ditches between rows to let the water soak in slowly and reach the roots. This works well for any vegetable best watered from below, such as brussels sprouts.
- Make sure the water is warm to the touch or plants will get a real shock in hot weather.
- Dig green manure, such as clover, alfalfa and vicia, into the soil in the autumn. This provides a natural source of nutrients.
- In late autumn, enhance the soil in harvested beds by adding mulch or digging in manure.
- Plant aromatic herbs or flowers around the vegetable patch, such as dill, French marigold, cornflower and alyssum, to attract useful garden visitors such as ladybugs and dragonflies.

KEEPING out invasive pests

- Pick off harmful pests such as caterpillars and snails individually. Snails tend to lurk in grass, so keep the lawn around the vegetable patch cut short.
- If bushes or hedges near the garden are infested with aphids, protect vegetables with garden fleece.
- Install chicken wire or netting over a freshly sown bed to keep cats and birds at bay. Once the tender shoots have emerged, use it to make a fence around them.
- Make a scarecrow by hanging shiny objects such as CDs or foil containers from branches or a forked pole stuck into the ground. They will reflect the sunlight as they move in the wind, helping to frighten away hungry birds.

A herbal extract for seedlings

1/4 cup (50 g) dried nettles
2 teaspoons (10 g) sage
2 teaspoons (10 g) rue
2 teaspoons (10 g) mugworts
4 teaspoons (20 g) ferns
4 teaspoons (20 g) onion peelings
10 quarts (10 L) water

Soak the herbs, ferns and onion peelings in water for 24 hours, then boil and strain. Dilute the completed slurry 10:1 and sprinkle on the seedlings to strengthen them. Repeat this application weekly.

Watering

Regular watering—not too much, not too little—is important for all plants. Collecting rainwater in a barrel or tank for use during dry spells is a long-standing practice that is just as useful today, even if your garden is small.

Collecting rainwater is not only a practice that is environmentally friendly, it is better for plants than using tap water, which may contain small traces of chlorine.

A SOAKER HOSE RELEASES WATER slowly but STEADILY.

HOW much water to apply

Look at a plant's leaves to see how much water to give.

- Small, leathery, thorny, shiny or fleshy leaves indicate a low need for water, as do leaves with a wax-like layer. Succulents or Mediterranean plants do well without a lot of water, as do ivy, amaranth, nasturtium, sage, French marigolds and zinnia.
- Plants with soft, large or thin leaves tend to be thirsty, as do all flowering plants and those with solid rootballs and shallow root systems.

WHEN and how to water

- Water plants in both the flower and vegetable gardens before 9:30 a.m. The leaves will dry off quickly, reducing the risk of a fungal infection. If you water plants at night in cool weather, the soil surrounding them remains wet, potentially causing the roots to rot—plus, the moisture could attract snails. But evening watering is highly recommended in hot weather as it reduces evaporation.
- Water infrequently but thoroughly. The pauses between watering leave time for a deeper, branching root system to form in the drier soil. Don't saturate plants in heavy soil—they will become waterlogged.
- Make an inexpensive soaker hose at home from an old garden hose. Drill some small holes into it, connect it to the main hose and you've got an effective, efficient watering system.

Water young plants carefully so they don't lose their foothold.

• Be particularly careful not to water the leaves of melons, peppers or tomatoes. If you have time, it's even worth shaking rainwater from their leaves to be sure fungal diseases don't set in.
• Don't water directly on flowers. In the sunlight, the little water droplets act like a magnifying glass, potentially burning delicate petals.
• During hot summer weather just spray the plants—but don't do it in bright sunshine.
• Young shoots need more water than plants that are several years old with deep root systems.
• Water thirsty plants at ground level so that maximum water gets to the roots.
• If you water intensively with a watering can every couple of days in the summer heat, repeat the process after about 30 minutes. The water will penetrate deeper into the soil.
• Water bushes and shrubs on the root area beneath the outer branches. During dry periods, large trees need plenty of water, especially fruit trees when they are flowering or when fruit is ripening. Water for several hours.
• Always water plants well before you move them, and again after they are in their new positions.

Watering aids

one Dig a hole about 6 inches (15 cm) deep next to a plant that needs lots of water.

two Place a flowerpot of the correct size into the hole, drain hole downwards, and cover it with a plate or piece of plastic. Disguise it with leaves or a little soil.

three Fill with water at regular intervals. It will trickle slowly into the earth and reach the roots directly.

Connect a rain barrel directly to the downpipe of the roof gutter. If the barrel is raised, it's easier to fill the watering can.

COLLECTING water

Most plants tolerate rainwater better than water from a spring or tap. Collected rainwater is usually warmer and free of fluoride, chlorine and lime. Water that is high in lime, leaves white spots on the leaves.
• Keep water clear by occasionally adding a little charcoal or activated carbon (for use in aquariums) to the rain barrel.
• Cover barrels so that small animals can't get in them.
• Collect the water in which vegetables have been cooked—which contains nutrients—for use in the garden.

OPTIMUM moisture

• Rake the soil regularly, including in the furrows. Loosening the soil gives water easier access to a plant's roots.
• After a heavy summer rain, loosen up the soil only on the surface or the moisture in it will evaporate too quickly.
• Spread a layer of mulch to hold the moisture in the soil longer and prevent plants from getting thirsty too quickly.

Weed control

"The best shade in the garden is the gardener's own shadow," counsels an ancient Chinese proverb, which is why our grandparents were out in the garden every day pulling weeds. But if you're pressed for time, here are a few preventive measures you can try to keep botanical invaders at bay.

Weeds are plants that grow and reproduce quickly and easily but aren't welcome in the garden because they edge out the more delicate flora and make the garden beds look untidy. However, if you take note of which weeds thrive you will be able to evaluate the composition of the soil, while their roots may ventilate the soil and enrich it with nutrients. Certain weeds serve as the basic ingredient in liquid fertilizers or compounds that are used to prevent and combat garden pests and diseases, while herbs such as dandelion, dock and sorrel are useful for their medicinal properties.

Be especially careful when hoeing weeds among single plants in a vegetable bed.

COMMON weeds

- Privet (*Ligustrum* spp.) has taken hold in many gardens and open spaces, as its berries are rapidly spread by birds. Its creamy-white sprays of flowers, which appear in spring, are also a major irritant for hay fever sufferers. Cut the tree off at ground level and spray the stump with glyphosate within 30 seconds. Repeat spray, if necessary, and remove any seedlings that come up.
- Wandering jew forms a dense ground cover, especially in damp, shady spots. Every piece of stem and root will regrow, so you need to be vigilant. Rake or roll up large areas, then go back over the area picking up any pieces left. Continue checking the area every couple of weeks. A thick layer of newspaper covered with at least a 2–4 inches (5–8 cm) layer of mulch can also inhibit growth.
- Wild onions grow in garden beds and lawns. It has light green, grass-like leaves, and in spring it sends up tall stems topped with white flowers. It is spread by the seed, and also when the bulb is disturbed. If you try to dig it up during active growth—spring and summer—the bulb instantly shatters, scattering tiny bulbils throughout the soil. The best time to try to remove it is in winter, when the bulb stays intact. Don't try to sift the bulb from the soil. Instead remove and throw away the handful of soil within which the bulb is contained. Break off flowerheads whenever you see them and snap off the leaves. Herbicides are generally not effective.

• Lawn weeds can make a lawn look unsightly, but they are usually easily removed by digging them out by hand before they flower.
• Purslane seeds can persist in soil for years, so pull young seedlings or cultivate older plants with a sharp hoe on hot, sunny days. Gather and dry plants in the sun before composting them. Crowd future growth with dense plantings.

WEED removal

Make sure that weeds are pulled out regularly, as they spread quickly and rob other plants of nutrients.
• Weed on dry days after a rain when the soil is loose, allowing plants to be pulled up easily.
• In dry weather, let the weeds decompose at the edge of the bed.
• Weed again a few days after breaking up the soil of a bed. When you turn the soil, the seeds of weeds lying on the bottom may come to the top and start to shoot.
• Cut off flowerheads or seedpods before weeding or hoeing to prevent seeds from getting into the soil. Place seedheads in the trash, not the compost, to prevent them from germinating.
• Make short work of weeds growing in cracks between paving stones or on house walls by pouring boiling water on them.
• Pour salt on lawn weeds or sprinkle them with a solution of one part vinegar and one part water.

PREVENTING weeds

Chemical weed and pest killers are a bad idea. The substances they contain harm the environment and run the risk of damaging the soil so much that the plants you have nurtured die, too. With so many natural ways available to control weeds, there is no need to use them.
• Plants that rob weeds of light and nutrients through their own growth are an environmentally friendly way to control weeds. Ground cover plants are especially useful.
• Use dense-growing ground cover plants such as wild strawberries, periwinkles and violets for shady areas.
• Prevent weeds from growing in sunny beds by planting sedums, euphorbias and ground cover roses.

Violets thrive in shady spots and their dense growth helps to banish weeds.

• Mulch between plants to prevent unwanted weeds from coming to the surface. For mulch, use freshly cut grass, wood chips, lucerne or sugar cane; in rock gardens you can also use gravel.
• Sow plants that nourish the soil. This also suppresses weeds and will later contribute to healthy growth in the flower bed.
• To prevent the growth of weeds in larger or inaccessible areas of the garden, cover thick layers of newspaper with mulch and cut crosses into the newspaper through which plants can emerge (or into which they can be planted).

GOOD TO KNOW

The culinary side of weeds

Weeds are generally despised as invaders, to be pulled swiftly from the garden. But many of our ancestors would have seen them as food. Daisies, fat hen (goosefoot) and chickweed are tasty in salads. Ground elder and sorrel make a delicious soup or you can serve them as a vegetable. Young dandelion leaves are a surprisingly tasty treat mixed into salads and stir-fries.

INDEX

C

D

E

F

G

M

N

W

Y

Z

ACKNOWLEDGEMENTS

Reader's Digest thanks the following for permission to use their images.

Front cover tr Shutterstock; bl Corbis; bc Shutterstock; br iStockphoto; back cover Friedrich Strauss; 10 iStockphoto; 11 Fotolia; 12 t iStockphoto, b Shutterstock; 13 Shutterstock; 14 t Getty Images, b iStockphoto; 15 Shutterstock; 16 t Shutterstock; 17 Getty Images; 18 Getty Images; 20 iStockphoto; 21 iStockphoto; 22 Shutterstock; 23 b iStockphoto; 24 tl Mauritius Images, br Mauritius Images; 25 t Mauritius Images, b Mauritius Images; 26 iStockphoto; 27 Mauritius Images; 28 iStockphoto; 31 Getty Images; 32 Mauritius Images; 33 SuperStock; 35 bl Mauritius Images; 36 Getty Images; 37 t Getty Images, b Mauritius Images; 39 Mauritius Images; 40 iStockphoto; 41 Getty Images; 42 t Shutter-stock; 43 Mauritius Images; 44 Mauritius Images; 46 Shutterstock; 48 Getty Images; 49 t Shutterstock, b iStockphoto; 50 SuperStock; 51 tr Getty Images, b Corbis; 52 iStockphoto; 53 Mauritius Images; 54 tl Getty Images, br Getty Images; 55 t Mauritius Images, b Shutterstock; 56 t Mauritius Images, b Shutterstock; 57 iStockphoto; 58 Corbis; 59 t Photolibrary, 60–61 Shutterstock; 62 t SuperStock, b Corbis; 63 t iStockphoto, r Getty Images; 64 t Getty Images, bl Shutterstock; 65 l Shutterstock, r Shutterstock; 66 tr Shutterstock, b Shutterstock; 67 t iStockphoto, b Shutterstock; 68 a1pix; 70 Mauritius Images; 71 iStockphoto; 72 Mauritius Images; 73 Getty Images; 74 t Getty Images, b SuperStock; 76 SuperStock; 77 br Shutterstock; 78 tl Shutterstock, br Phavoir; 79 t iStockphoto; 80 tl iStockphoto.com, br Corbis; 82 iStockphoto; 84 Getty Images; 85 iStockphoto; 86-87 t Shutterstock, b Shutterstock; 88 iStockphoto; 90 iStockphoto; 91 iStockphoto; 92 istockphoto; 95 iStockphoto; 96 iStockphoto; 97 Getty Images; 98 Shutterstock; 99 tr Corbis; 100 iStockphoto; 101 iStockphoto; 102 l Mauritius Images, r Corbis; 103 l Getty Images, r Masterfile; 106 Mauritius Images; 108 Getty Images; 110 PhotoAlto; 111 Shutterstock; 112 b Shutterstock; 114 Corbis; 116 Shutterstock; 117 Getty Images, t Corbis; 119 Shutterstock; 120 iStockphoto; 122 Getty Images; 123 iStockphoto; 124–125 Shutterstock; 130 Corbis; 131 iStockphoto; 133 bl Shutterstock; 134 Shutterstock; 136 Mauritius Images; 137 iStockphoto; 138 t Mauritius Images; 138–139 c SuperStock; 140 Getty Images; 141 tl Shutterstock, br iStockphoto; 142 iStock-photo; 146 tr Getty Images, bl Getty Images; 147 Getty Images; 148 Getty Images; 149 Getty Images, bl Mauritius; 152 tl Getty Images; 153 b Getty Images; 154 tr iStockphoto, bl iStockphoto; 155 iStockphoto; 156 Getty Images; 157 tl Shutterstock; 158 Mauritius Images; 159 Getty Images; 160 Mauritius Images; 161 l Corbis, r Corbis; 162 tl Corbis, br Mauritius Images; 163 t Getty Images; 164–165 Shutter-stock; 166 Getty Images; 167 Shutterstock; 168 t www.gapinteriors.com/David Cleveland, b www.gapinteriors.com/Tricia Giovan; 169 Shutterstock; 170 Getty Images; 171 Getty Images; 172 SuperStock; 173 iStockphoto; 174 Shutterstock; 175 www.gapinteriors. com/Dan Duchars; 176 Shutterstock; 178 www.gapinteriors.com/Graham Atkins Hughes; 179 t Shutterstock; 180 Getty Images; 181 Getty Images; 182 www.gapinteriors.com/House & Leisure; 183 t iStockphoto, b Corbis; 184 Artur Images/Angelika Klein; 185 t Mauritius Images, b www.gapinteriors.com/Caroline Mardon; 186 Mauritius Images; 187 www.gapinteriors.com/ Piotr Gesicki; 188 Corbis; 189 Chromorange -Photostock; 190 TIPS Images; 191 tr www.gapinteriors.com/House & Leisure, bl iStockphoto; 192 Corbis; 193 t Getty Images, bl Getty Images, br Corbis; 194 Corbis; 195 iStockphoto; 196 Picture Press; 197 Picture Press; 198 Picture Press; 199 Heinrich Heine; 200 Picture Press; 201 t Getty Images, b SuperStock; 202 & 203 tr www.gapinteriors.com/Trai Giovan; Shutter-stock; 280–334 bl (flowers silhouette) iStockphoto; 206 Friedrich Strauss; 207 b Reinhard-Tierfoto; 208 tr Friedrich Strauss, br PhotoAlto; 209 Getty Images; 210 Getty Images; 211 Getty Images; 212 Friedrich Strauss; 213 Getty Images; 214 bl Mauritius Images; 215 Friedrich Strauss; 216 Gap Photos; 217 tl Friedrich Strauss, br Getty Images; 218 Getty Images; 219 Gap Photos; 220 tr iStockphoto, b Shutterstock; 221 t Gap Photos, b Getty Images; 222 Gap Photos; 224 iStockphoto; 225 t Gap Photos, br Friedrich Strauss; 226 Gap Photos; 227 tl Getty Images, tr Mauritius Images; 228 Gap Photos; 229 tl Gap Photos, br Shutterstock; 230 Gap Photos; 231 t Gap Photos, b iStockphoto; 232 Gap Photos; 233 t Getty Images, b iStockphoto; 234 tl & br Shutterstock; 235 Friedrich Strauss; t Corbis; 239 t iStockphoto, b Friedrich Strauss; 240 b Corbis; 241 Getty Images; 242 t Reinhard-Tierfoto, l Getty Images; 243 Gap Photos; 244 t iStockphoto, b Getty Images; 245 Shutterstock